IMAGES of America

TEMPLETON

IMAGES
of America

TEMPLETON

Harry Aldrich Jr. and Brian P. Tanguay
for the Narragansett Historical Society

ARCADIA
PUBLISHING

ISBN 978-0-7385-3610-5

Published by Arcadia Publishing
Charleston, South Carolina

Library of Congress Catalog Card Number: 2004103633

For all general information, contact Arcadia Publishing:
Telephone 843-853-2070
Fax 843-853-0044
E-mail sales@arcadiapublishing.com
For customer service and orders:
Toll-free 1-888-313-2665

Visit us on the Internet at www.arcadiapublishing.com

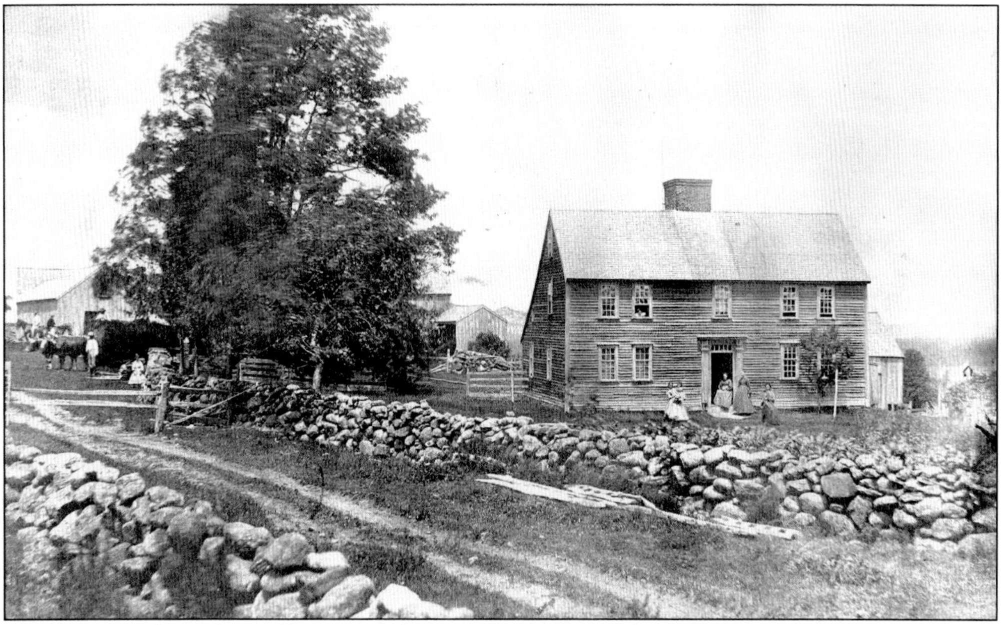

Templeton's oldest framed house was built in 1760 by Zaccheus Barrett at the foot of Dolbear Hill about a mile south of the center on what is now South Road. The Barrett families stayed for three generations, the Dolbear sisters, granddaughters of Mr. Barrett, were the last in the family. Since then, the house has gone through several owners undertaking many changes. It is still standing and in a very good state of preservation. The original shape is the same, but the inside has changed. Robert Young and family now own the home, under the name of Dolbier Hill Farm.

Contents

Acknowledgments

During the September 2003 meeting of the Narragansett Historical Society, Harry Aldrich Jr. suggested writing a book on Templeton in the Images of America series along with Brian Tanguay, who has a collection of glass-plate negatives that once belonged to Oren Williams of Baldwinville. We got together in October 2003 and started compiling the information we had, along with images in the historical society's collection. Our focus was on the images taken by both Oren Williams and Wallace Underwood from 1880 to 1940. Some of the photographers are not identified, and many of the images we discovered were not labeled. Those may some day become part of a new book, as we will continue to collect images and information for years to come.

We would like to thank the Narragansett Historical Society officers, directors, and members who supported this effort. Particularly, we thank Ralph C. Henshaw, who allowed us to enter the society building on short notice to find more information, and the Boynton Public Library, for allowing their collection to be utilized in filling in missing pictures and historical information. Especially, we thank the individuals who gave us their time and pictures that we needed to make this book a success. They are Janet Haley, John Brooks, Karen Olivari, Russell and Carol Stanley, Ray and Judy Page, Patrick Mullins, Bayard and Shirley Peabody, the Narragansett Regional School District, and Barbara Decoff.

We thank our family members for supporting our endless nights of research, especially our wives, Phyllis Aldrich and Tina M. Tanguay.

This book does not claim to be a complete history of Templeton; it is merely a collection of available images and information gathered from many different documents and books. Most of the history came from *The Story of Templeton* (1946) by Elizabeth Wellington Lord and *The History of Templeton to 1888* by Hosea F. Lane, to which we are indebted.

We hope this book is received in the spirit in which it was written. We hope to spark the interest of new historians and feed the hunger of those searching for facts about Templeton's past.

INTRODUCTION

In 1733, the township of Narragansett No. 6 was laid out. Zaccheus Barrett began by building the first frame house in 1760. Templetown was incorporated on March 6, 1762, through a bill enacted by Sir Francis Bernard, governor of Massachusetts. After 1764, the spelling changed to Templeton, and this was used in all warrants and became the spelling of record. By 1789, the town was divided into nine districts, each having a school for which it was responsible. In 1869, the district system was given up, and the town became the owner of every schoolhouse.

Located in central Massachusetts, Templeton now consists of four villages, or precincts: Templeton Center, East Templeton, Otter River, and Baldwinville. The town is situated 1,200 feet above sea level and covers about 20,000 acres. In the late 1800s and early 1900s, Templeton was made up of many farms. In 1887, there were 429 horses and 450 cows listed by the assessors. In 1885, the population was 2,627, with 1,302 males and 1,325 females. Of these people, 2,293 were born in America and 334 were immigrants.

The Otter River powered many factories and flowed through Baldwinville and Otter River, Templeton's northern precincts. In Otter River, there was a woolen mill, a paper mill, and a brickyard. The bricks, many of which exist today, were made with the word "Otter" cast into them. The Lord and Stone foundry, also located on the Otter River, produced cast-iron kitchenware and wood stoves.

Baldwinville was a thriving manufacturing area with many factories lining the Otter River. Local townsfolk worked for companies that produced chairs, children's toys, furniture, paper, boxes, machines for chair making, and household furnishings. The biggest manufacturer was eventually named the Temple Stuart Company.

Taverns were located in various parts of the town along stagecoach routes. John Brooks built Brooks Tavern along the route from Worcester to Greenfield in Brooks Village. It was a favorite stop to rest for the night and have a fresh team of horses ready in the morning. The Narragansett House in Baldwinville, built in 1832 by Capt. Joseph Davis, sat on the Fitzwilliam turnpike and was built with a high pointed roof, two or three stories higher than others surrounding it. It was a popular place for sleighing and school parties. The Templeton Hotel, located in Templeton Center, was destroyed by fire in 1888 and replaced by the Templeton Inn, built by Moses Richardson. A miniature reproduction of the Templeton Inn is on display in the historical society building. In the center of Templeton are churches, the Boynton library, the Narragansett Historical Society building, a country store, and John Boynton's tin shop.

This collection of images is a wonderful walk in and around Templeton in the late 1800s through the 1900s. Thankfully, these photographers were insightful enough to preserve the past. This book contains a few of the many images on display in the Narragansett Historical Society building.

One

Templeton Center

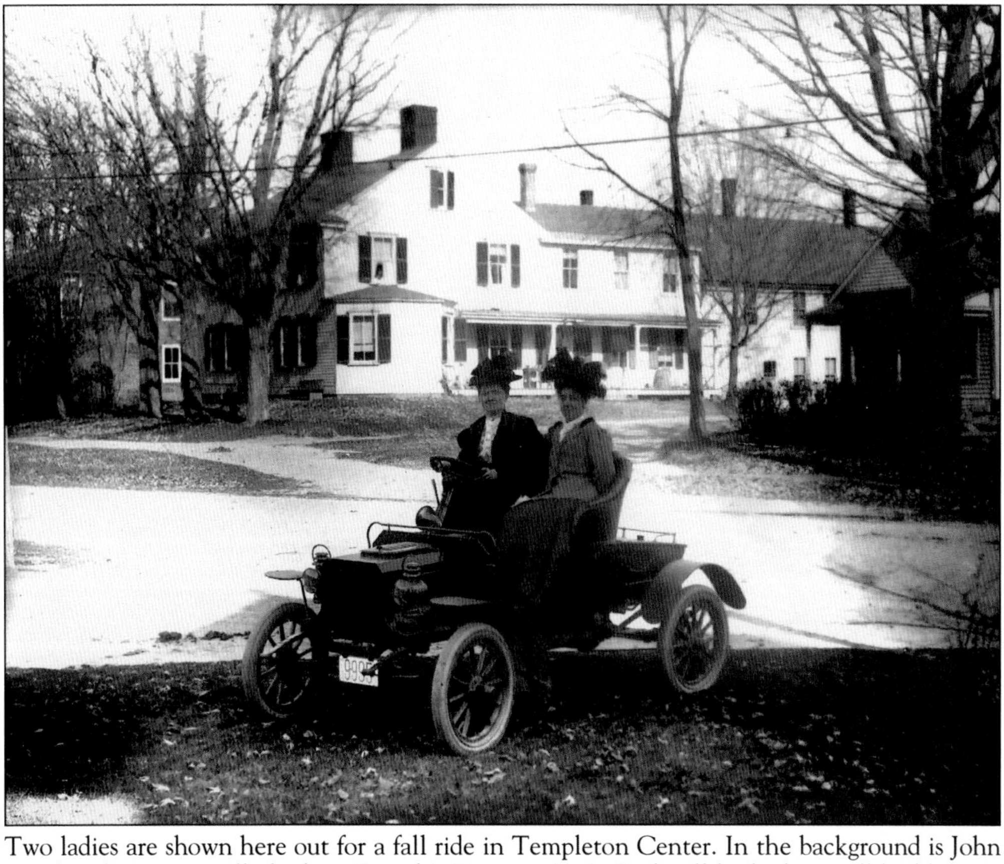

Two ladies are shown here out for a fall ride in Templeton Center. In the background is John Brooks's farm, originally built as French's Tavern. A. G. Bushnell built the small building on the right for use as a print shop. Bushnell was responsible for starting the *Gardner News*.

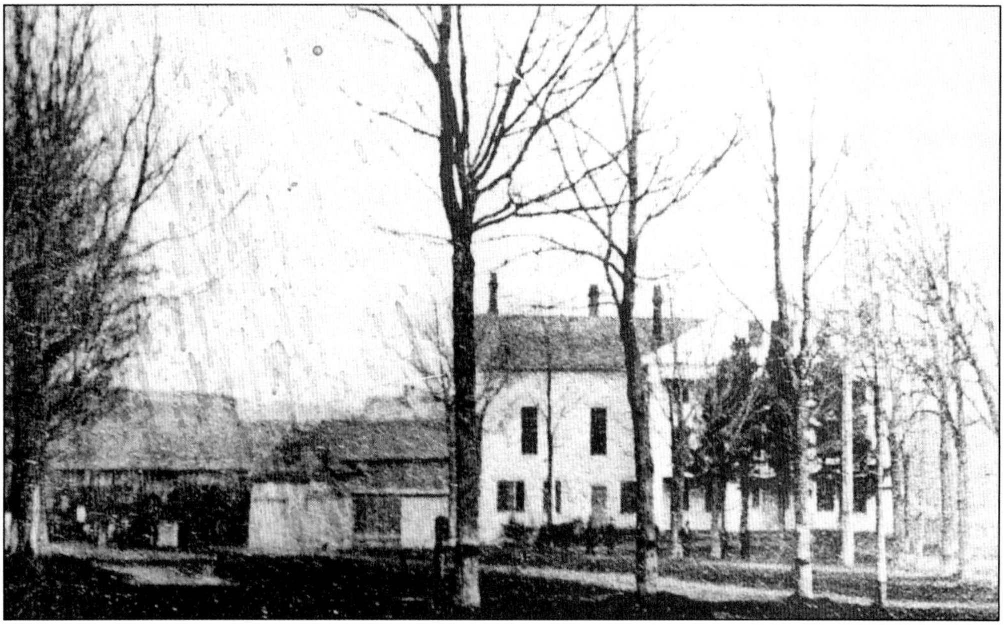

Built in 1820 on the common, the Templeton Hotel was destroyed by fire in September 1888. Hotelkeepers during its life were Charles E. Ellis, Lipha French, Calvin Townsley, Levi Pierce, and Francis Twitchell.

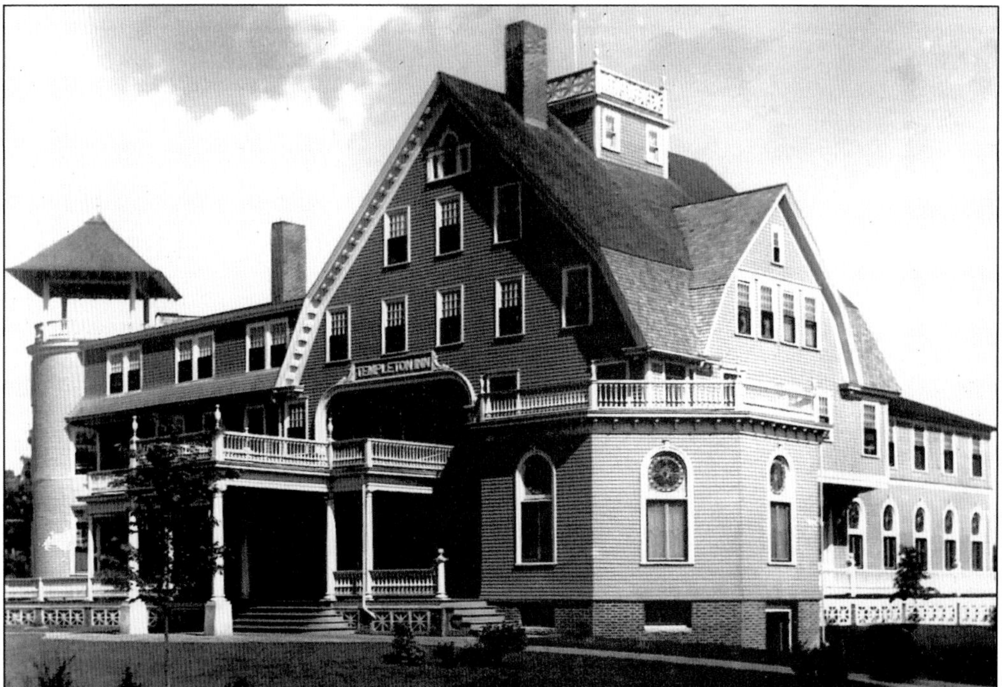

The Templeton Inn, better known as the Landlords Inn, was built in 1900 on the former site of the Templeton Hotel. Templeton native Ernest Maynard, who was also the architect of Keith's Theatre in Boston, drew up plans for the inn. When it was initially constructed, there were a total of 40 rooms.

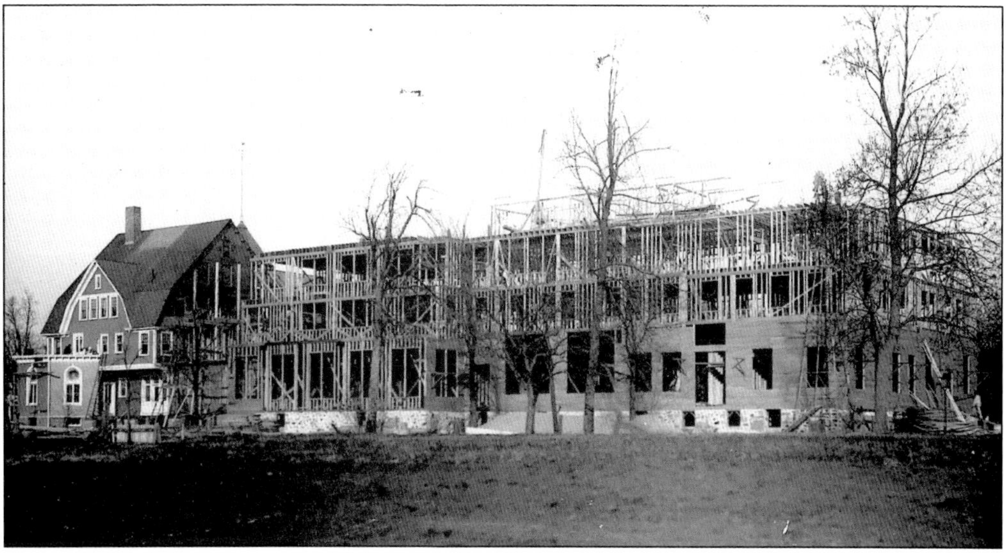

An additional 60 rooms were built onto the Templeton Inn c. 1910. A water tower was also constructed to the rear of the building to provide adequate water for guests and fire protection. The inn offered two rows of garages across the street for guests to rent.

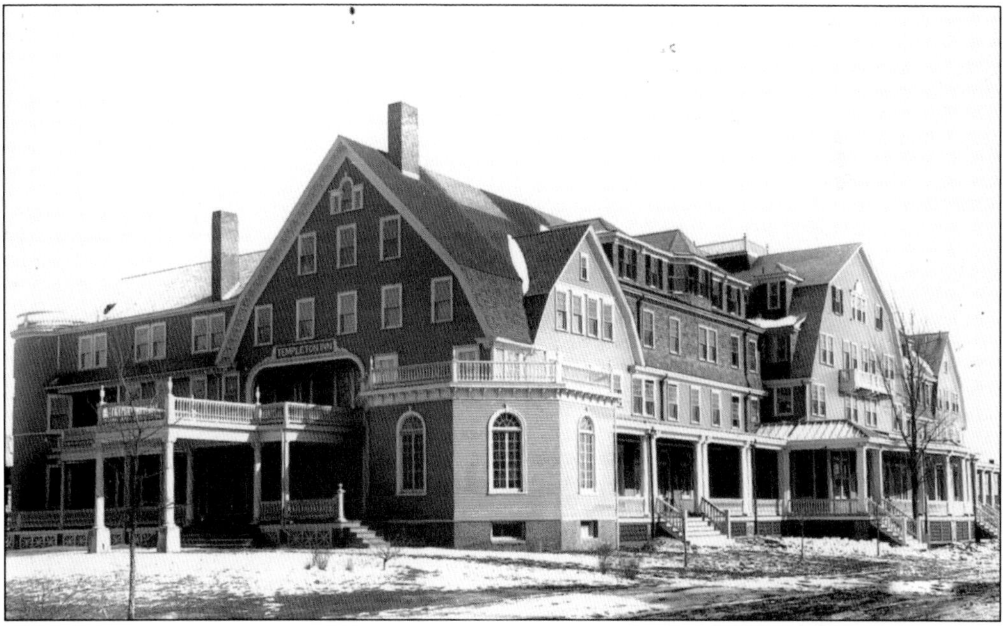

Taken from the front of the Blodgett Building on South Road, this image offers a view of the inn after the expansion. It was said to be the finest inn throughout all of New England. A scale model constructed by former resident Charles Burpee is on display in the Narragansett Historical Society building.

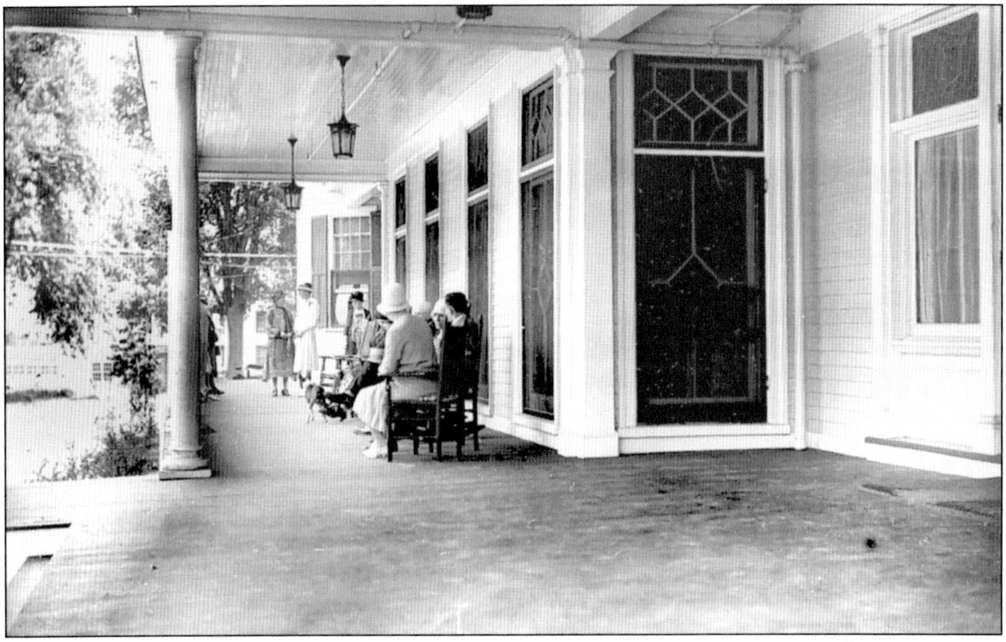

Some of the guests of the Templeton Inn are shown here enjoying a summer day, conversing and relaxing on the front porch. To the left in the picture, one can see some of the garages that were available to the guests. One can also see a small building that was formerly the Clover Farm store and is now Nygards Veterinary Clinic.

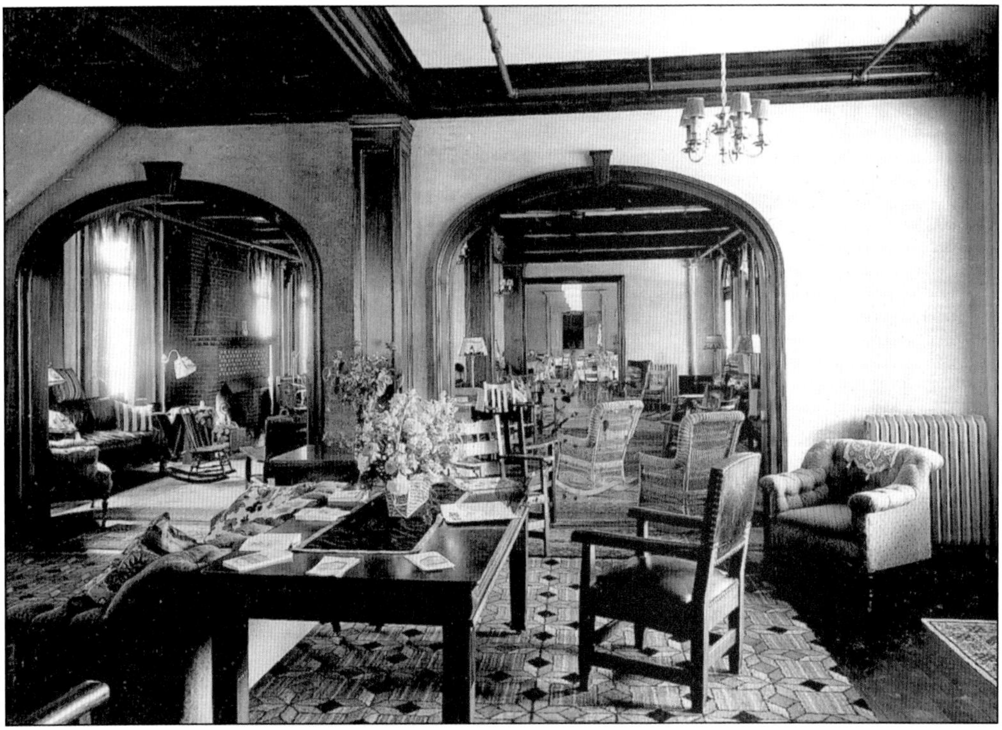

This view shows one of the sitting rooms of the Templeton Inn. Several guests could enjoy a conversation with friends or sit back and read the paper on a Sunday morning.

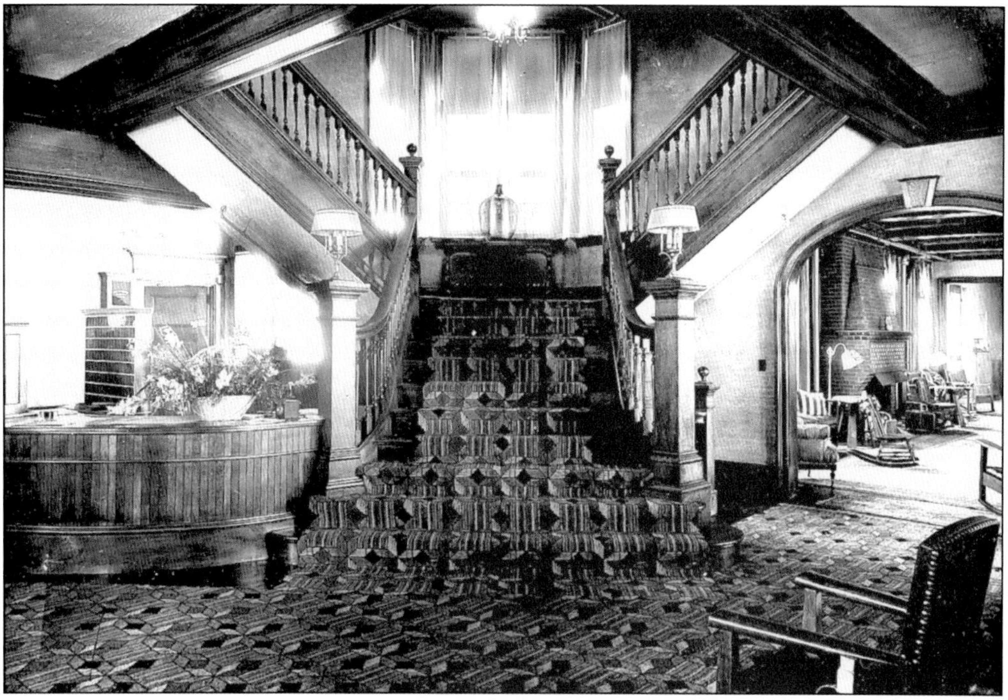

As one enters the Inn, one views this beautiful staircase; to the right is one of the sitting rooms, and on the left is the front desk. In the 1900s, one might have had the pleasure of being greeted by Grace E. Blodgett.

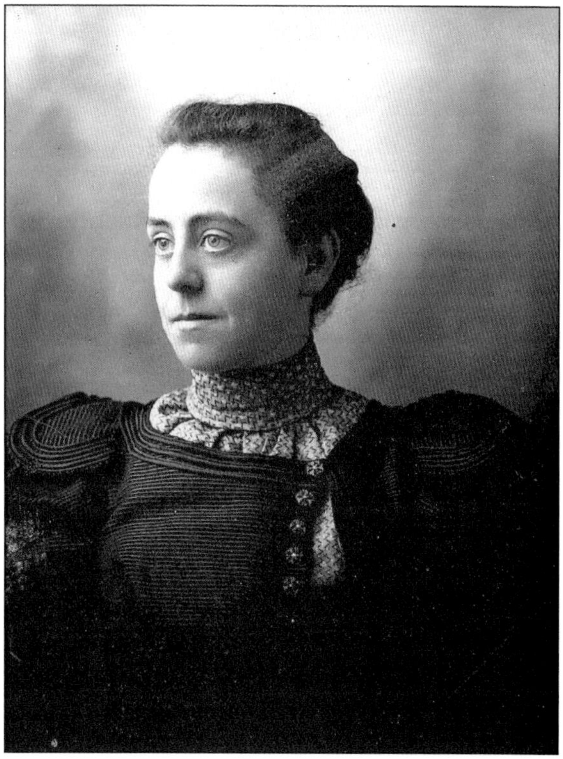

Grace E. Blodgett was born on April 23, 1870. The daughter of Percival and Georgietta Blodgett, she was very active in Templeton from childhood on. Grace worked in her father's grocery store and later was a clerk in the Templeton Inn when her father was the proprietor. She then worked for the Boynton Library as a librarian. Grace was a teacher and then the principal of Templeton High School until 1901. She helped form the first group of Campfire Girls in 1916 with 10 girls. Although 30 girls were on the membership list by 1920, Blodgett was forced to relinquish guardianship due to an illness in her family; no successor could be found and the group disbanded. When a Girl Scout troop organized in 1936, a number of the former Camp Fire Girls and sponsors became part of the new organization. Grace was an inspiration and leader to many of the young people in Templeton.

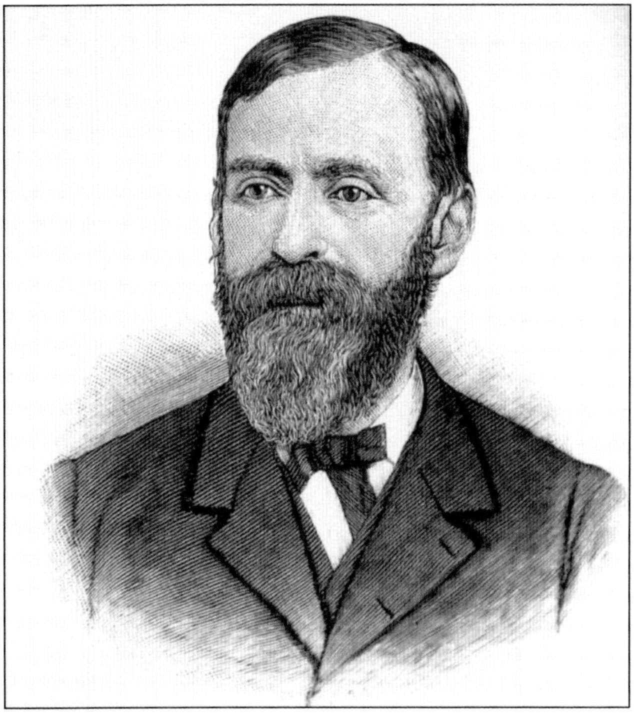

Percival Blodgett was born in 1841 in Orange. He came to Templeton in 1861 to teach school and stayed for several terms. In 1865, he went into the mercantile business under the name of Dudley and Blodgett. By 1870, he was ready to go into business alone and purchased the Colonel Lee building, where he set up a grocery store and residence. After retiring from the grocery business, Blodgett became proprietor of the Templeton Inn and active in community affairs.

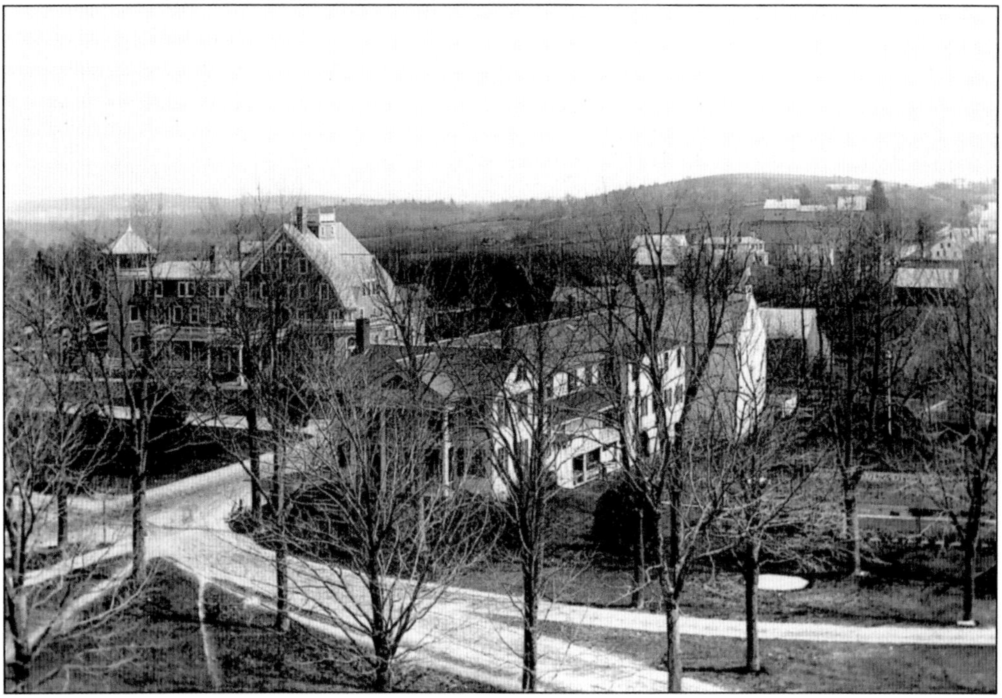

This is a bird's-eye view from the First Church's belfry, looking east toward Dolbear Hill on South Road. Col. Artemus Lee's former residence—P. Blodgett's at the time of this picture—is in the center of the photograph, and the Landlords Inn is across the road. The small white spot in the lower right of the picture is the old fire well.

Shown in this photograph is Col. Artemus Lee, born November 2, 1793, in Barre. At the age of 17, he came to Templeton in 1810 and served as a clerk in the Union Store, owned by John W. Stiles, now the historical building. In 1829, he erected a building on the southerly side of the common, which today contains several businesses and apartments. Colonel Lee served several terms as a state representative and a senator. He was a Republican delegate for the national convention of 1868.

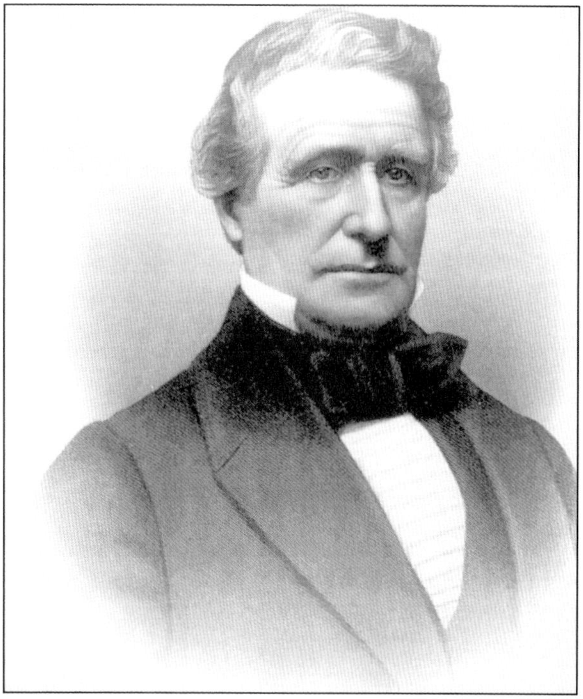

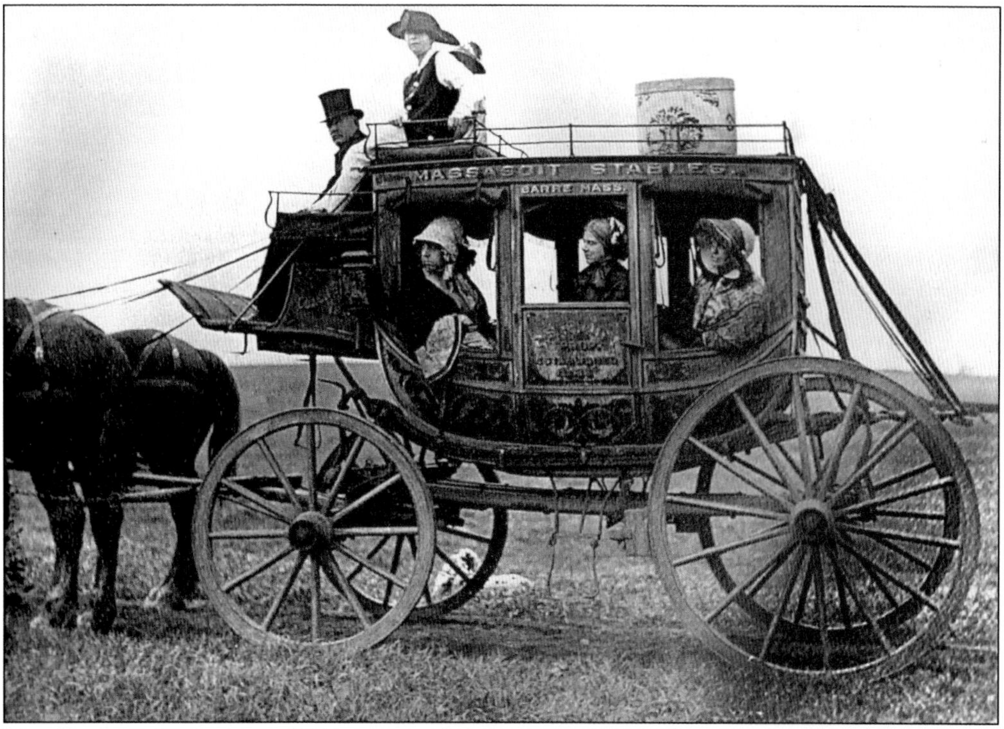

This Barre stagecoach would have passed through town traveling to New Hampshire. Well-known driver of the stagecoach Ginnery Twitchell was the brother of Francis Twitchell, a keeper at the Templeton Inn. Ginnery Twitchell eventually owned more than 200 horses and became a pony express rider.

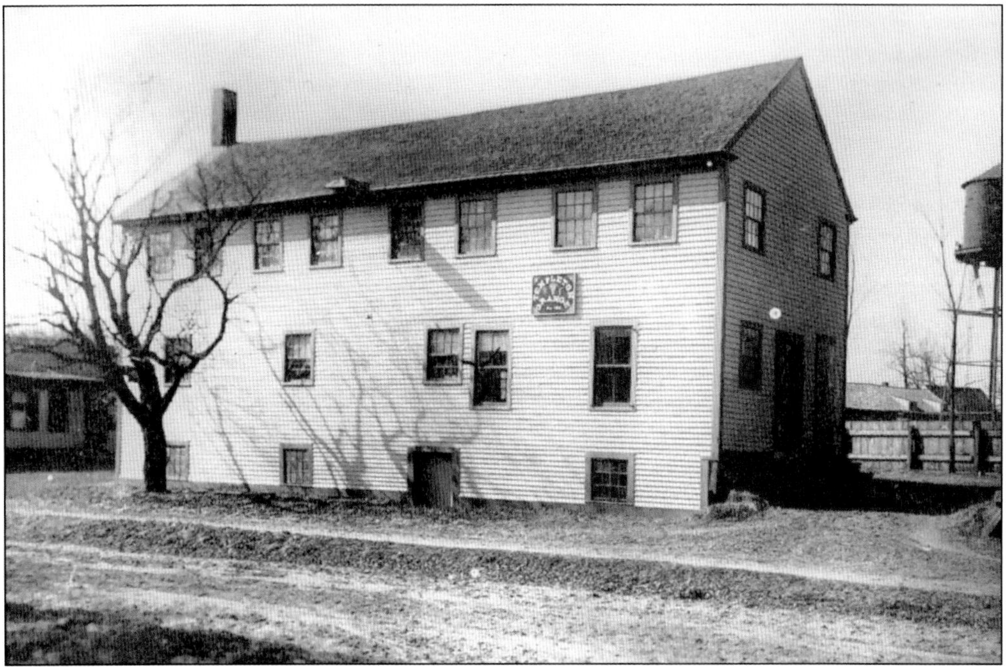

The Templeton Grange held its first meeting on March 16, 1885, with 35 members. The Grange was a social group that discussed current events, farm problems, and other relevant issues. They purchased grain, coal, flour, and other goods by the carload to get a better price and divided it amongst the members. The members purchased this building in 1897 to serve as their meeting hall. Membership dissolved in the late 1900s. The building was donated to the Narragansett Historical Society. The wooden water tower in the rear was the first tank used by the Templeton Inn.

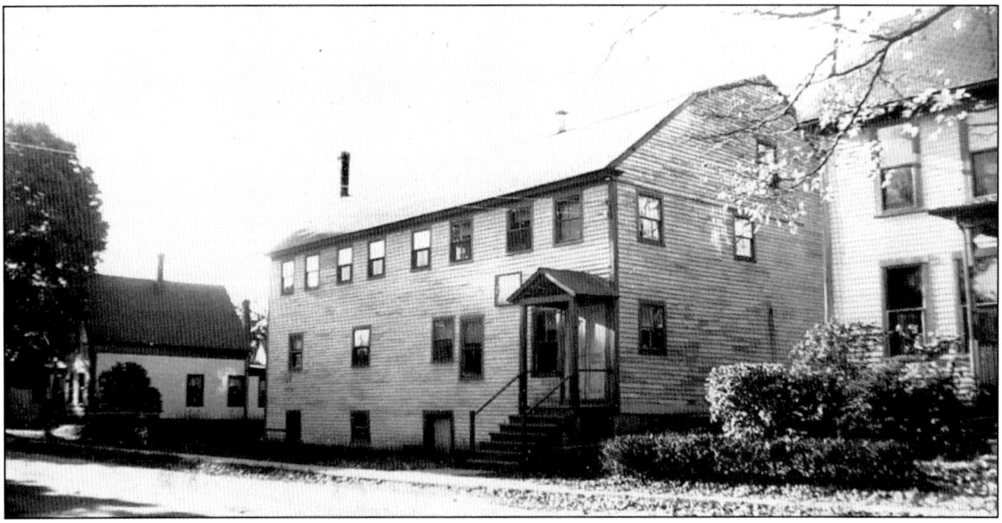

This picture of the Grange hall on Hubbardston Road shows that some changes have been made. The door has been moved to the front from the end, and the roof has been redesigned as a gambrel. The date of this picture is unidentified. John Boynton and David Whitcomb originally used this building as a tin shop.

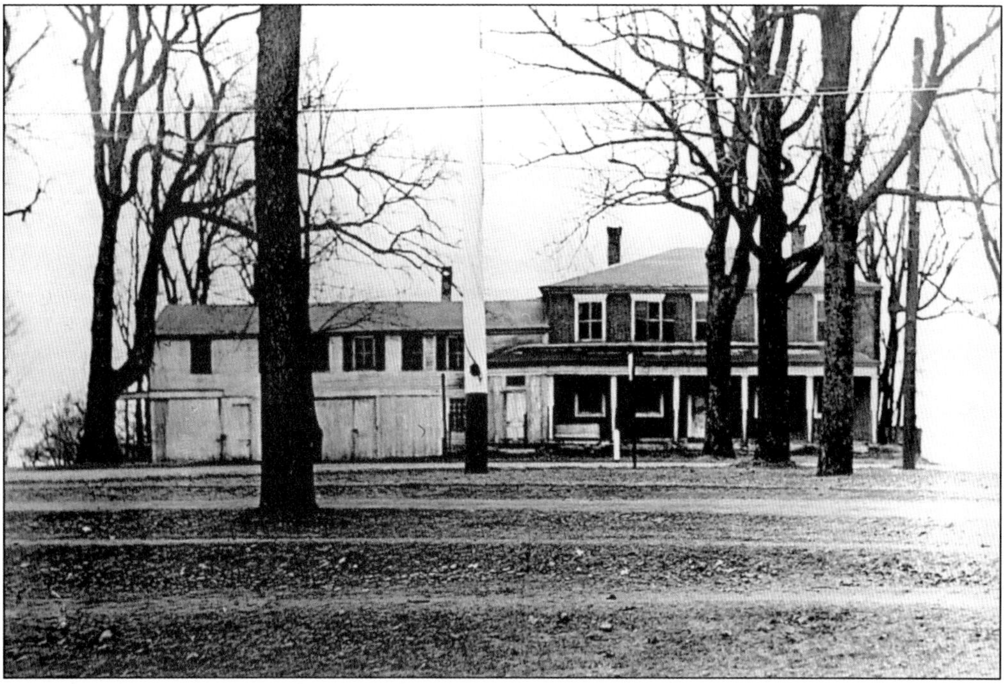

The Narragansett Historical Society building is shown here as it looked *c.* 1933, when it was first purchased by the society. It was restored, the porch was removed, and the shed was rebuilt to look as it does today. It was dedicated in October 1934.

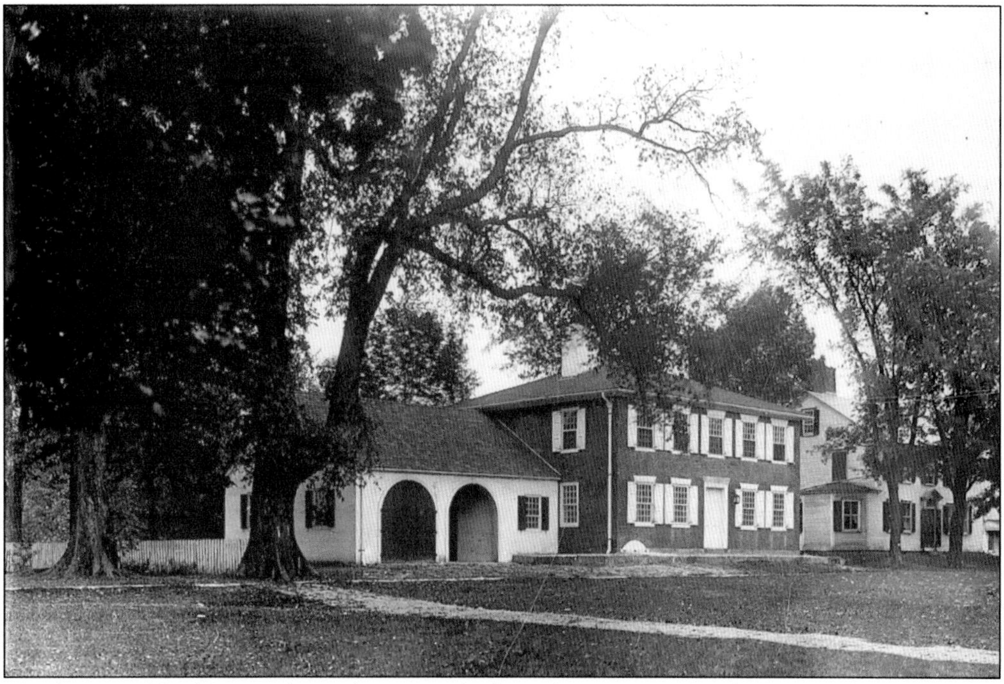

The historical building is shown here as it looks today. Society members recently restored the garage doors. Two stones rest on the front lawn: one is dedicated in memory of Gladys Salame and the other lies in honor of the township, which was laid out in 1734.

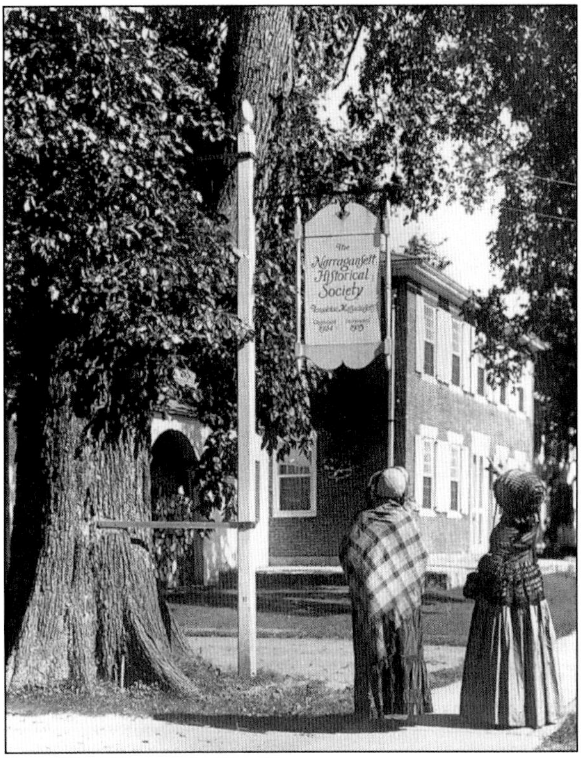

The Narragansett Historical Society sign stopped these ladies on their walk. The sign still hangs in the front as a reminder that the society offers an enormous number of historical artifacts and an occasional Saturday morning tea party.

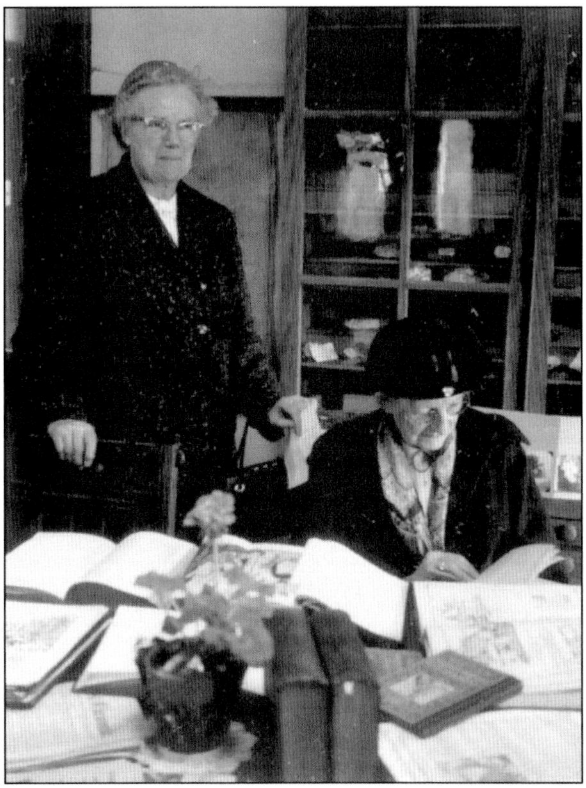

Mildred Henshaw and Lucy Baker are shown here working at the Boynton Public Library c. the mid-1900s. As lifelong residents of Templeton, they worked at the library for many years. Mildred Henshaw's husband was Charles R. Henshaw, a farmer in town known for being a dowser and for his knowledge of the town boundaries.

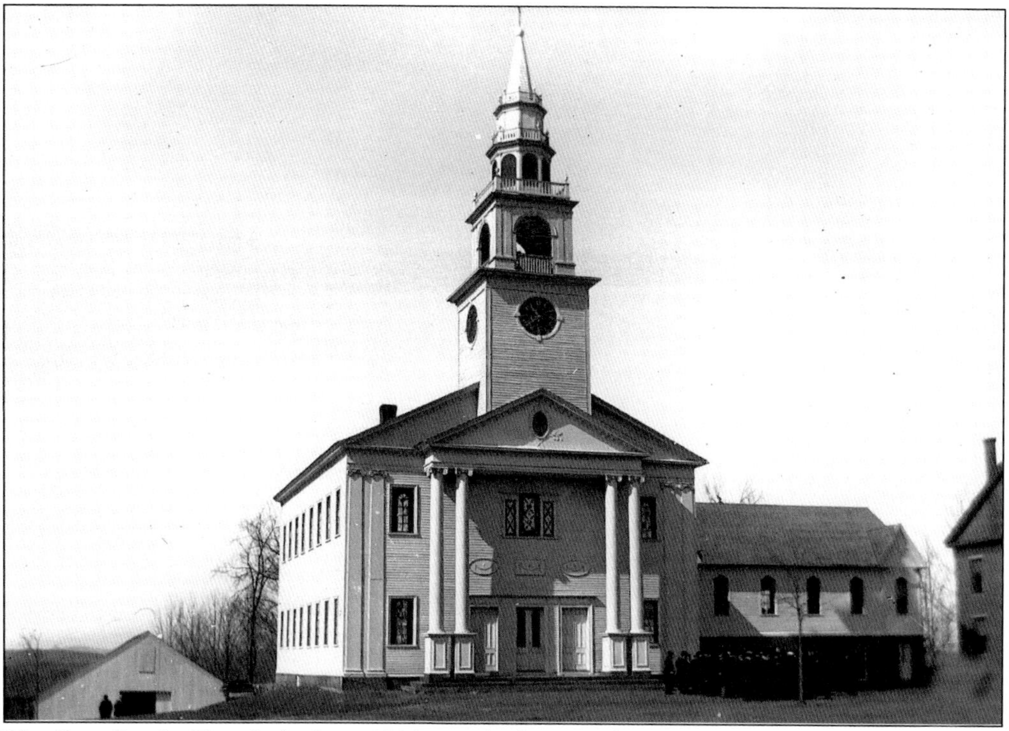

The First Parish Church, built in 1811, overlooks Templeton Center. The chapel was added in 1872. The brick building housed the school on the ground floor, the town hall on the upper floor, and the town hearse, driven by Moses Chamberlain, in the basement. The school abandoned the building in 1942, and it was then used by the Scouts until it was torn down in 1948.

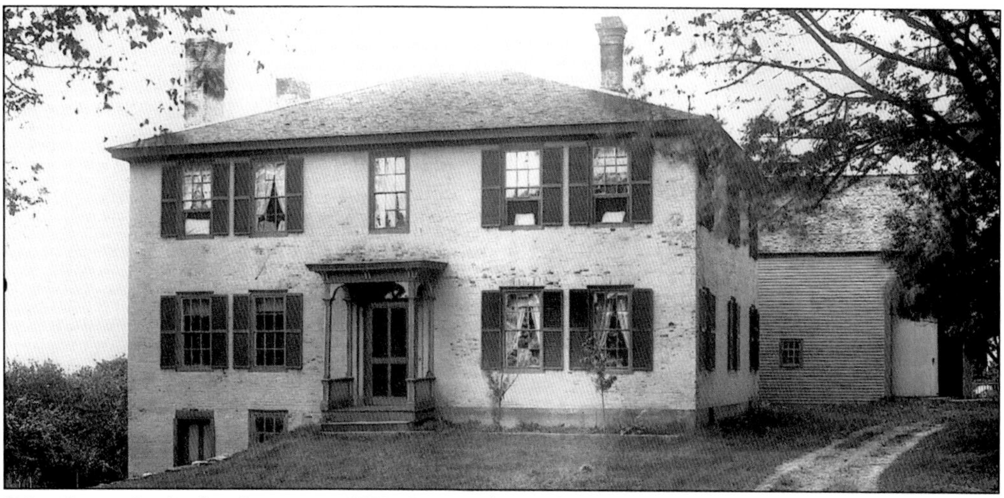

Silas Stone built this house in 1770. It was the only house in the center of town built with bricks. Imported from England, the bricks were used as ballast on a ship. It was once known as the Joseph Upham Tavern. It was used as a private boys school until 1837, and then town physicians Dr. Spencer and Dr. Tobin lived here. Elsa Stone, who tutored students, later owned the house. Today, the building houses a business operated by the Whittle family called the Country Mischief.

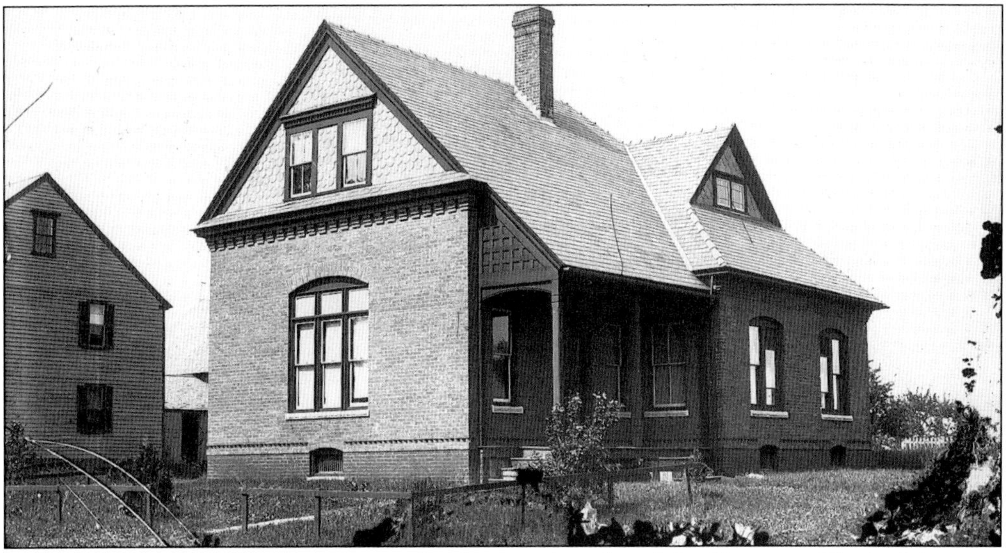

The Boynton Public Library was named in honor of resident John Boynton. The building was constructed in 1885 with $2,000 that was appropriated by the town. The library was originally opened in 1873 with funds given to the town by Boynton's partner, David Whitcomb Esq., with the stipulation it be a free public library. For 12 years, the library had been kept in rooms on the upper floor of the Col. Artemus Lee building. The library was moved when construction of the Boynton Street facility was completed.

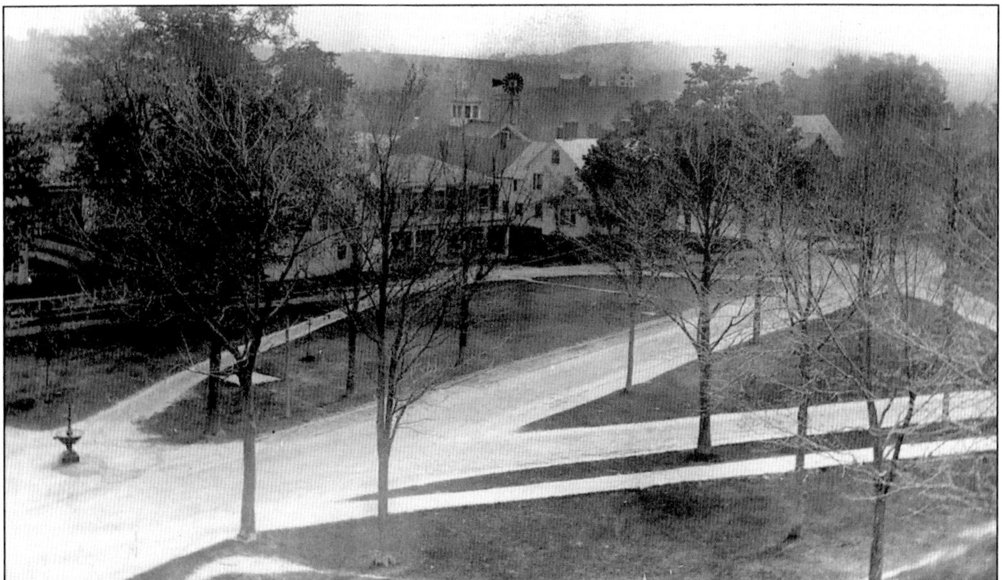

Taken from the belfry of the First Church early in the 20th century, this picture shows two prominent structures on the common. The large house and barn next to the windmill was built by Lipha French in 1820 and was a tavern until it was sold to John Work in 1855. Then Henry Smith took over in 1865. The Twitchell family owned it until 1895, when it was purchased by John Brooks and operated as a dairy farm. It was then purchased by Roger Couillard and his wife in 1963 and is still in the family today. The Narragansett Historical Society building can be seen to the left.

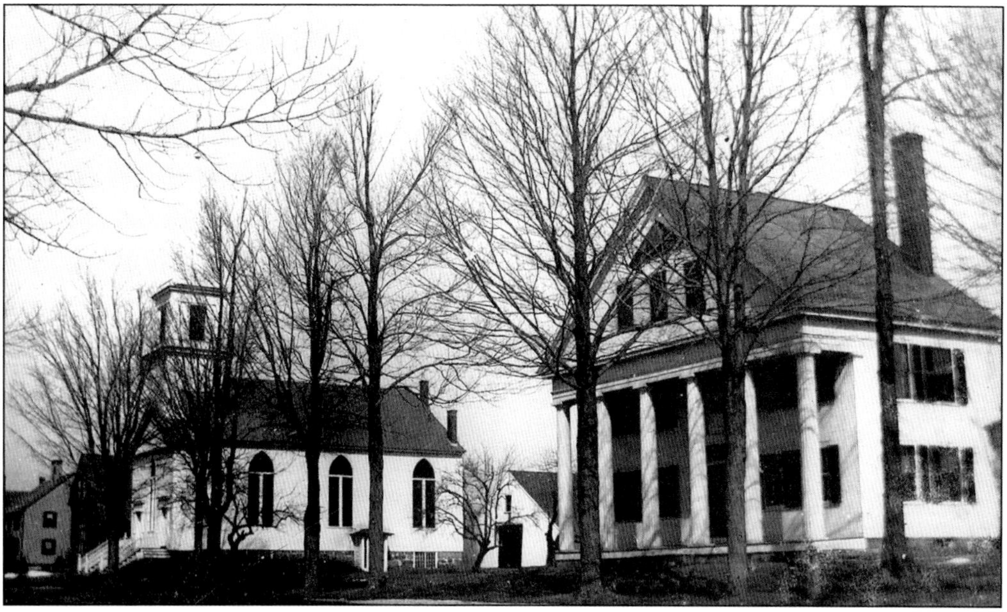

Shown here are the First Church parsonage and the First Trinitarian Church of Templeton; the house was built by John Boynton, founder of the Worcester Polytechnic Institute. Although Boynton never lived in the house, his business partner, David Whitcomb, did. Boynton, who left a front door on the second floor without a veranda, never completed it. He became so aggravated by the suggestion of a passerby to build the veranda, he vowed never to built it.

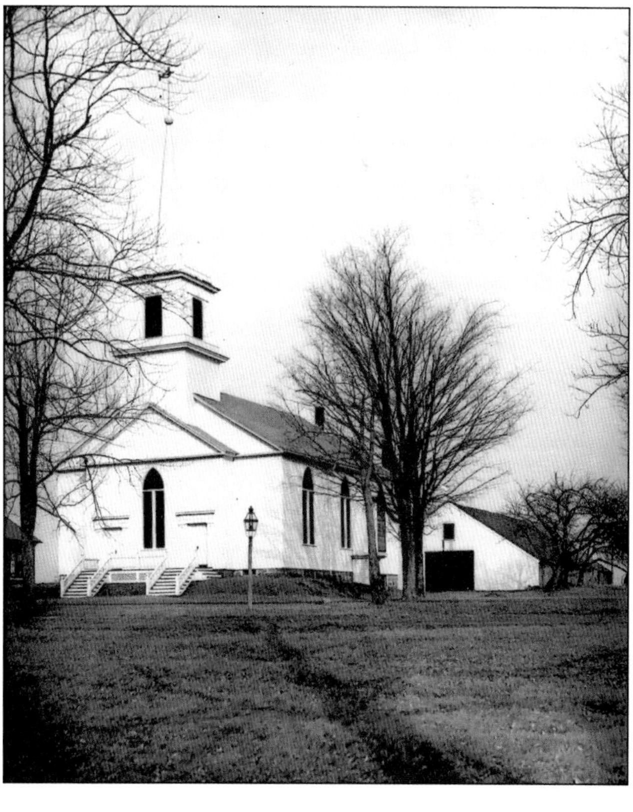

The First Trinitarian Congregational Church of Templeton is located between the Boynton Public Library and the parsonage. Built on land donated by Dea. Benjamin Hawkes, the church was started in 1832 by a group of individuals who had separated from the First Church. The two churches eventually merged again into one church, and the Trinitarian Church was taken down in the mid-1900s.

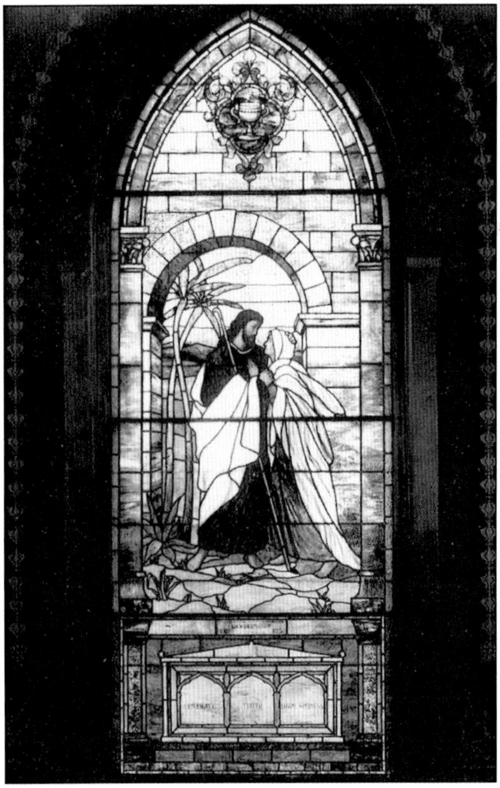

Moses Richardson donated this stained-glass window in memory of his mother, Lucy. After the church was torn down, the J. P. Martin Construction Company gave the window to the First Church, on the common.

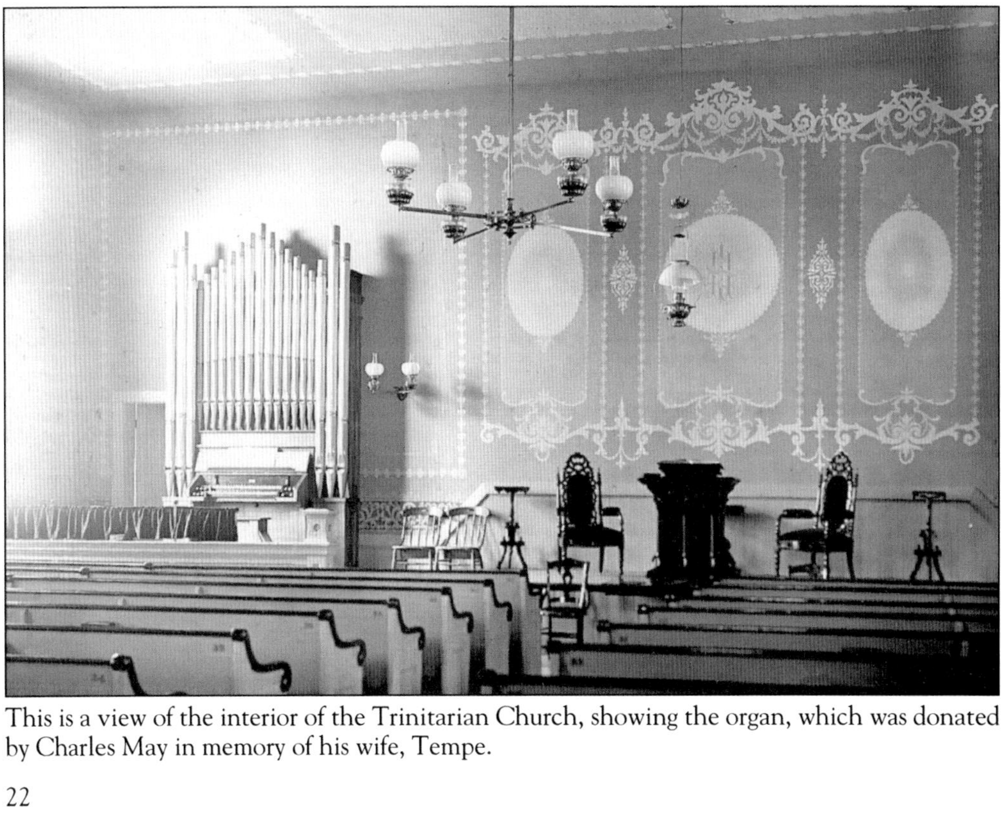

This is a view of the interior of the Trinitarian Church, showing the organ, which was donated by Charles May in memory of his wife, Tempe.

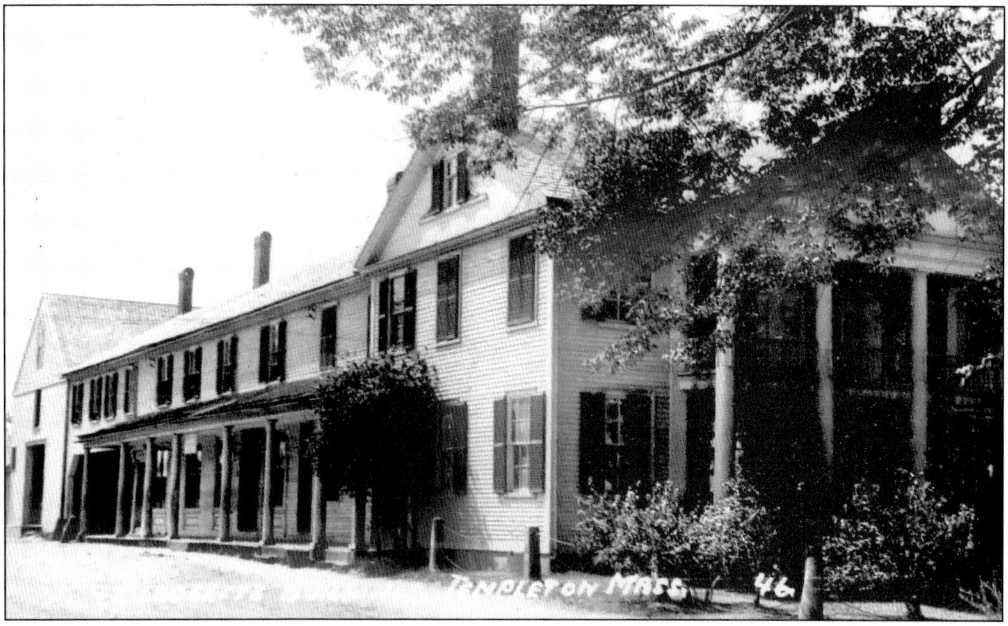

Col. Artemus Lee's residence was built in 1829 at a cost of $11,000. The building is located on the corner of South Road and Dudley Road. Colonel Lee sold the property to Percival Blodgett in 1870, and it has changed hands several times since then. The building has been home to many stores and businesses over the years, including a clock shop, the United Co-op Farmers Store, a barbershop, a grocery store, and apartments for many tenants. At one time, Templeton's post office and the Boynton Public Library were housed in this building.

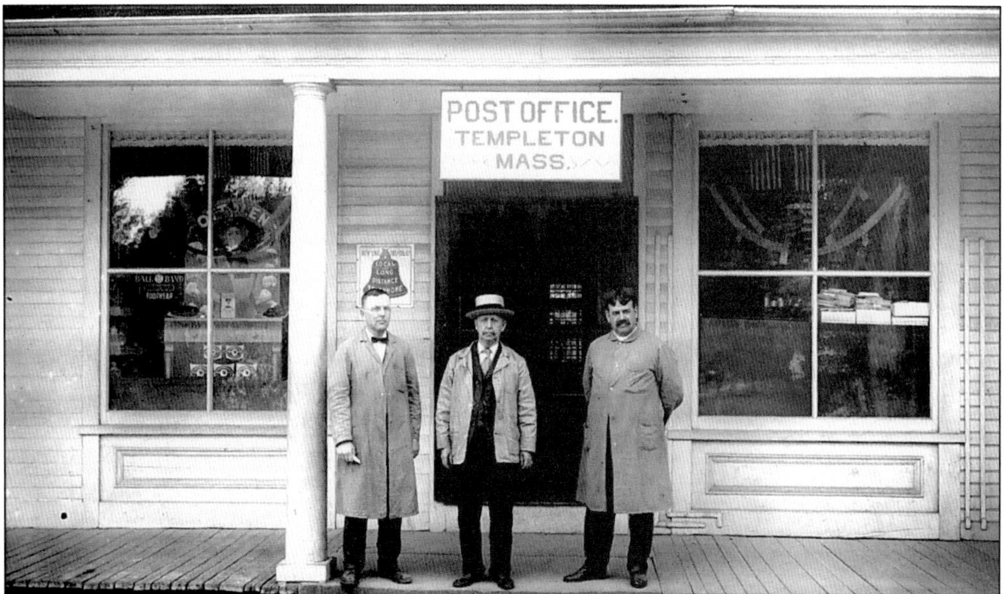

Employees Moses Winch, Eugene Lincoln, and Frank Johnson pose in front of the Templeton Center post office and Johnson's store, located in Artemus Lee's building on the common. The building still stands, housing the Templeton Country Store, the Ice Cream Bar, the Henshaw and Haley Company, and apartments.

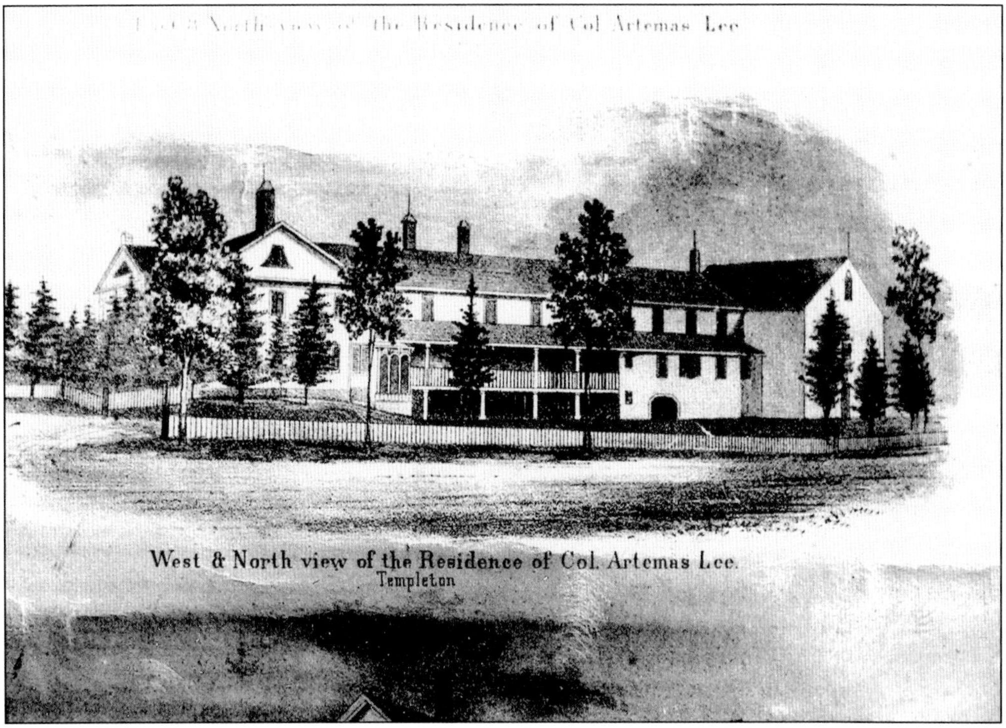

This is the view of Col. Artemus Lee's residence from Wellington Road; it is one of Templeton's largest homes. The present owners are building an addition on this side that will include a three-car garage.

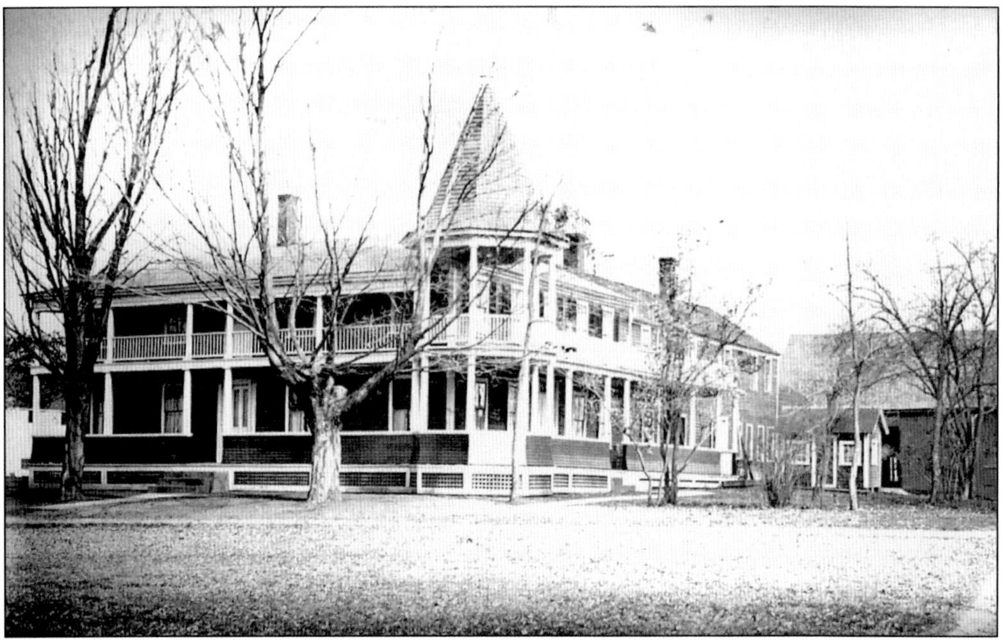

Located on Boynton Street, this was the home of Alice Tobien in 1887. George Bourn purchased it and then William Hawkes. Rudolph Sundstrom owns the house today.

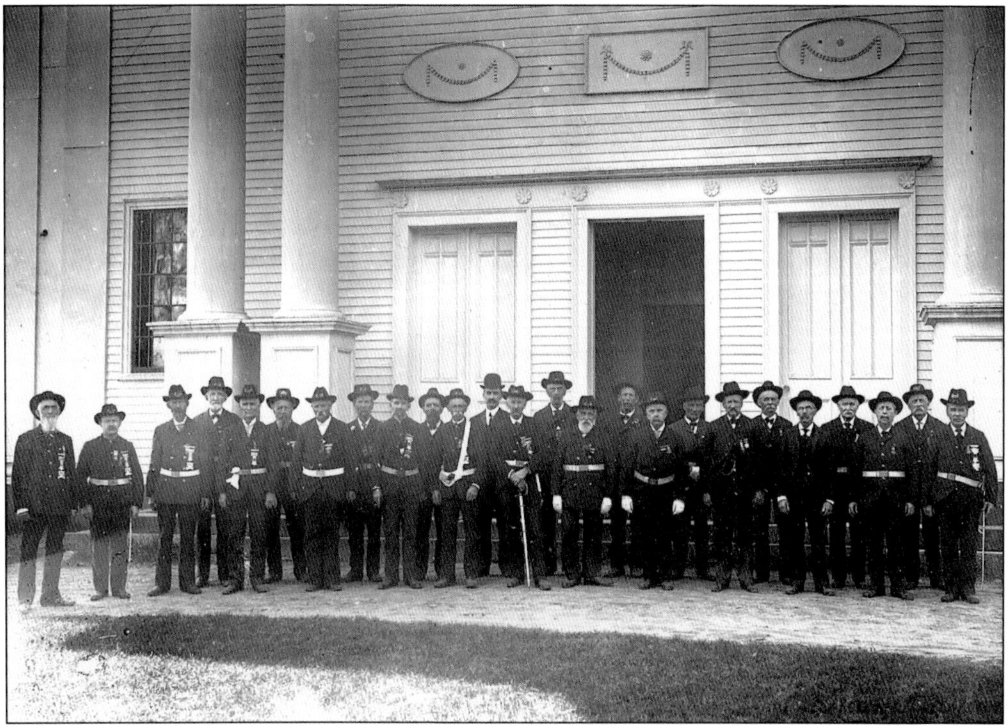

Veterans line up in front of the First Church of Templeton for memorial services for Pres. Abraham Lincoln. Templeton held this service on April 18, 1865, four days after the assassination.

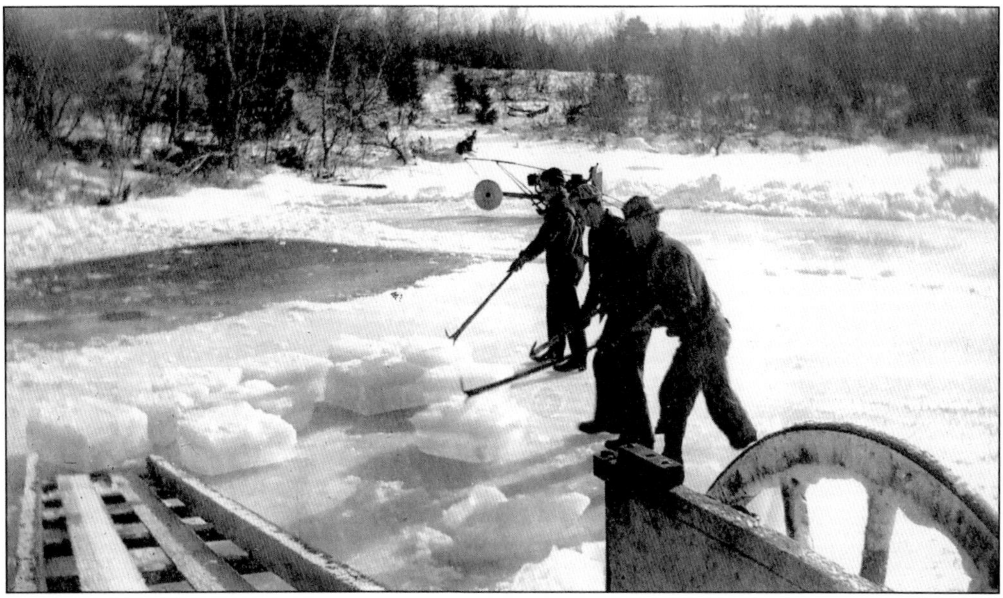

Possibly the Bourn Hadley Pond is where these men are harvesting ice. This was performed every winter, as refrigeration had not yet been invented. The ice was cut from local ponds, stored in barns, and packed in sawdust for insulation.

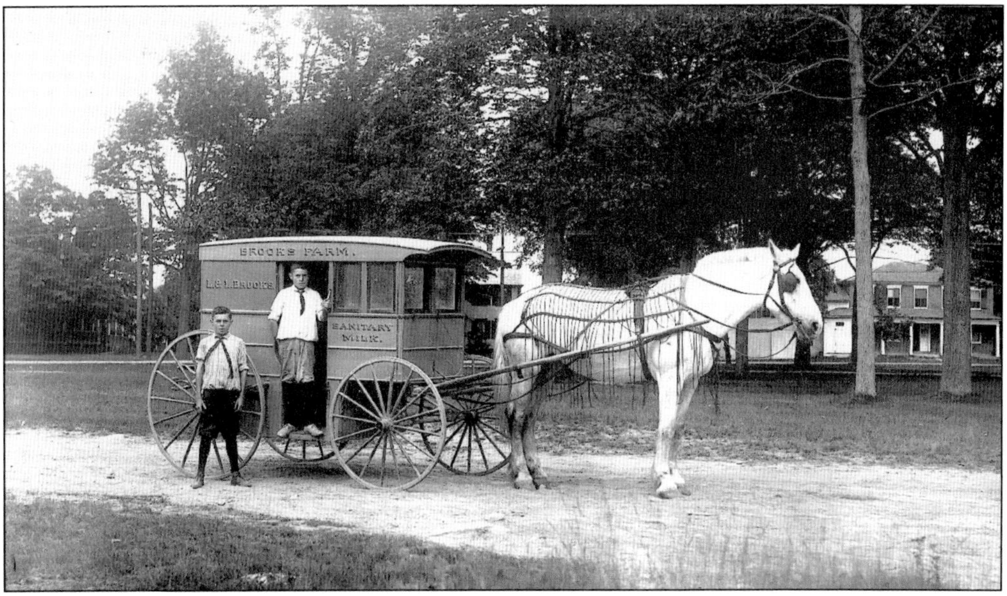

Twins Lawrence and Leonard Brooks, age 15, are shown here in 1915 on their father John Brooks's milk wagon. Brooks owned and operated a dairy farm in Templeton Center, raising Guernsey cattle. He owned the farm for more than 50 years. John W. Works, and later Francis Twitchell, had owned the farm in the mid-1800s. Roger Couillard and his wife later purchased the farm, and the family still owns it today. The barn in the picture was taken down many years ago.

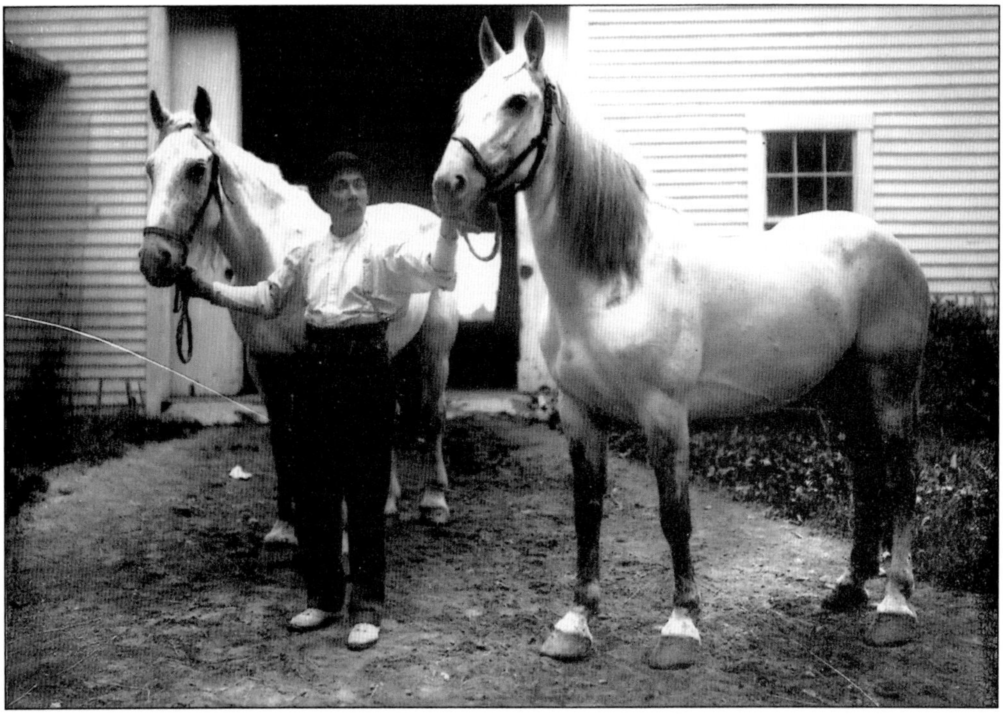

John Brooks is shown here with his horses on the farm in Templeton Center. The horses were used to pull the milk wagon, mow the hay fields, and bring the hay to the barn.

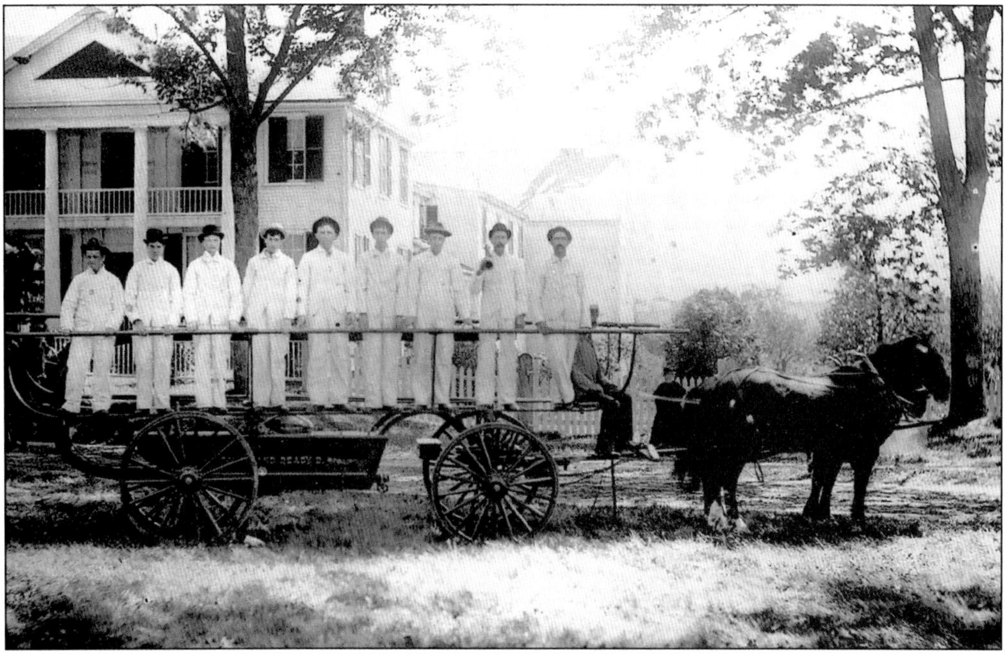

All dressed in white, the crew of the Rough and Ready pose on the common in front of the Col. Artemus Lee building.

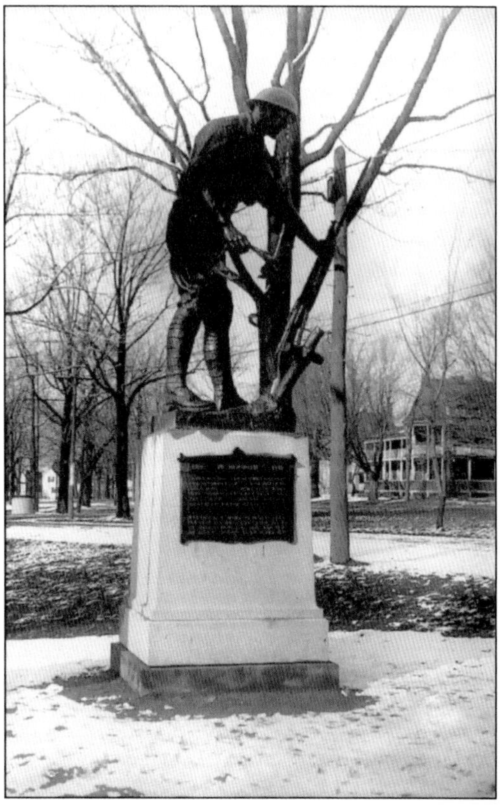

The World War I memorial was purchased and erected by the town in 1921 in memory of veterans from Templeton. The monument is located on the common.

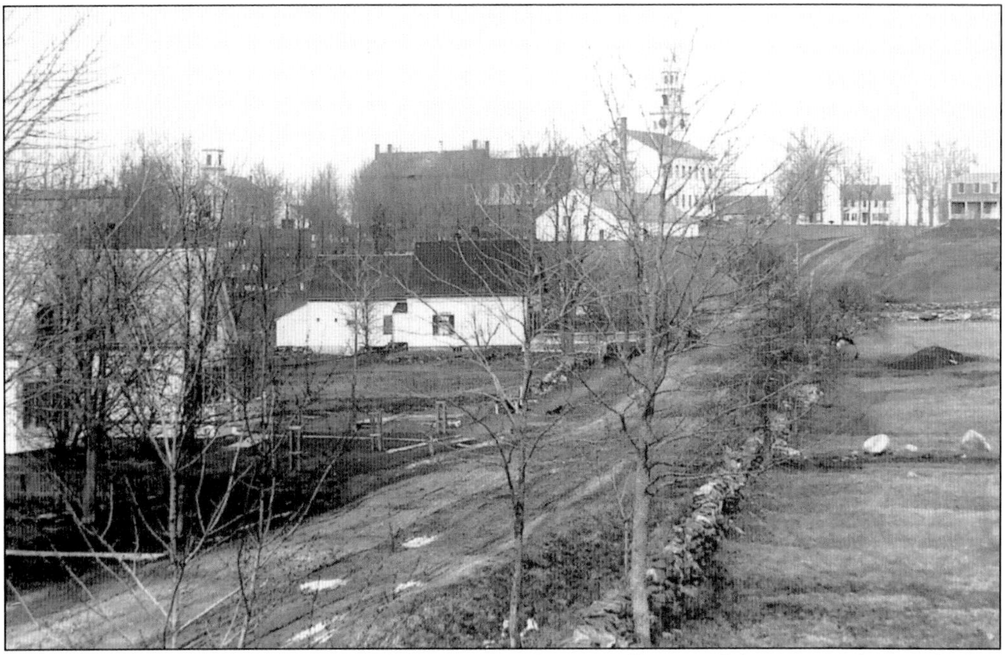

This is a view looking toward Templeton Center from Dudley Road (Route 101). On the left is the Trinitarian Church without its steeple. Shown to the far right is a house built in 1807 by Cyrus Brown. The First Church of Templeton can also be seen in the center of the photograph with the old carriage shed—which was destroyed by a fire in the early 1900s—behind it.

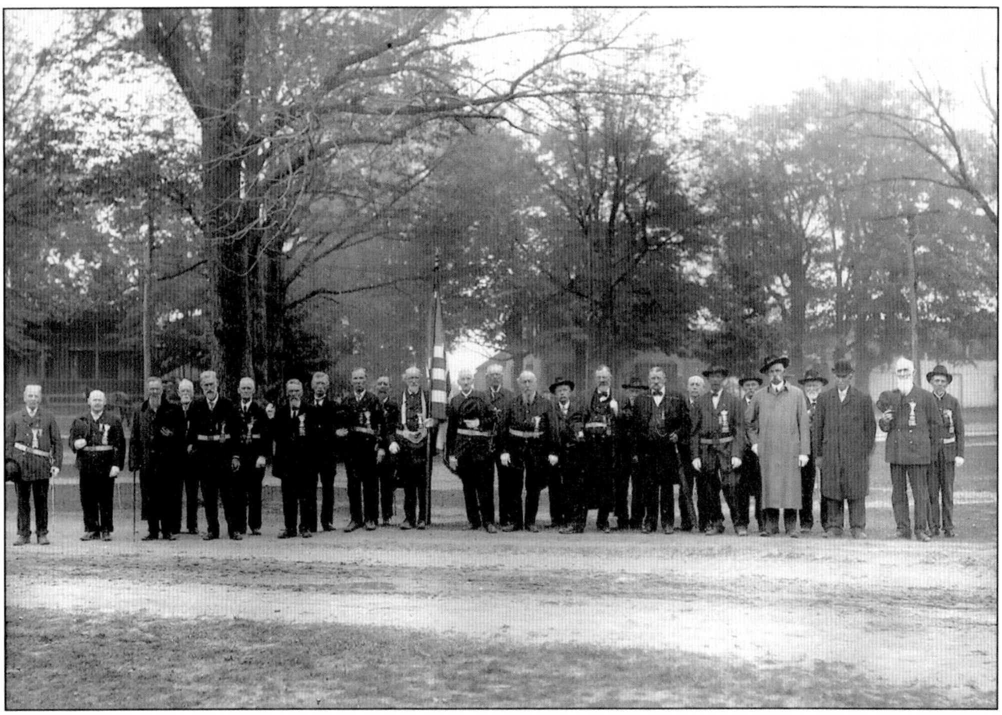

This appears to be a group of veterans (possibly the Knights of Honor) who had their hall in the Colonel Lee building. This photograph was taken on Templeton Common.

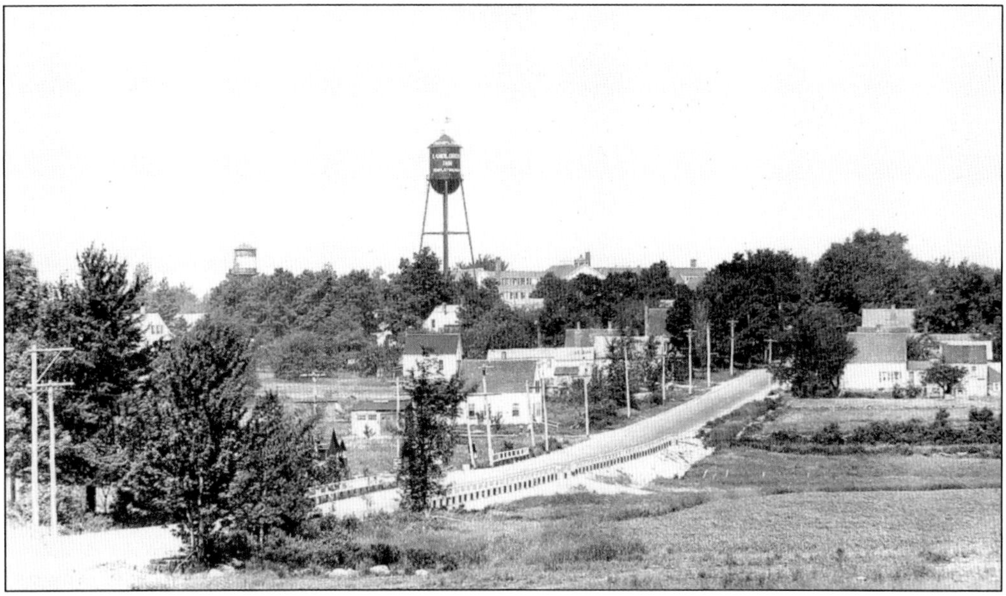

In this scene from east of the village on Route 2A, one can see the inn and the tower that provided water pressure for fire protection. The smaller wooden tank to the left was the original. The first white house on the left was the home of Girard Bushnell, a longtime town official. The Greene family now owns the home. The first house on the right is the home of the Ford family.

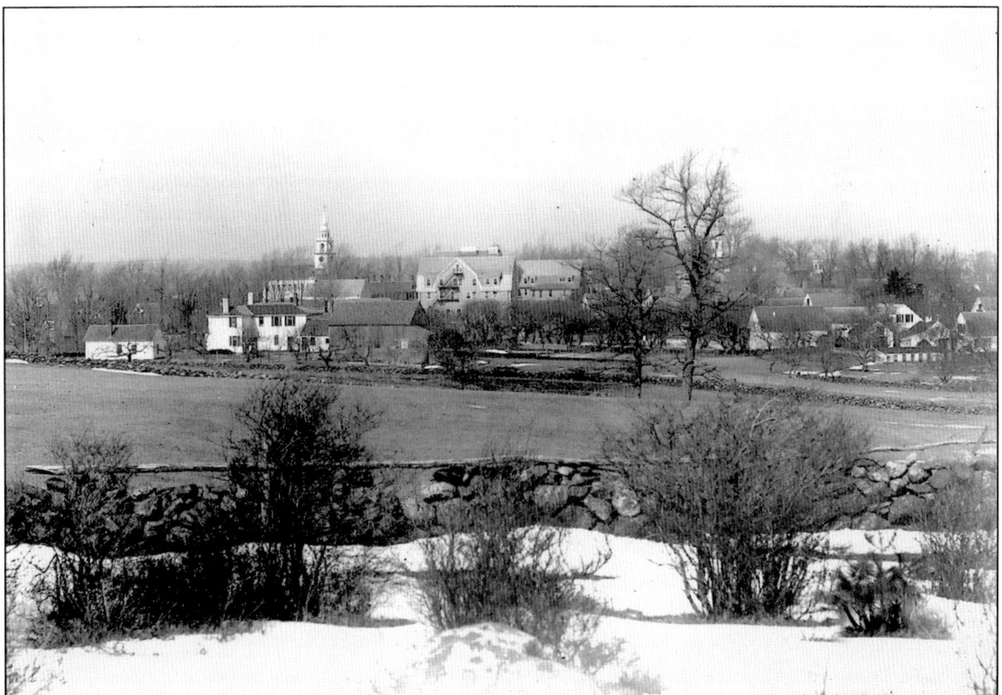

This is a view looking down into Templeton Center from the field of Isaac LaClair on South Road. The First Church and Templeton Inn are in the background.

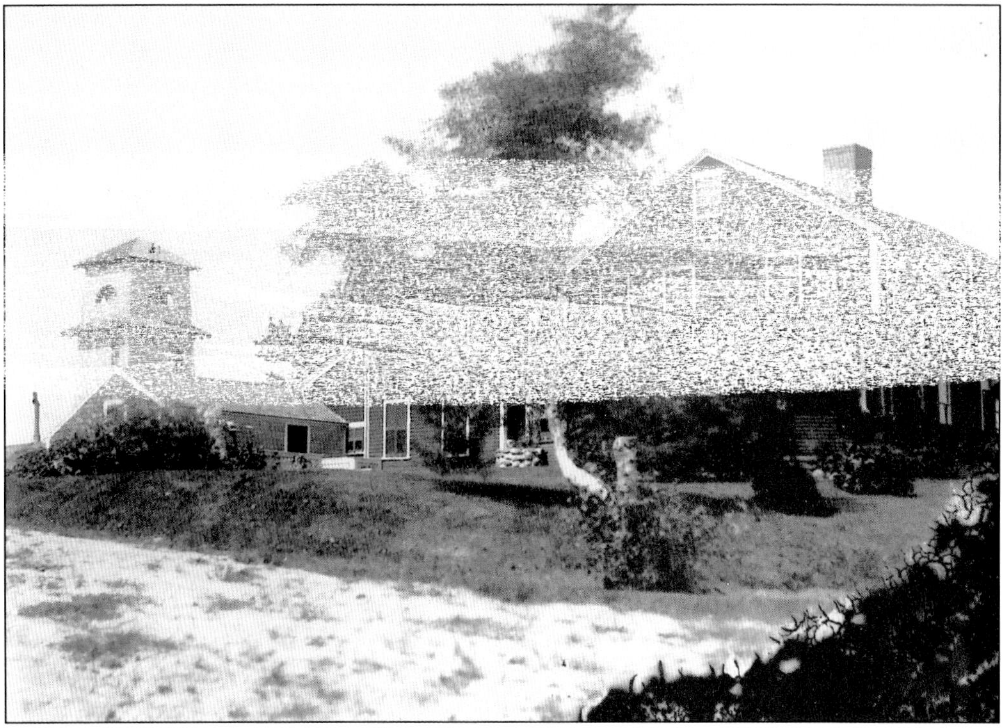

Aaron Jones kept his farm on Partridgeville Road. The tower was a tank for water storage. Built in the early 1800s, the house is now owned by the Mark Moschetti family.

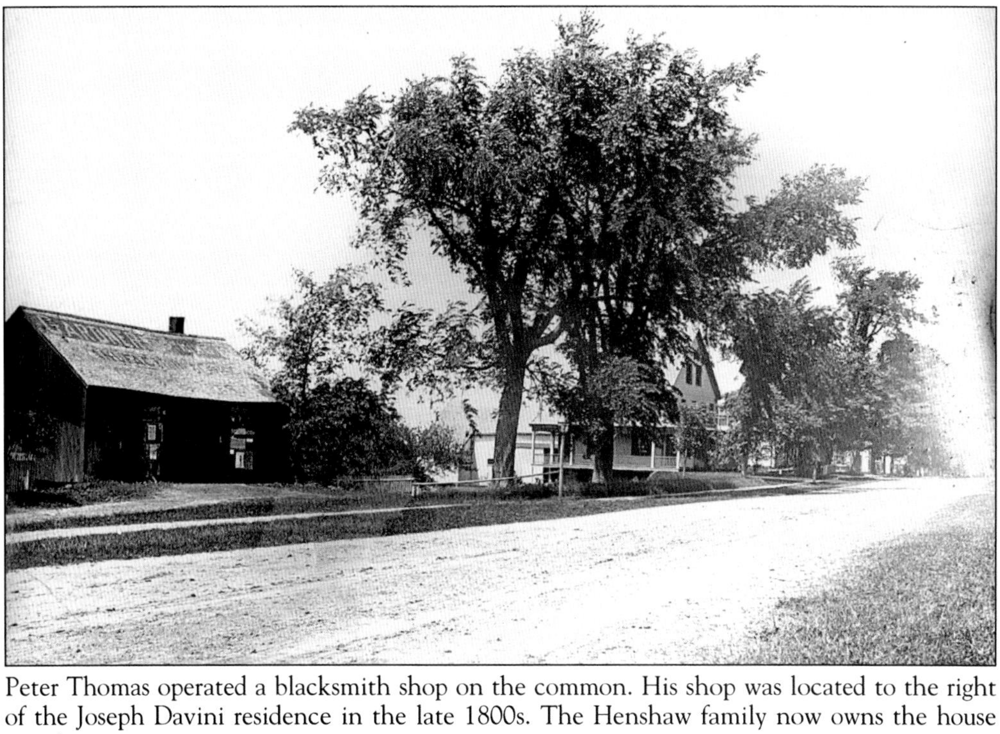

Peter Thomas operated a blacksmith shop on the common. His shop was located to the right of the Joseph Davini residence in the late 1800s. The Henshaw family now owns the house seen here.

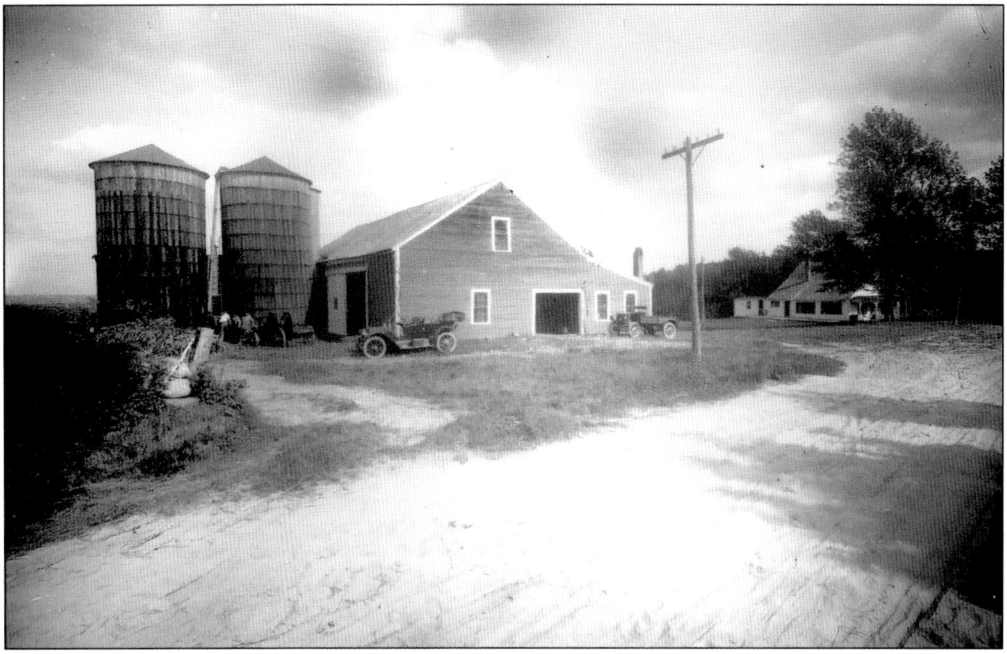

George Couillard owned this farm *c.* 1920. It was sold to Robert Young in the mid-1900s and is still in operation today. The farmhouse is featured as the first framed house in Templeton. Both of the silos and the barn are now gone. The house remains.

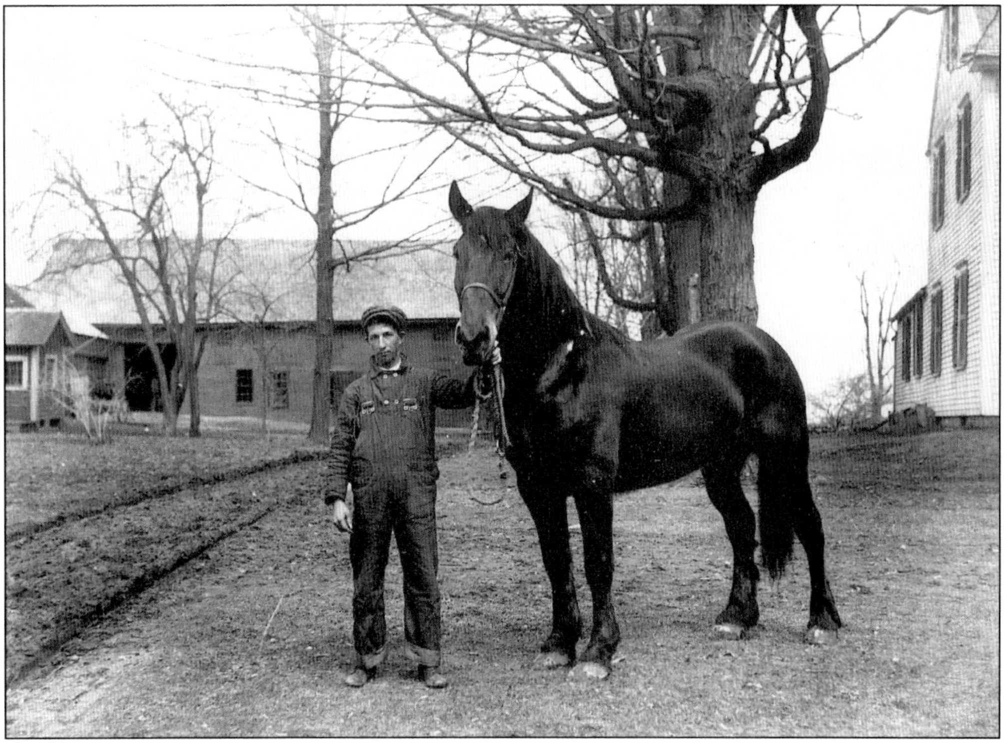

Marcus Hawkes and his horse stand in a driveway between houses that were owned by William Hawkes.

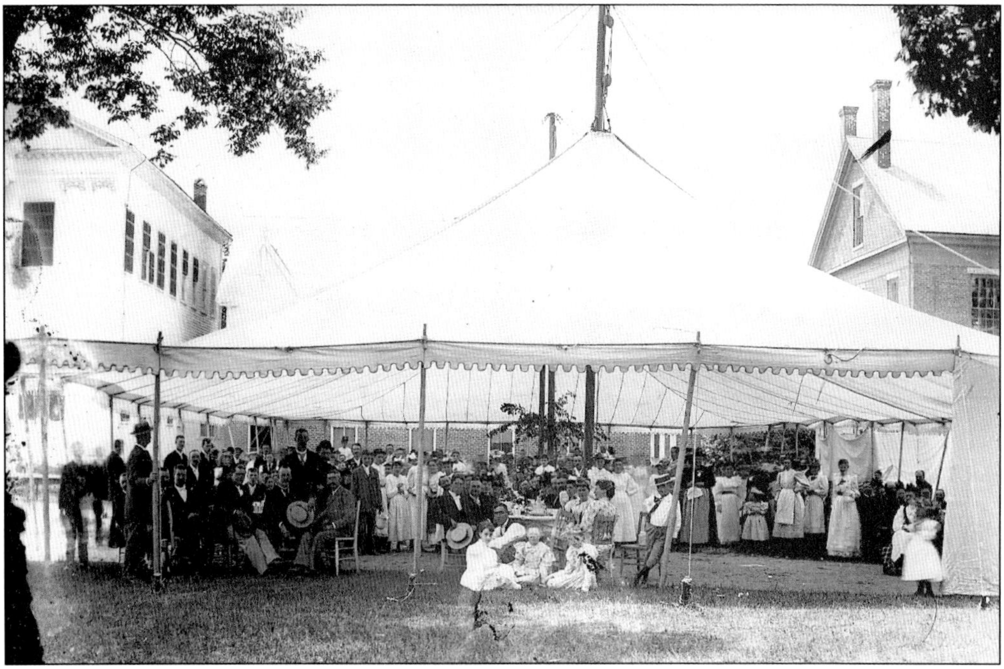

Parishioners gather in front of the First Church for their annual summer banquet. The building to the right of the tent is the old town hall and school, which was taken down in 1948. Country fairs and church functions were popular in the early 1900s, providing residents of the village an opportunity to get acquainted with others outside of the village and to swap stories with one another.

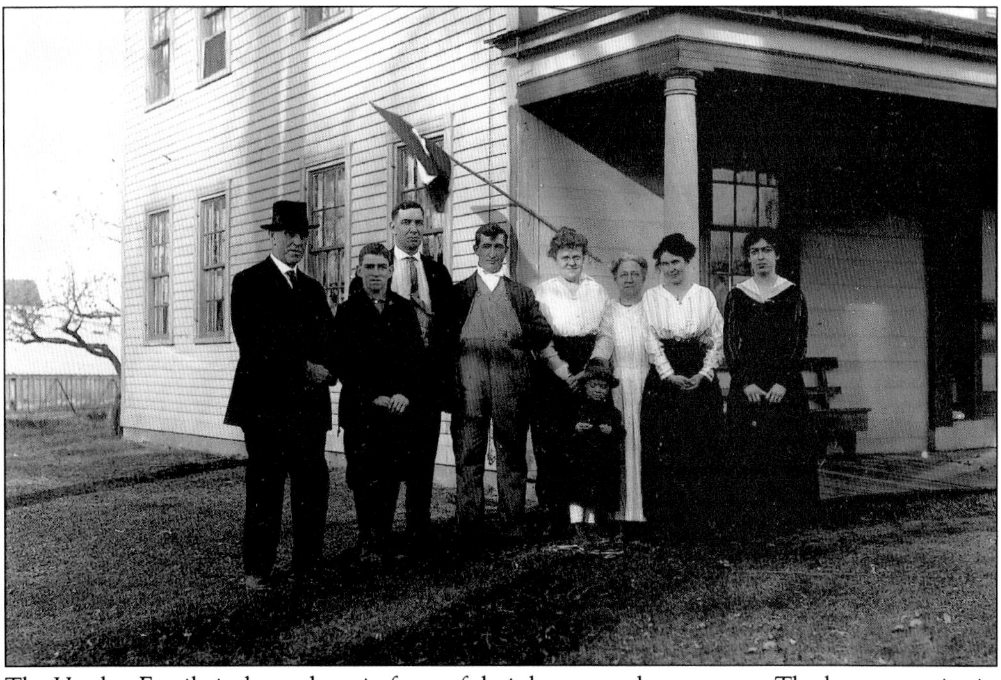

The Hawkes Family is shown here in front of their home on the common. The home remains in the same family today, owned by Michael Morgan and his wife, Adrian.

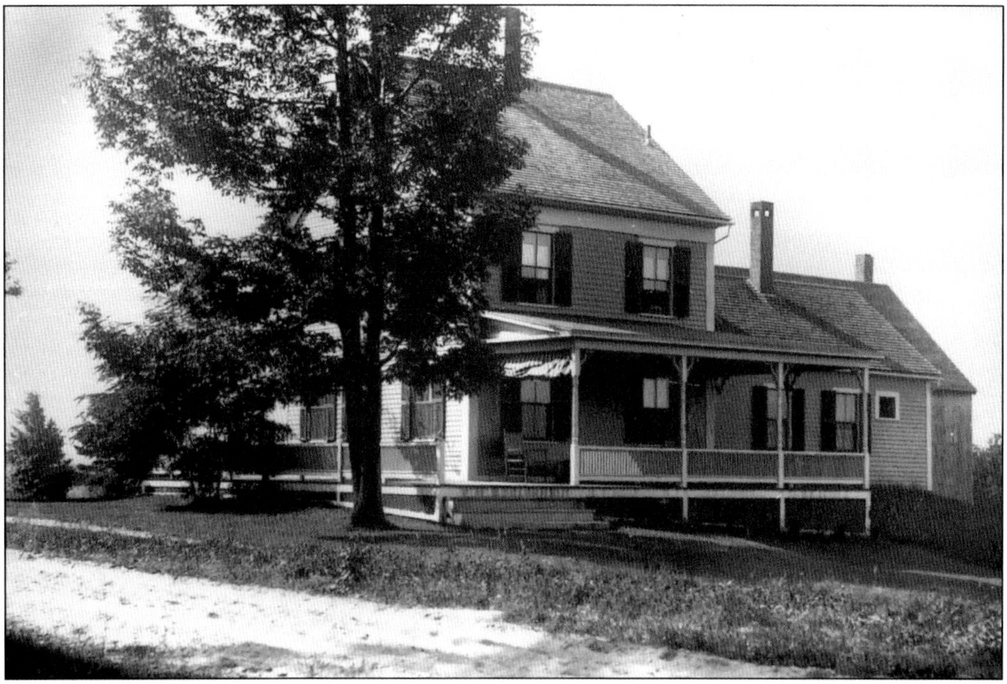

Elizabeth Wellington Lord, author of *The Story of Templeton*, once lived in this home on Baldwinville Road.

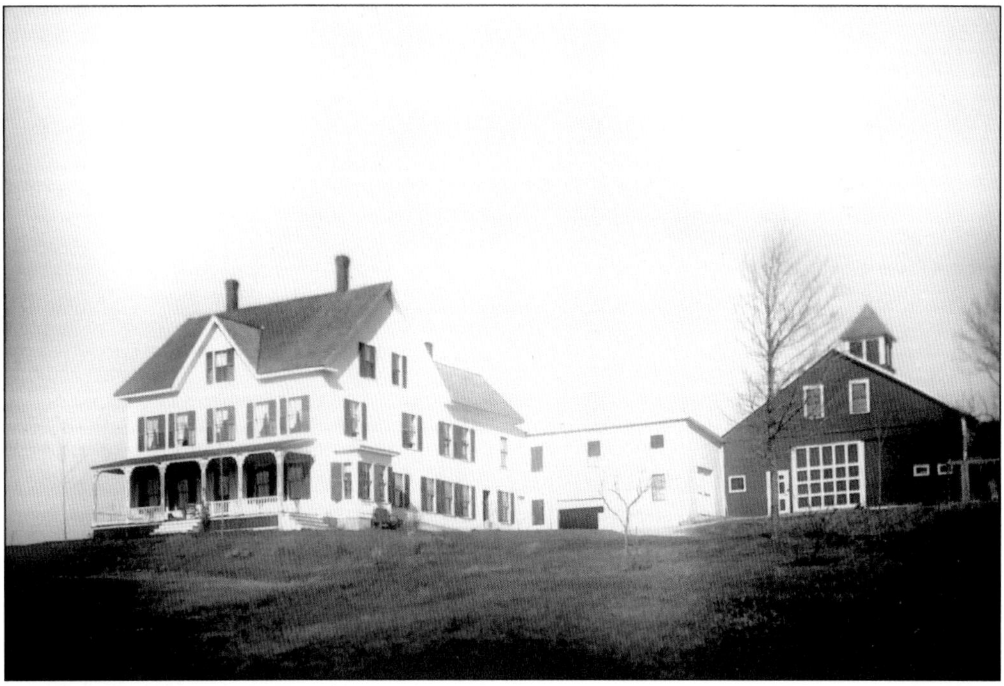

Hill Crest farm was once owned by Emil Hendrickson. It was destroyed by fire on June 19, 1916. Hendrickson rebuilt the home and later sold it to Sigfrid Johnson. Johnson's daughter and son-in-law, Arthur Carl, later owned it. Richard M. Wilson and family now own the land and home.

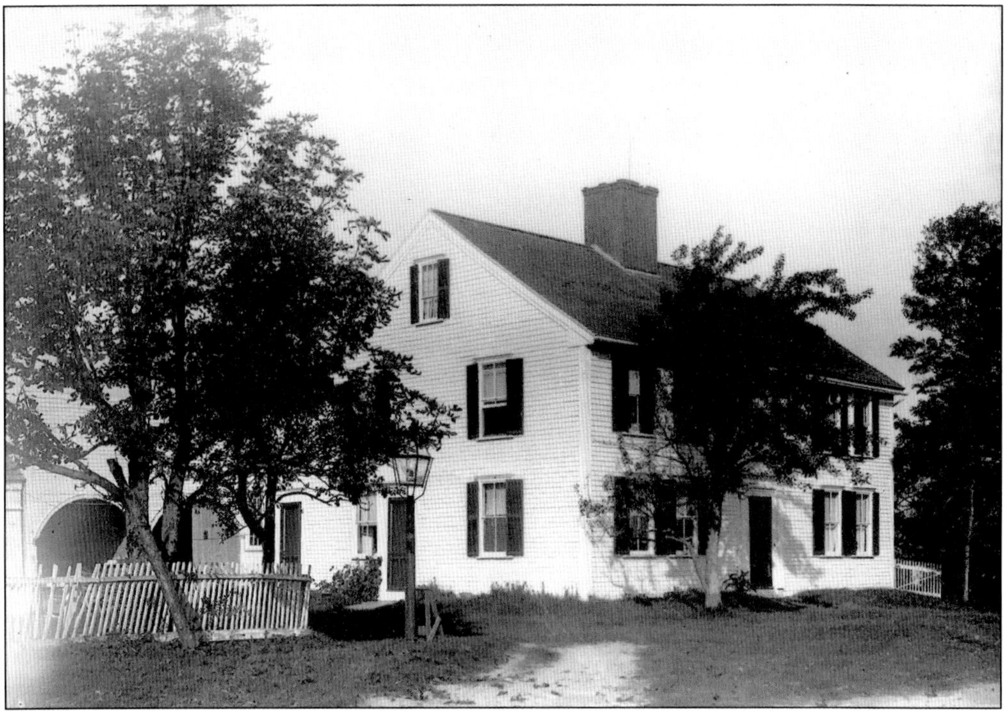

Built by Jonathan Cutting in 1790, this house on Baldwinville Road is now the home of Dr. David Bell and family.

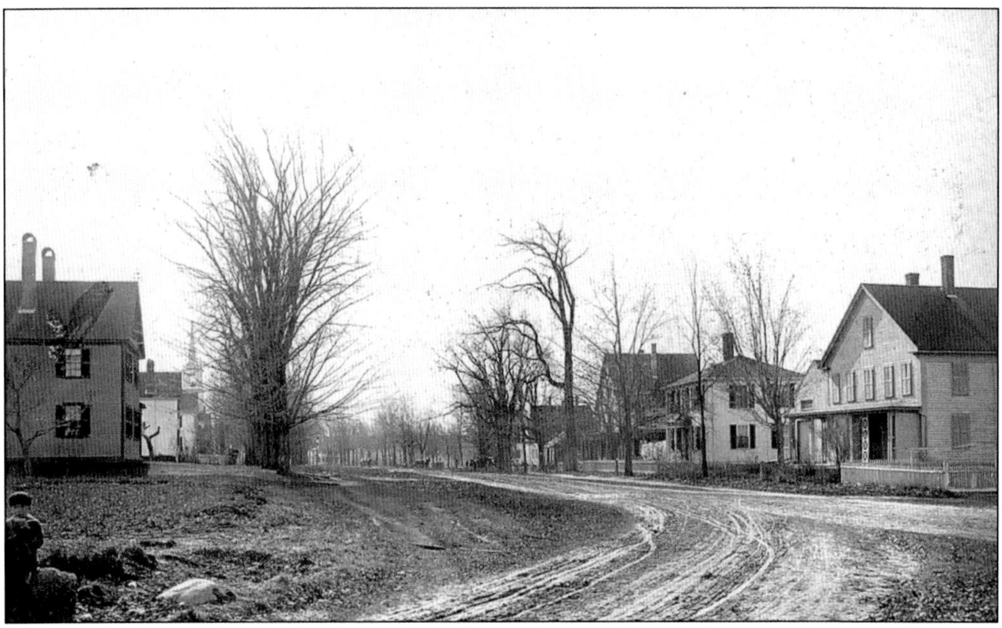

This is an early view from the intersection of Otter River Road and Baldwinville Road looking toward Templeton Center. The house on the left is that of Col. George P. Hawkes. The house on the right was originally the home of Margaret W. Stone; later it was converted into a business run by Adams Printing, and today it is known as the Country Mischief. The house next to the Stone house was the home of H. F. Lane and was taken down in the mid-1900s.

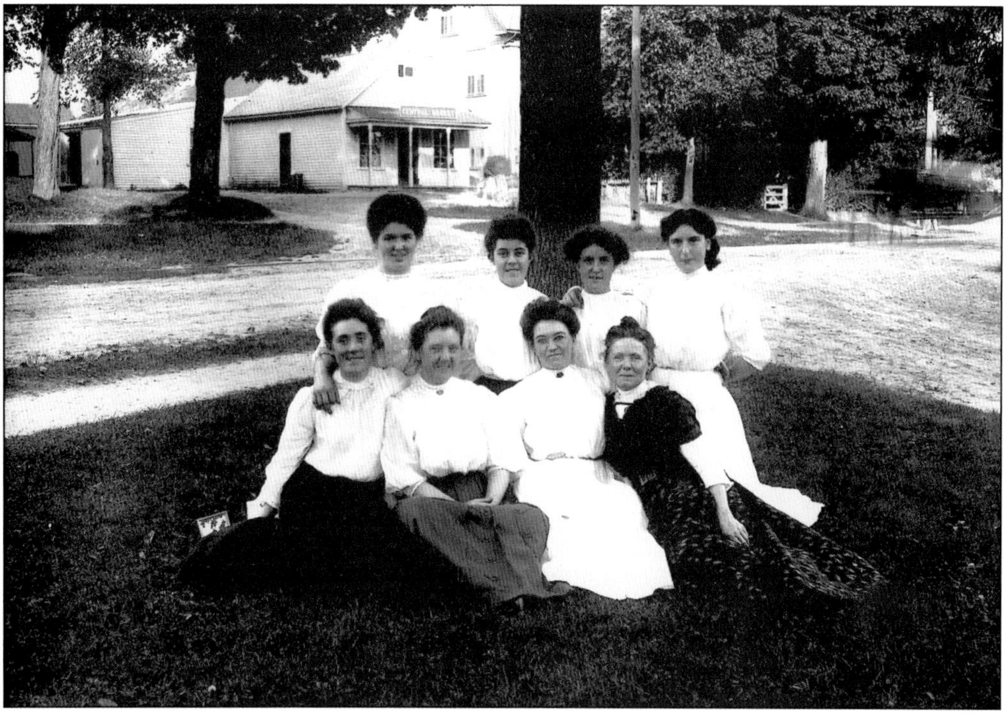

On Templeton Common, a group of ladies pose for a picture. The building in the background is the Central Market. In later years, the building became Templeton Center's post office.

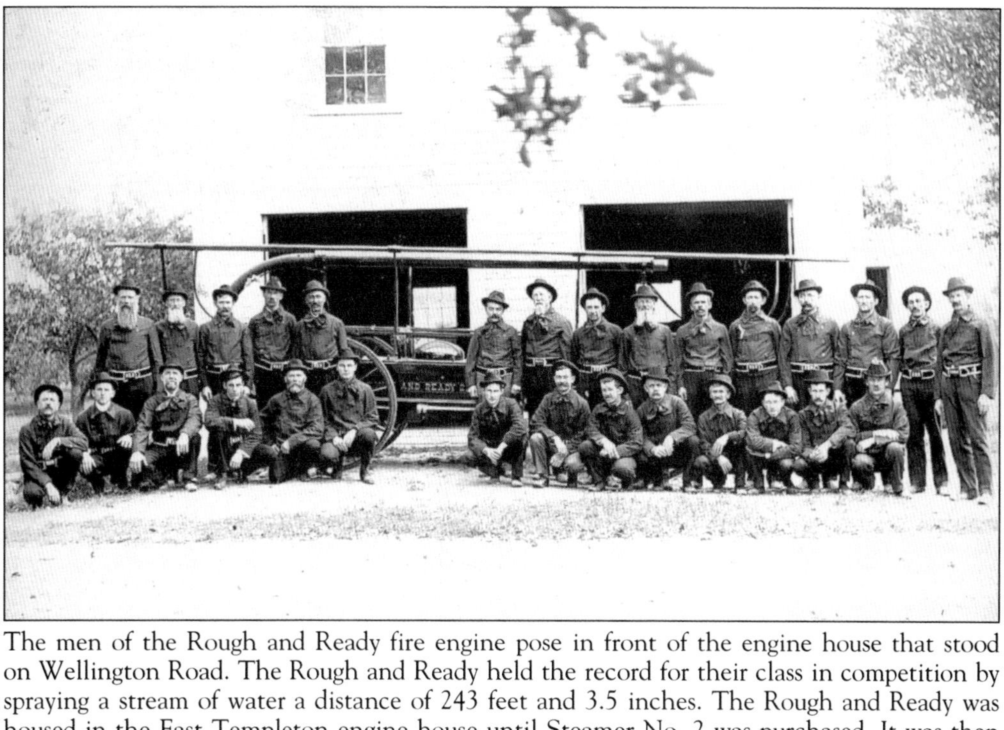

The men of the Rough and Ready fire engine pose in front of the engine house that stood on Wellington Road. The Rough and Ready held the record for their class in competition by spraying a stream of water a distance of 243 feet and 3.5 inches. The Rough and Ready was housed in the East Templeton engine house until Steamer No. 2 was purchased. It was then transferred to Templeton Center. The engine house was taken down in the 1960s.

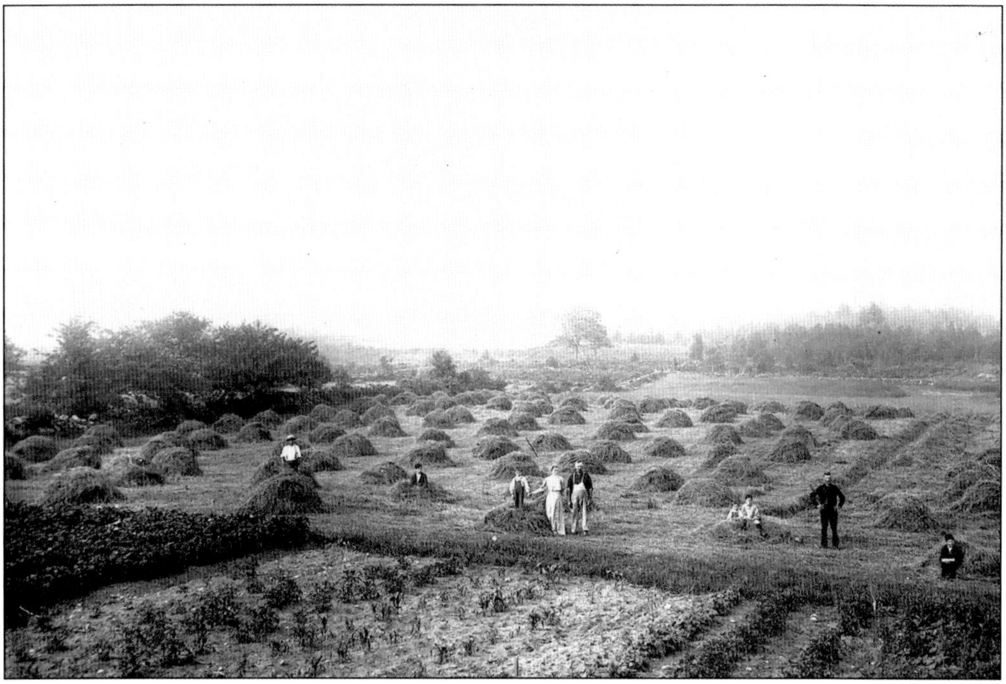

The job of harvesting hay to feed the livestock for the winter was a family operation. The hay had to be cut and raked by hand, and then loaded on the wagon with pitchforks. It was then piled in the hayloft or barn by hand. There were no machines available during this period in time. The children's job was to climb on top of the pile and pack it down to make room for more.

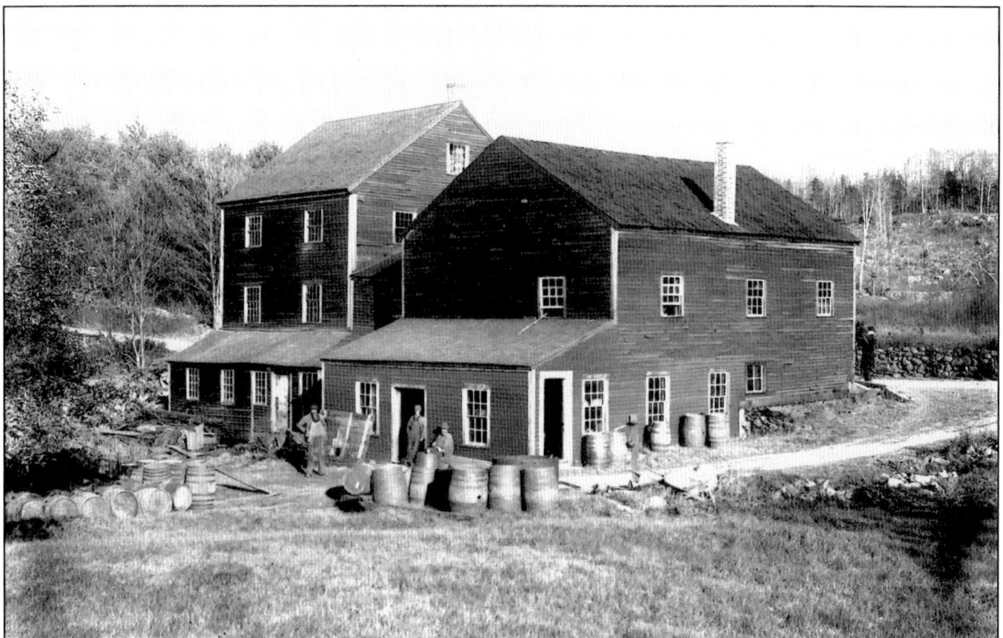

Near the Rollin Woodbury Farm, an old cider mill operated on Barre Road in the early 1900s. It was owned and operated by William and Catherine Wheeler.

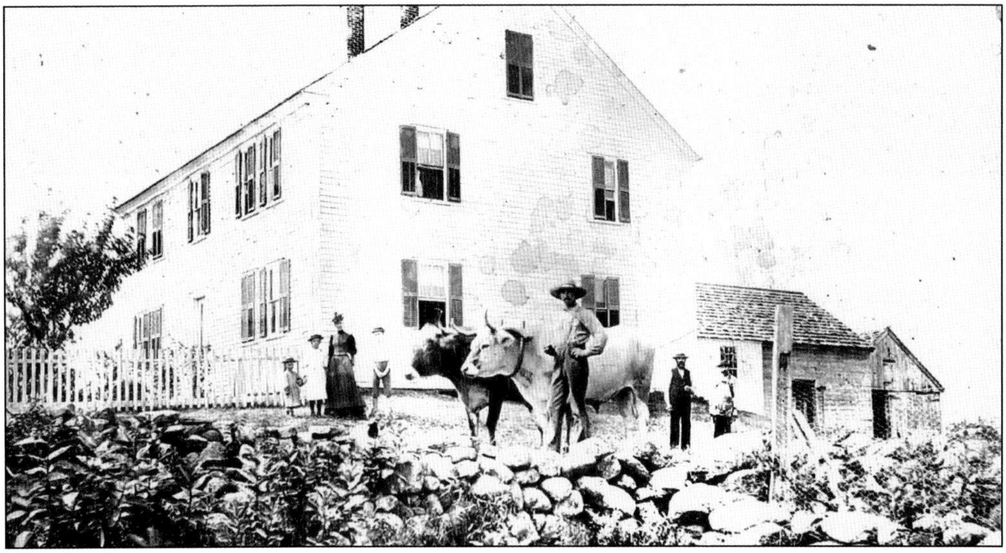

Henshaw Road, located just off Barre Road, is the location of this farm, still in the Henshaw family. This photograph dates from 1899. Behind the ox and in a vest is Josiah I. Henshaw, along with family and farm hands. This is the farm that has been used in the Civil War reenactments held over the past 5 years in the spring. To see what it was like back then, take a ride by this untouched farm. Ralph and Mildred call the farm home after putting many hours of restoration into it. The main house was built in 1810, and Josiah purchased it in 1886. Henshaw farm was known for owning the largest herd of Brown Swiss Cattle in Massachusetts.

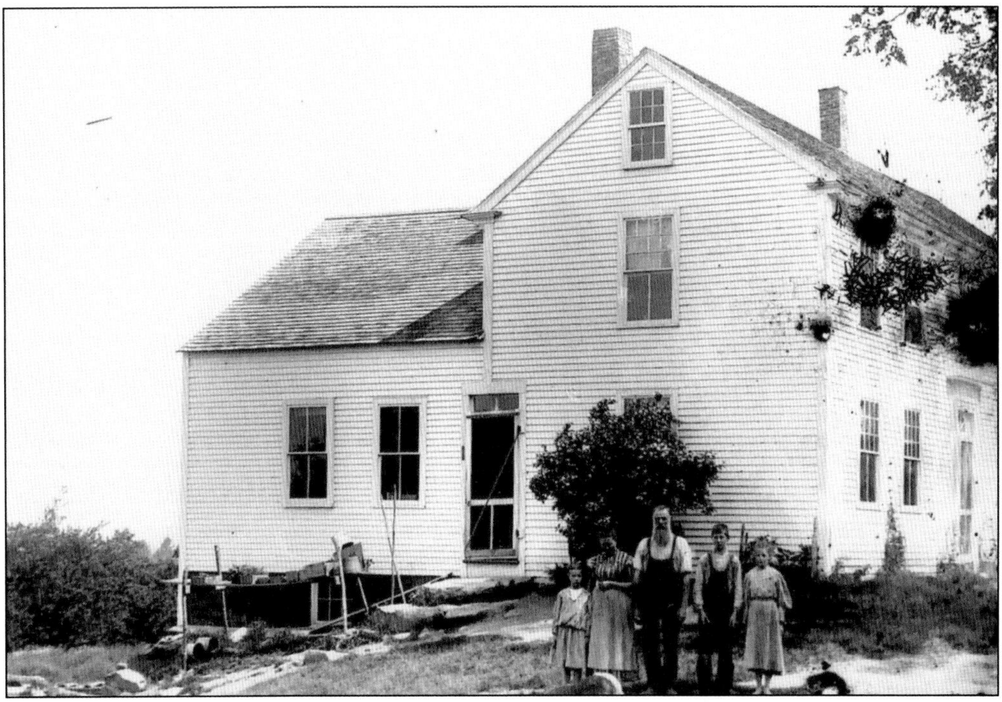

James Woodbury and family are shown here standing in front of their home on Barre Road. Roy Woodbury, on the right of his father, later owned and operated the family farm. Today, the Arthur LeClerc family owns this farm.

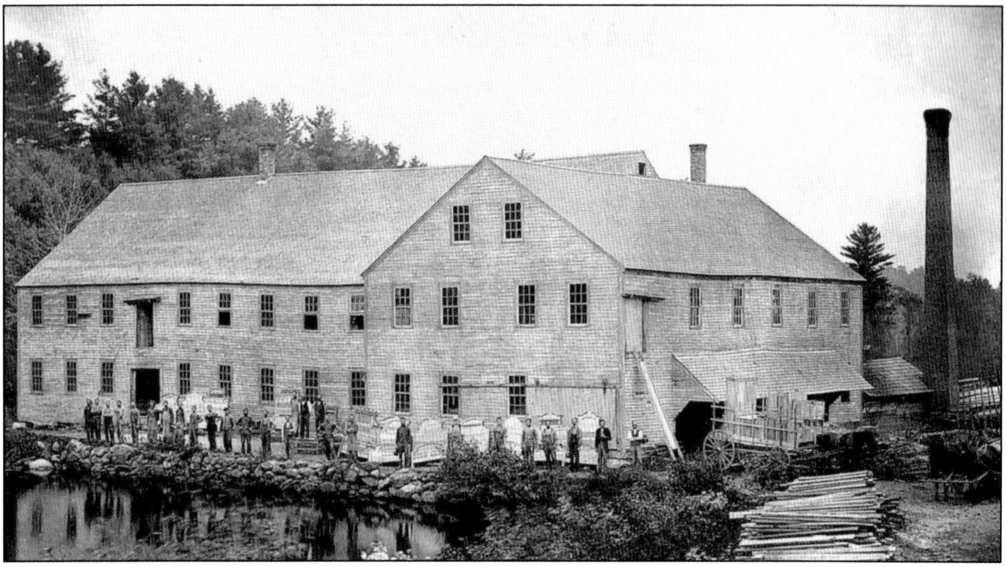

The original Bourn, Hadley, and Company factory is shown here, located in back of the Candlelight Pond near Pine Grove Cemetery. Benjamin Hawkes and his sons, George, James, and Edwin, started the factory in the early 1800s. Isaac Bourn and John Brooks operated it as the Bourn and Brooks Company until 1879, when John sold his share of the company to Lucian N. Hadley. It then became known as the Bourn, Hadley, and Company. On August 5, 1890, a fire destroyed the factory. The erection of a new factory was underway two weeks later when townspeople showed their appreciation for the value of the company and a plot of land on which to rebuild was presented.

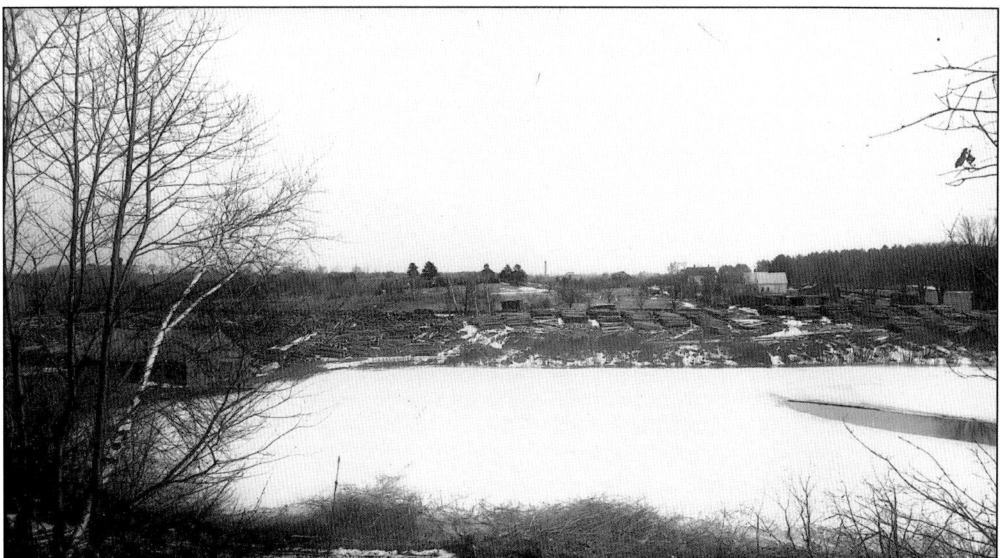

Bourn Hadley Pond was named after the company on its banks. The company used pine to make bedroom furniture. Later, they switched to chestnut, then ash, and finally oak.

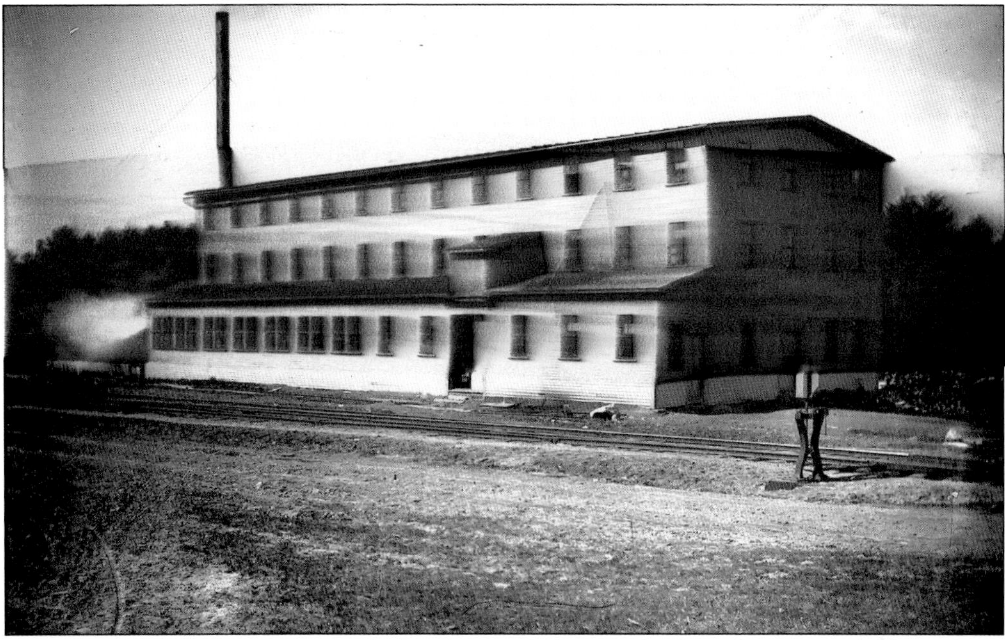

Bourn, Hadley, and Company built this factory following the fire of 1890. With the railroad track next to the building, they were able to load the cars more easily, saving time and money on horses and carts.

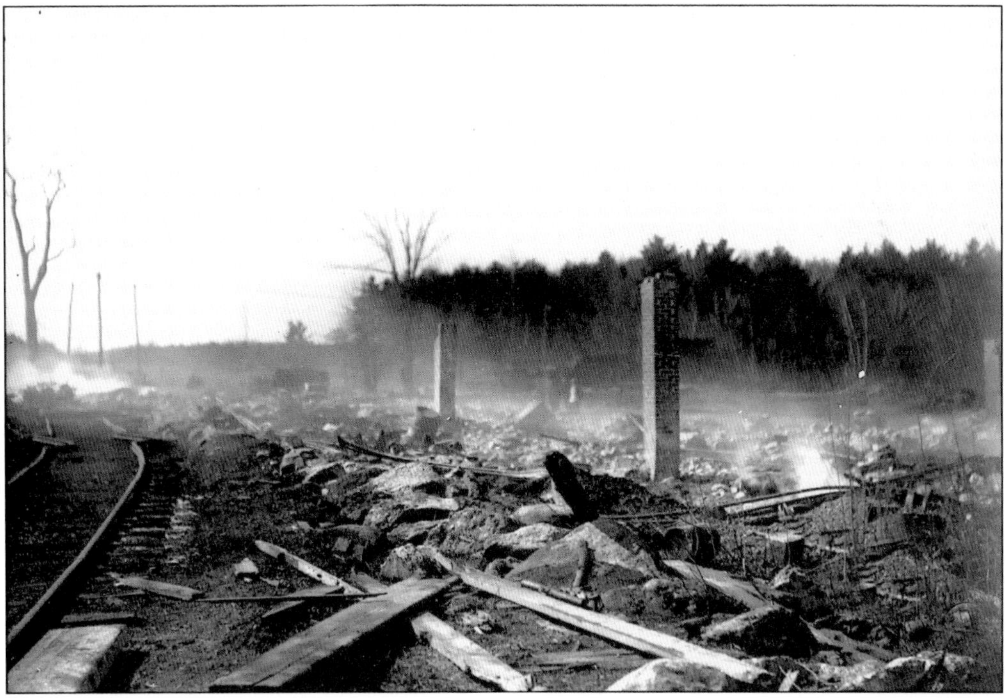

Shown here are the ruins of the Bourn, Hadley, and Company factory following its second fire in September 1903, which started from sparks of an engine passing by on the Ware River railroad tracks. In November 1903, the company sued the New York Central and Hudson River Railroad Company for $27,000 in damages resulting from the fire.

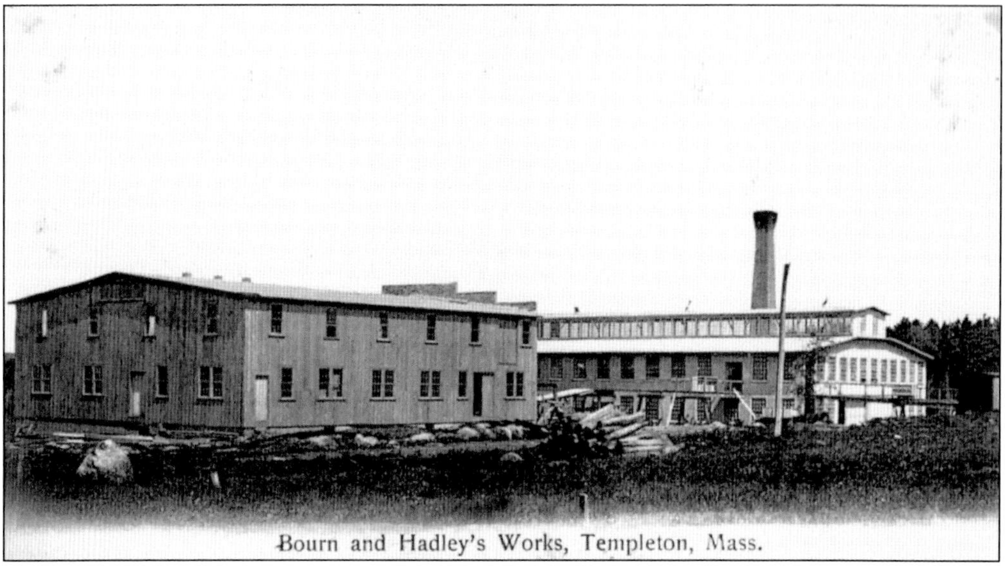

The Bourn, Hadley, and Company factory is shown here in 1929, when it was sold to the Conant Ball Company in Gardner. This is the new factory rebuilt following the 1903 fire. The Conant Ball Company operated its business here until the late 1900s, when the company closed down this Templeton plant and continued their operation in Gardner. The factory building was later taken over by the Glenwood Kitchen Company, which still manufactures kitchen cabinets.

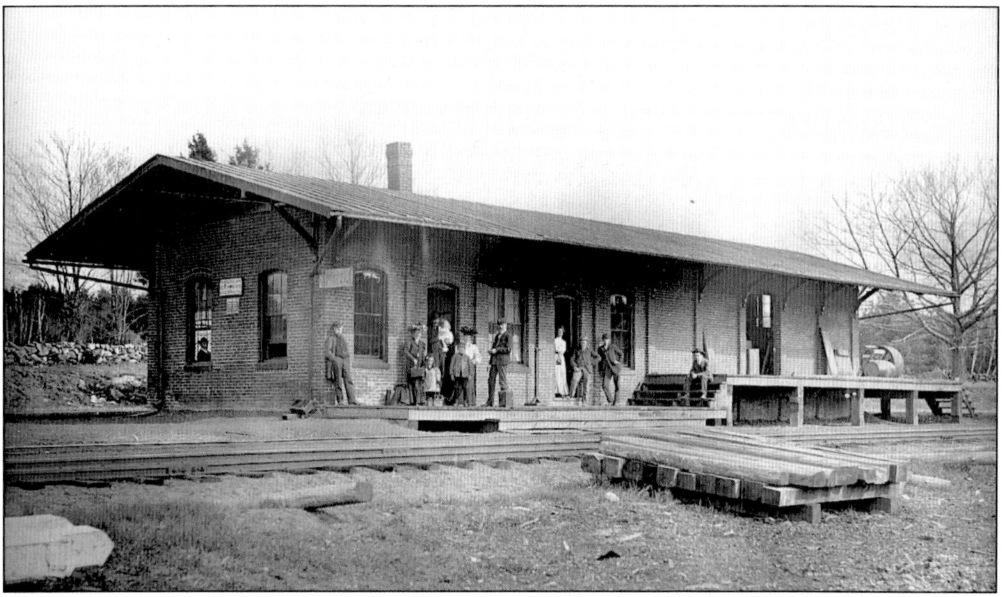

The Ware River Railroad Freight Station was located off Patriots Road in the area of the former Conant Ball Company. Serving the industry in Templeton and East Templeton, the railroad started running through this area in 1873. The railroad tracks were removed in the 1960s, and the station was abandoned. It was used briefly by the R. T. Curtis Company as a terminal for ready-mix concrete and later taken down in 2002.

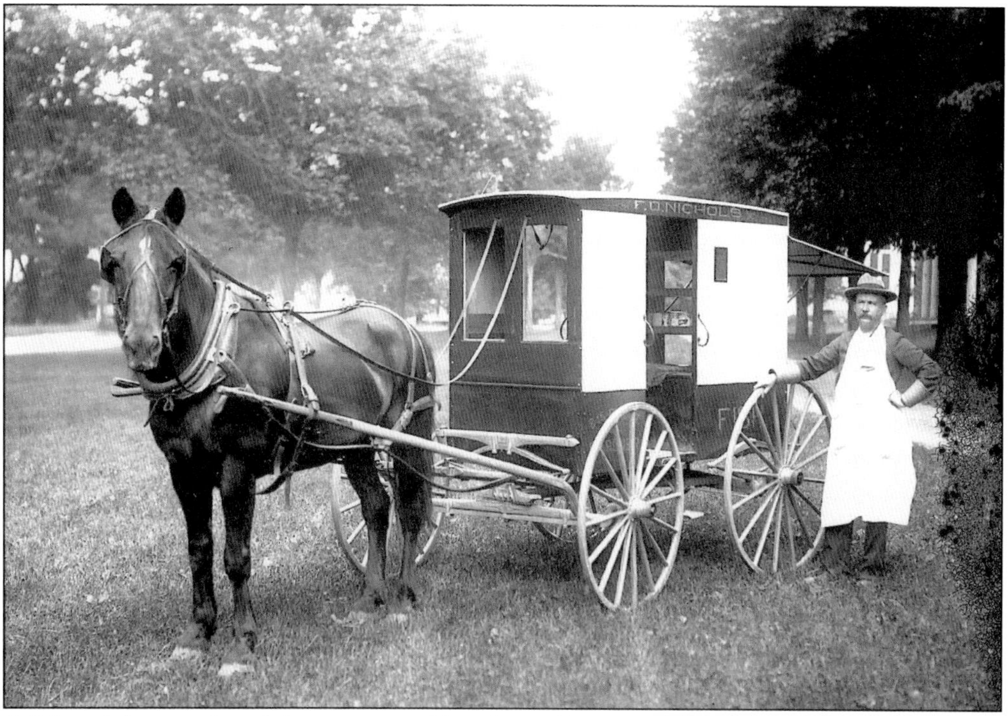

A fish peddler stands with his wagon on Templeton Common. The name on the wagon is F. O. Nichols and it is assumed that this gentleman is Mr. Nichols.

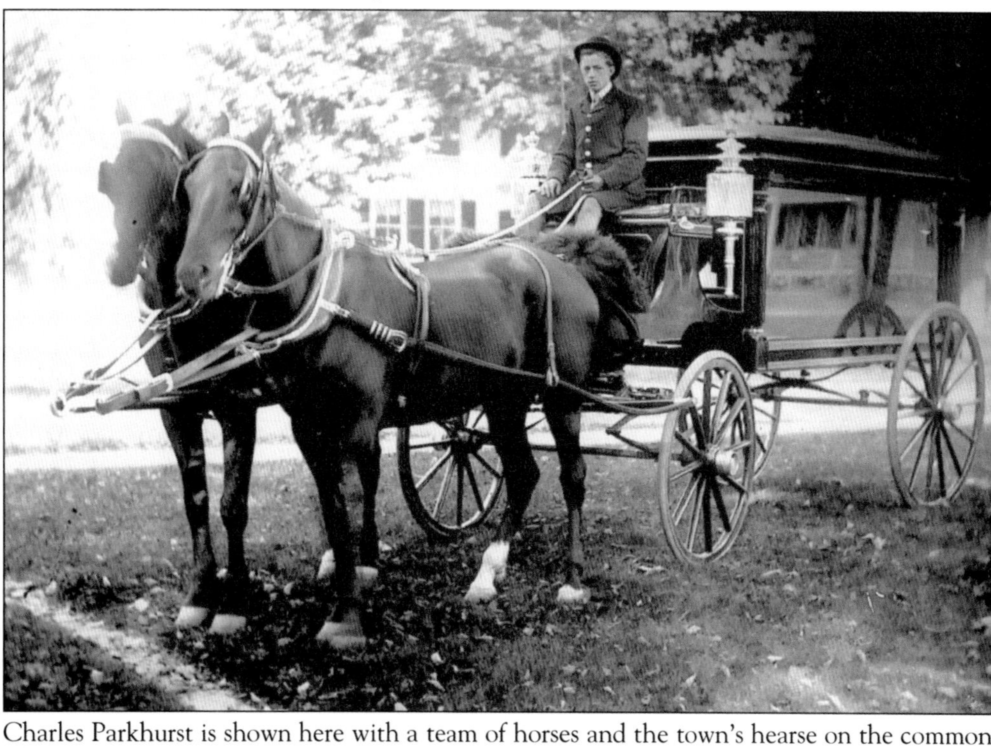

Charles Parkhurst is shown here with a team of horses and the town's hearse on the common. The hearse was stored under the town hall and school.

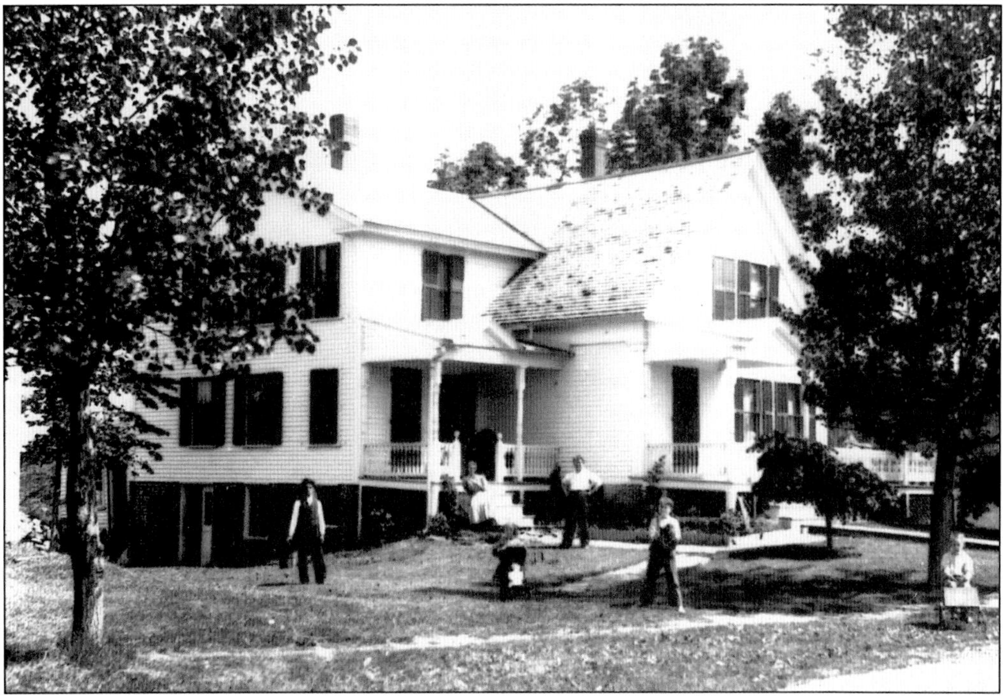

Robert T. Bourn and family lived here in 1905. The boys are playing in the yard, while Carrie E. Bourn takes a break from her duties and enjoys a sunny day. Today, John Quarella and his wife, Eleanor, own the property.

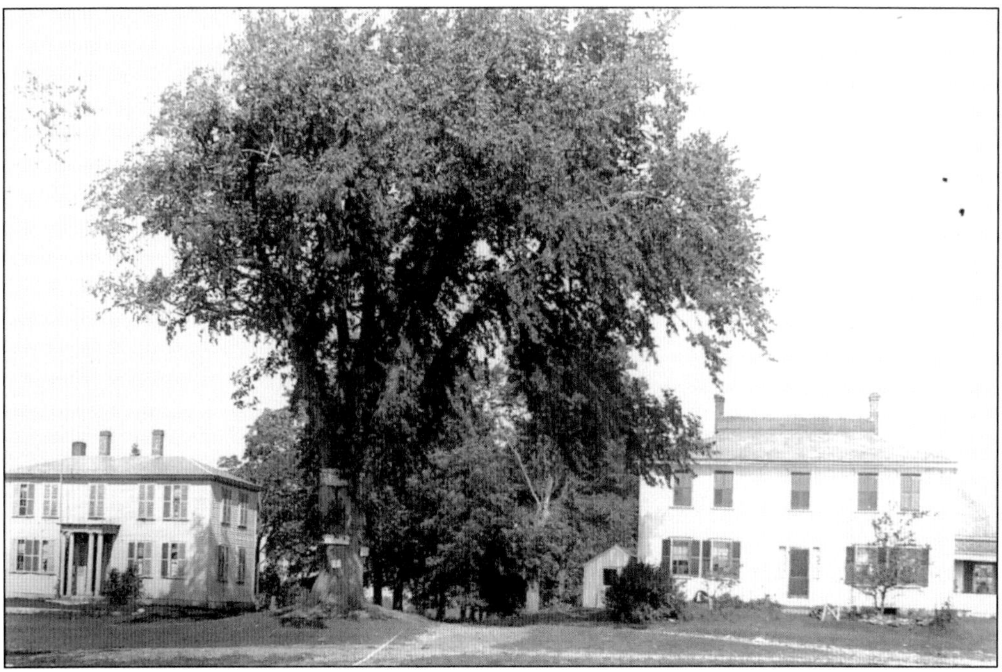

On the right is John Brooks tavern, located in Brooks Village Center. Originally built by Isaac Bourn, the tavern was a stop for stagecoaches. D. W. Spear owned the house to the left, and it stands today. The tavern is gone.

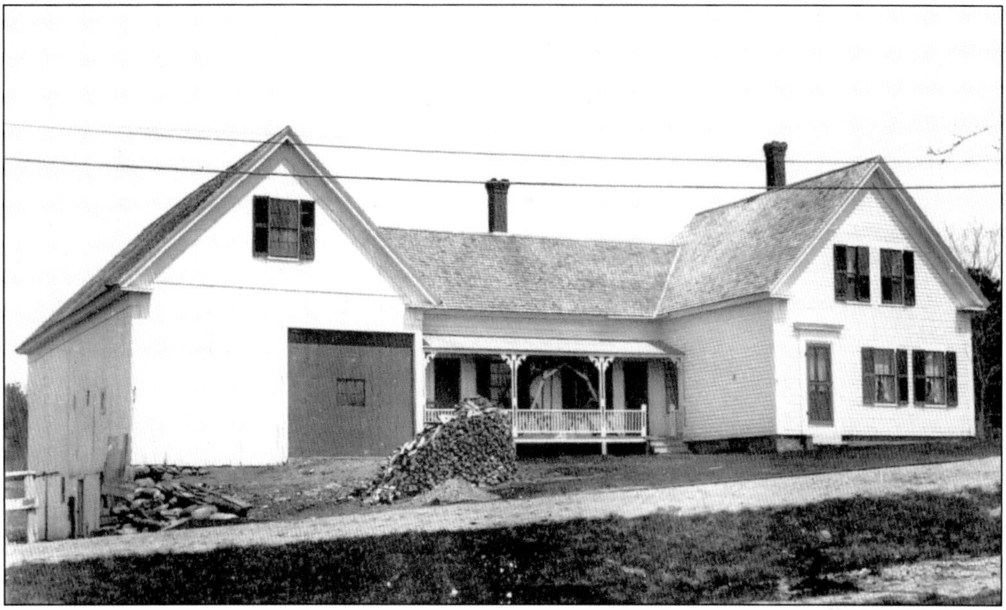

This house, located at 569 Patriots Road, was built *c.* 1870. It was the home of Edwin Brooks, a timber cruiser and buyer for the firm of Bourn and Brooks, which became Bourn, Hadley, and Company and later Conant Ball Company. For many years, it was the home of William Haley and his wife, Dorothy.

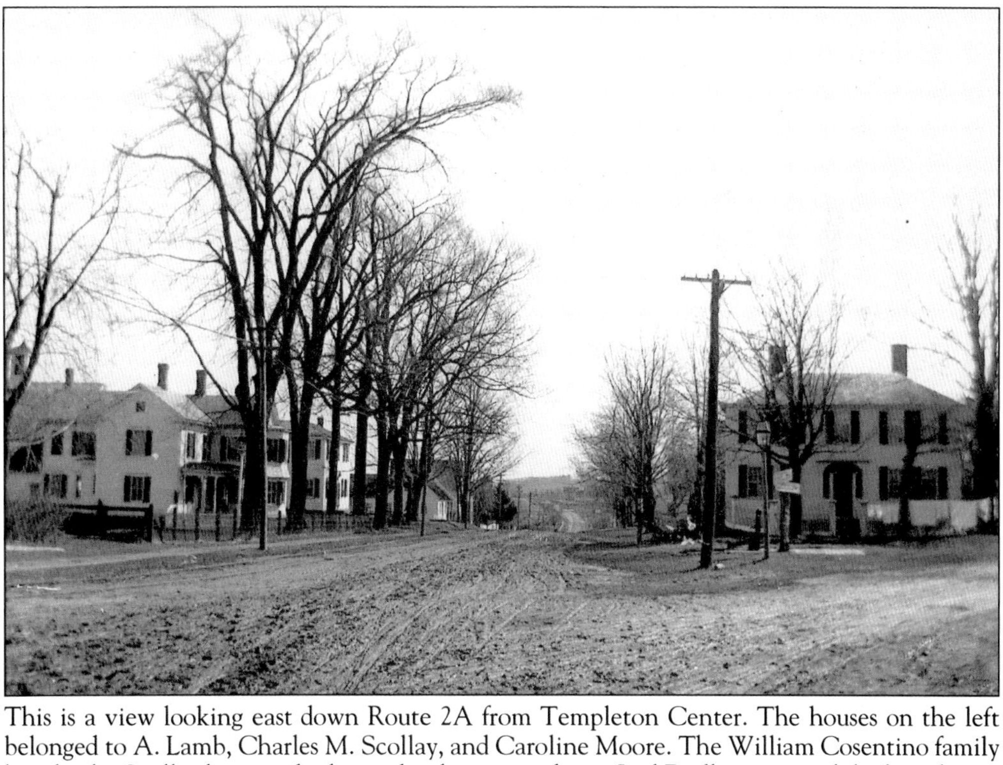

This is a view looking east down Route 2A from Templeton Center. The houses on the left belonged to A. Lamb, Charles M. Scollay, and Caroline Moore. The William Cosentino family bought the Scollay house, which now has been torn down. Joel Dudley occupied the large house at the intersection.

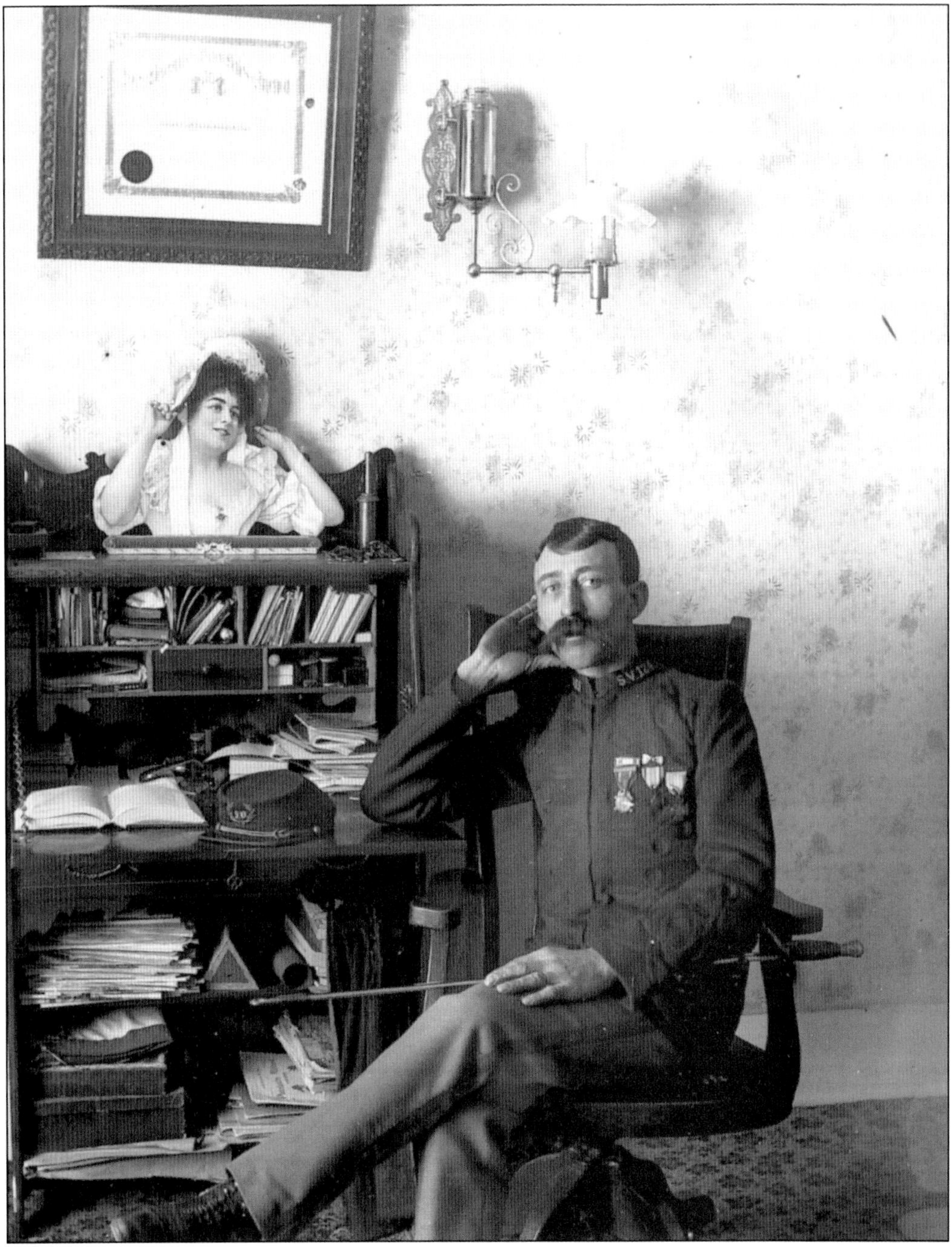

The following chapter is dedicated to Oren R. Williams, photographer, woodworker, fireman, Spanish-American War veteran, tax collector, and town clerk. Shown here at his writing desk, Oren spent many hours taking pictures of Baldwinville and Templeton. Half of the glass-plate negatives are stored in the historical building. Brian P. Tanguay has a private collection of 200 plates that were recovered from an estate sale in Fitchburg. Included in the collection was the original camera used by Oren. To complete Oren's original collection, 55 glass plates were found in the basement of Dr. Louis Fletcher's home. All of these images are now on display in the historical society; the best were picked for this chapter.

Two

BALDWINVILLE

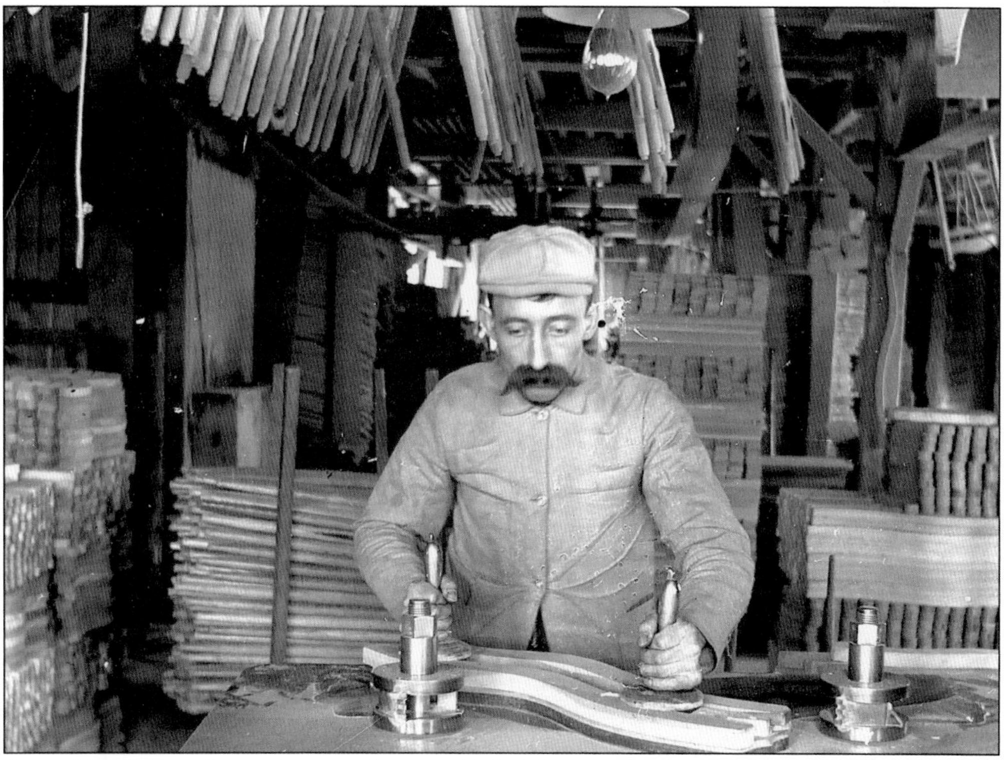

Oren Williams is shown here working at E. L. Thompson Chair Company, below the dam in Baldwinville. This photographer moved to the other side of the camera for a rare picture, probably taken by his brother. Oren Williams left this job and continued as a woodworker for the Waite Chair Company while he was the chief engineer at the Baldwinville fire department. In 1923, Oren replaced Dr. C. A. Fletcher as town clerk.

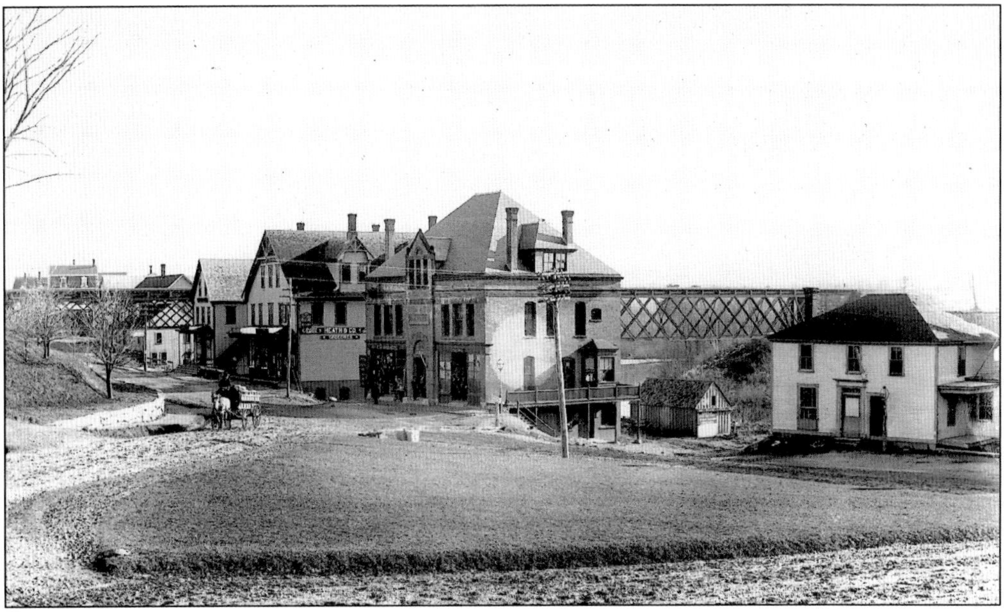

This is a view of Central Street from Memorial Street, looking at the Bank Building before fire destroyed its third floor. The Odd Fellows used the top floor for their meetings. To the left of the Bank Building is the Cady Block. At this time, the Cady Block was rented to Heath and Company, which sold boots, shoes, and groceries. Upstairs in the building was a real estate and insurance company. At one time, a pool hall was located on the third floor of the building.

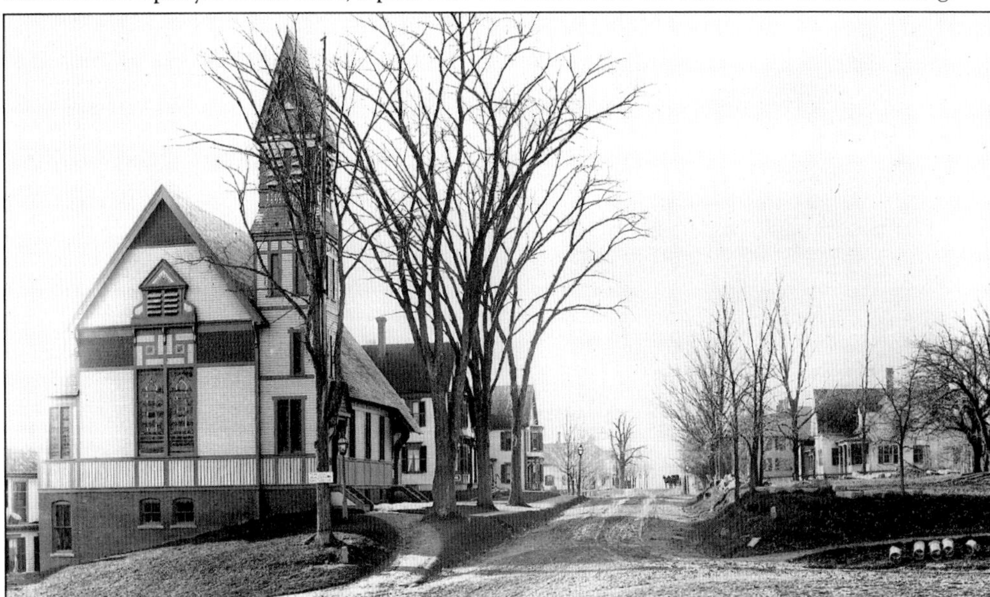

This is an image of the First Congregational Church, located on the corner of Elm Street and Memorial Street. Many factory owners of this time lived on this street. Behind the church is L. O. Day's residence. Across the street is E. L. Thompson's home. Dr. L. Baker lived next to his father Rev. W. Baker. One of the last houses on the left side was owned by H. M. Small. Memorial Street at the time of this picture continued all the way down to the river and crossed over to Maple Street.

The Baptist Church is shown here in its present location on the corner of Pleasant Street and Route 202 (across from Cumberland Farms). Originally built on the corner of Baptist Common and Baldwinville Road in 1799, the church was first moved to a site presented by Capt. Eden Baldwin and owned by Joshua Hosmer between Baldwinville and Otter River on Old Gardner Road. This site proved inconvenient, however, and the church was moved again to its present location in Baldwinville. A spire was added to the church, and its interior was refurbished in 1869. Later, the people of the village gave the church a clock for its tower. Between 1879 and 1880, a chapel was added by the Ladies Social Union, which had formed in 1867. The spire on the church was destroyed by the 1938 hurricane. It was never replaced, although a clock dial was saved and installed in the front of the church.

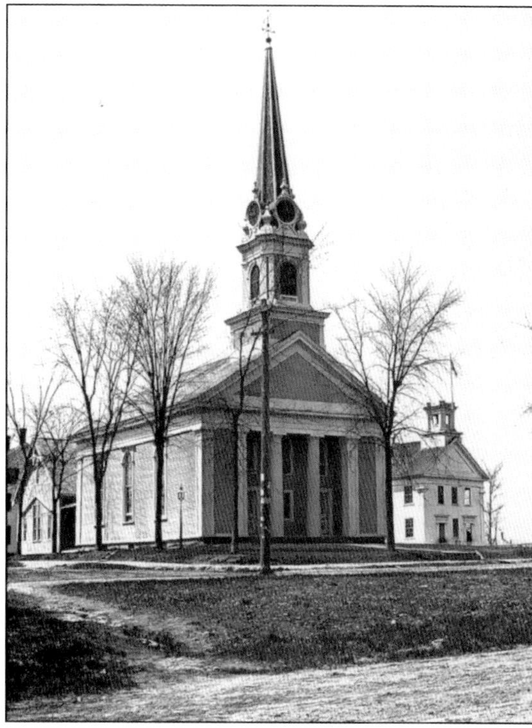

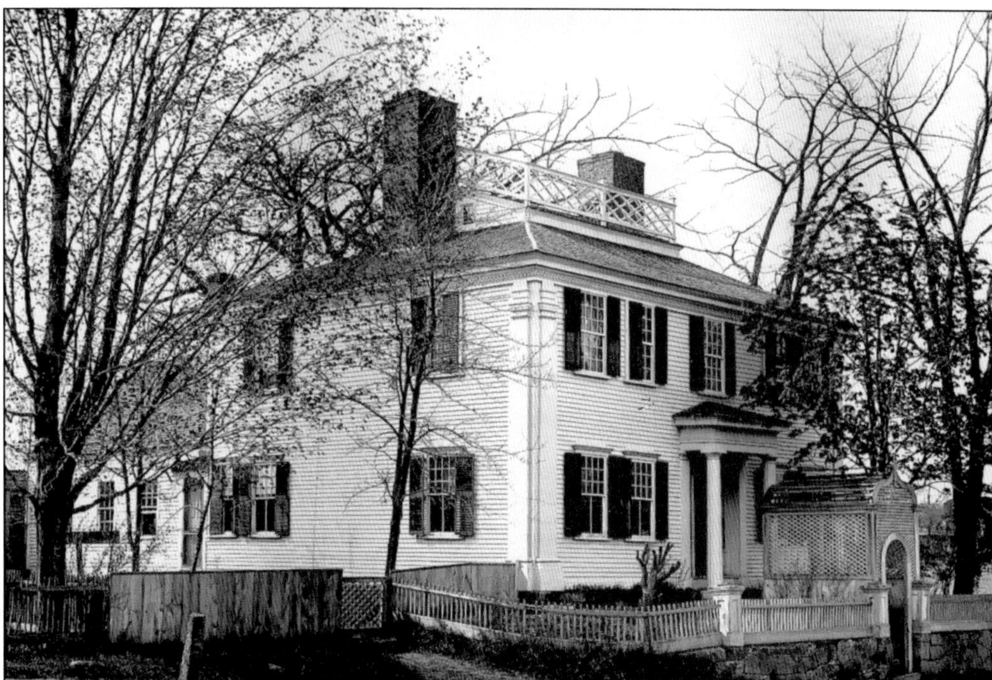

The oldest framed house in Baldwinville is located on the corner of Maple and South Main Street (now Baldwinville Road and Route 202). Built in 1797 by Eden Baldwin, the home was the birthplace of Eden's son Christopher Columbus Baldwin in 1800. Christopher Baldwin became well known in the state as a lawyer and historian.

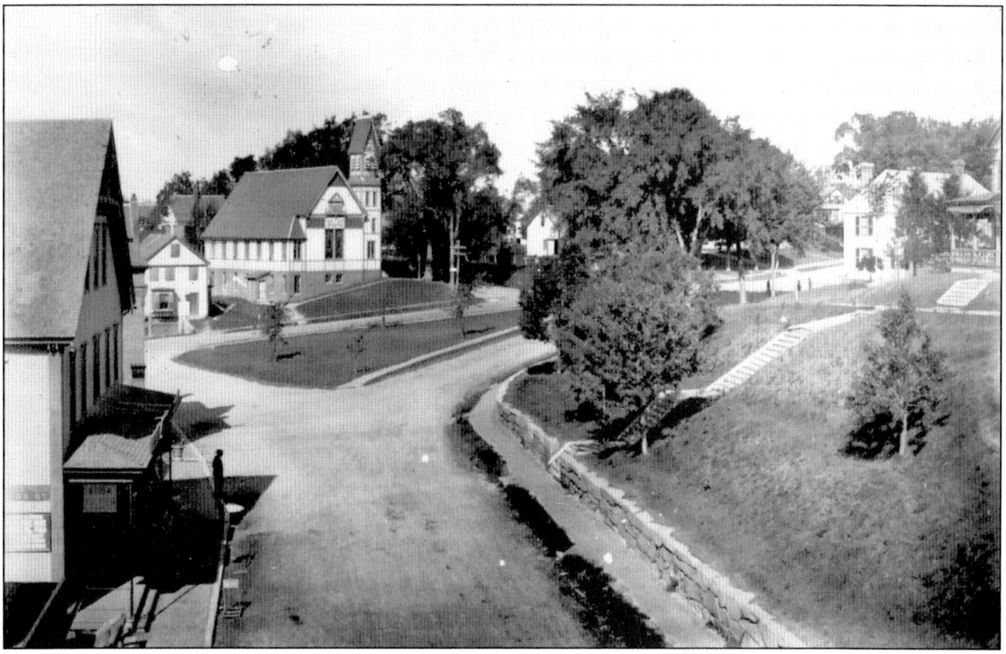

This view is looking down at Baldwinville from the trestle of the Ware River Railroad. To the left is the Cady Block; to the right are stairs leading to C. A. Perley's house and greenhouses. Perley was known for his cucumber houses and being the son of the well-known manufacturer Charles A. Perley of Thompson, Perley, and Waite.

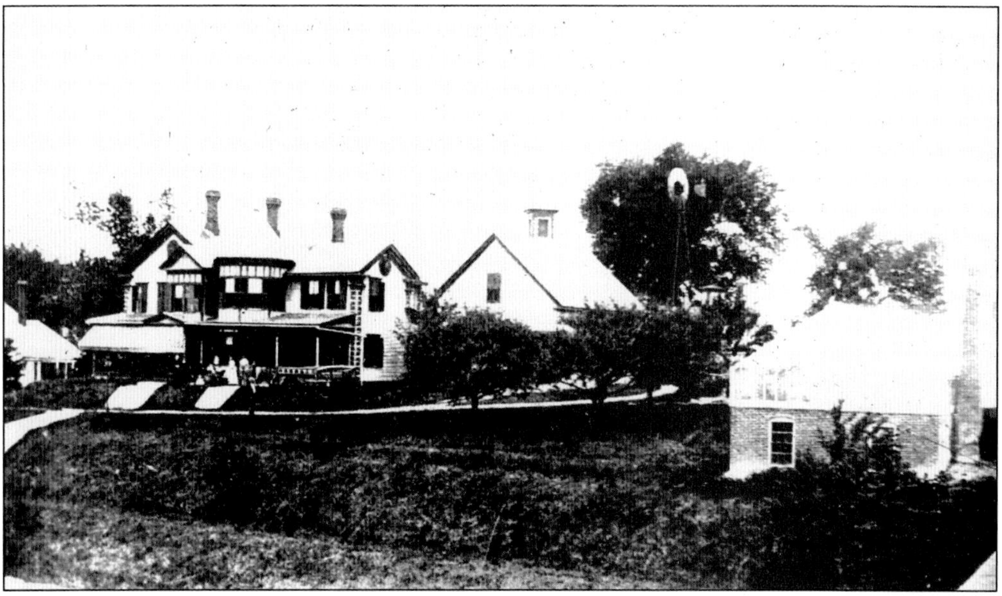

Charles A. Perley's home overlooks Central Street. C. A. Perley was born in Gardner on September 15, 1826. He was in the chair manufacturing business in Baldwinville; he was a member of the firm Baker, Sawyer, Thompson, and Perley. The company was later renamed Thompson, Perley, and Waite. He was the president of the Templeton Savings Bank for several years and a state representative in 1885. Charles Perley died on February 2, 1887. The current residents of the home are Barry and Jean Morse.

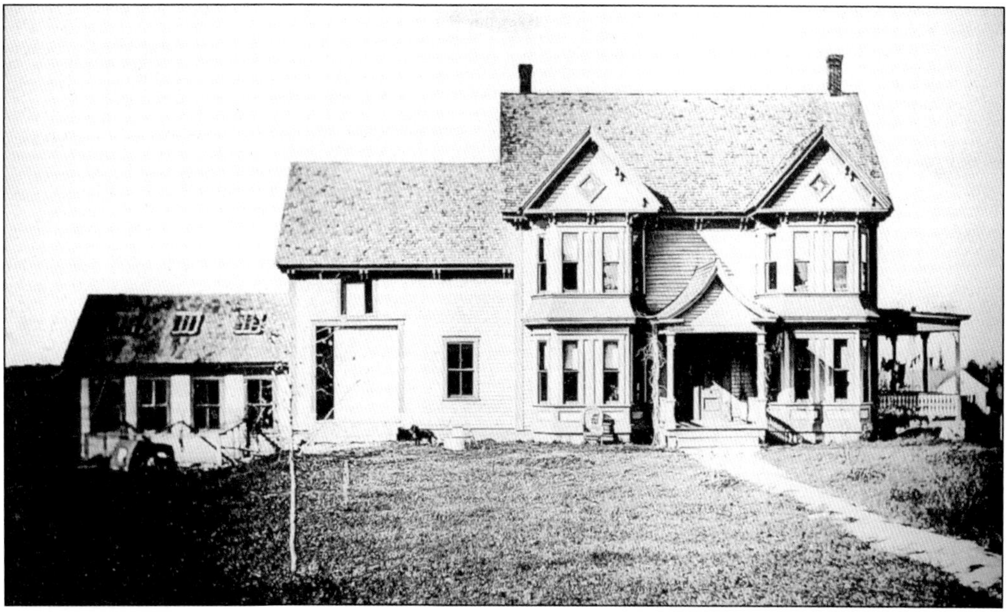

Shown here is J. Wyett Coolidge's home on Lamont Street, across from Reservoir Street. Coolidge was the editor of the *Cottager*, a local monthly newspaper established in 1882. In 1885, the *Cottager* became the *Cottager and Ready Record*, dissolving its connection with the Hospital Cottages for Children. The Hospital Cottages Women's Board established its own paper at this time, named the *Cottage Friend*. J. W. Coolidge was a great supporter of the hospital and one of Dr. Baker's personal friends.

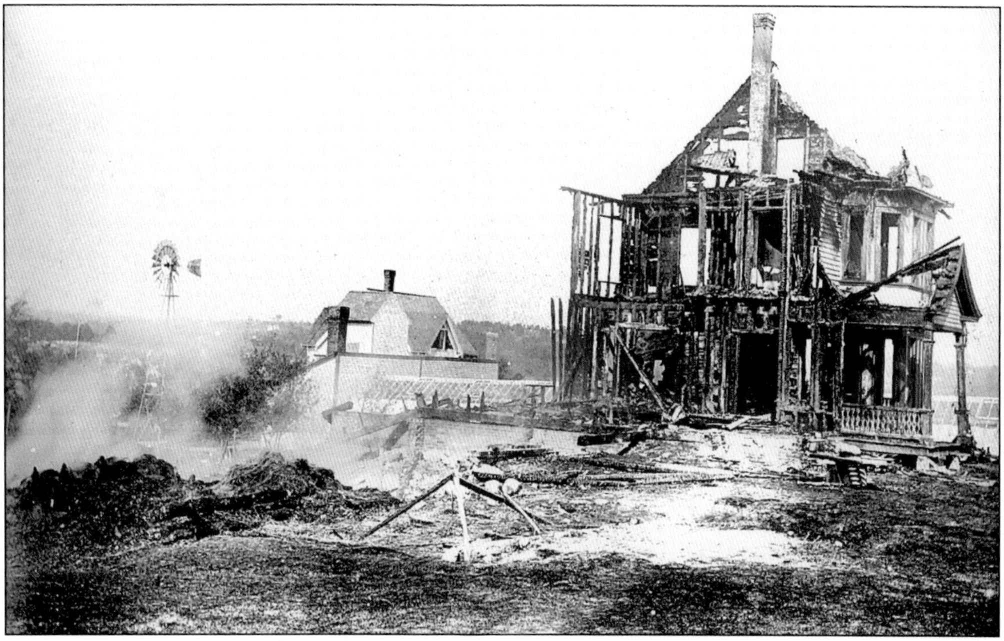

Devastated by fire, the editor's house was a complete loss. It is not known if J. W. Coolidge rebuilt on this location or simply bought a new house in a different location. The map from 1898 lists F. F. Gleason as the owner of this house. No record has been found to verify or finish this story.

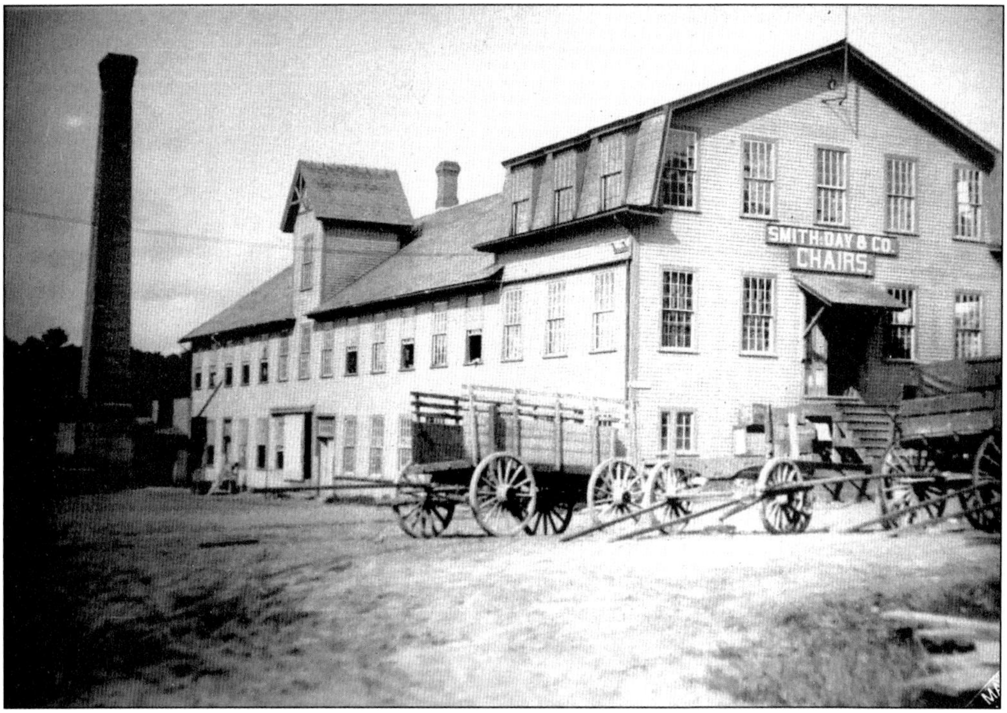

In 1871, two co-workers of a local chair company walked home to dinner and agreed to start their own chair company. That was the beginning of Smith, Day, and Company. C. A. Smith and L. D. Day were soon to by joined by Charles Day. They quickly had 50 hands in the Baldwinville factory and owned a plant in Detroit, Michigan, where 40 hands were employed.

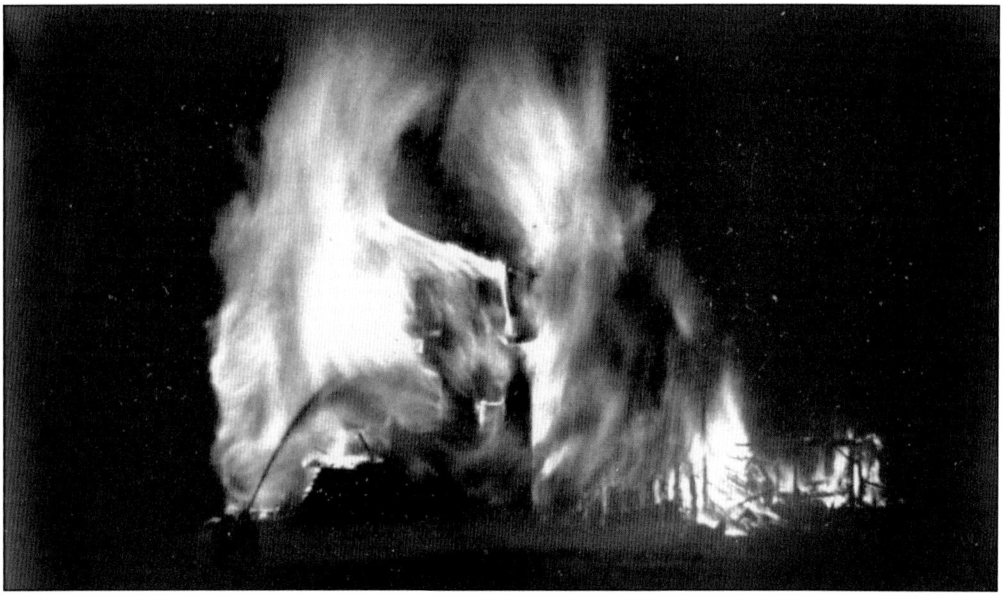

Completely engulfed in flames in this image, the Smith, Day, and Company building was a complete loss. The firemen from Baldwinville got the new steamer working to try to save the factory. Shown at the left of the photograph, two firemen sprayed a heavy stream of water on the flames.

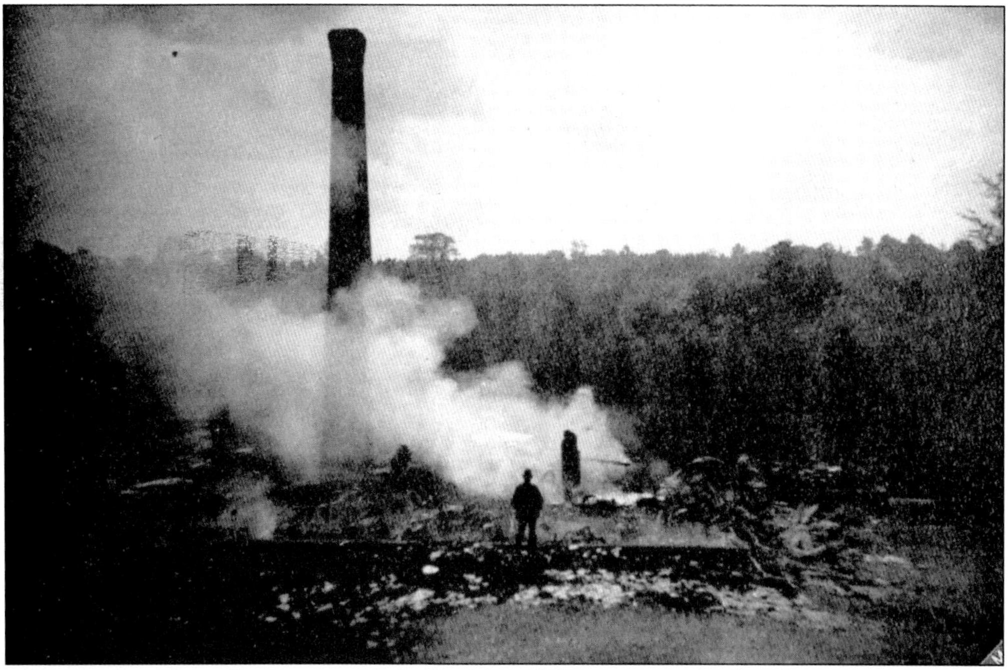

After the fire, the other tenants of the building did not continue their businesses, so Smith, Day, and Company built a fine new shop with 15,000 square feet of floor space. They produced about 100 different kinds of cane-seat chairs. The goods made by this firm have a reputation for good quality.

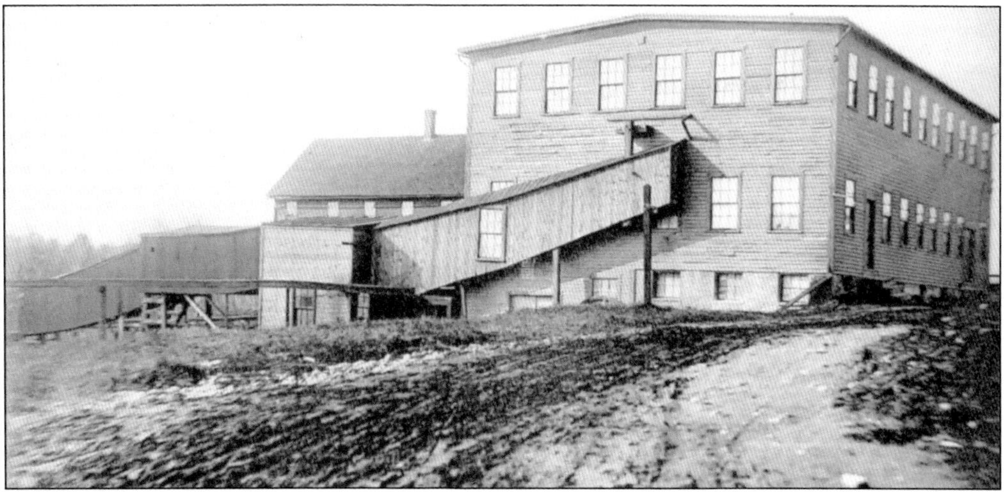

Across Mill Street from the Smith, Day, and Company building was H. M. Small's asbestos building, started in 1875 under the name of Small, Gould, and Company. It was not long before Irving Gould died by accident. In 1886, Small bought the interests of his partners and continued operations under his name solely. His company produced finished products of packing, spun and woven goods, steam-pipe coverings, and various products. The products were shipped all over the United States, Germany, and Great Britain. Small held many of the town offices and sacrificed his private interests for the public good. As a corporator and trustee, he was one of the first prominent supporters who was identified with the growth of the Hospital Cottages for Children.

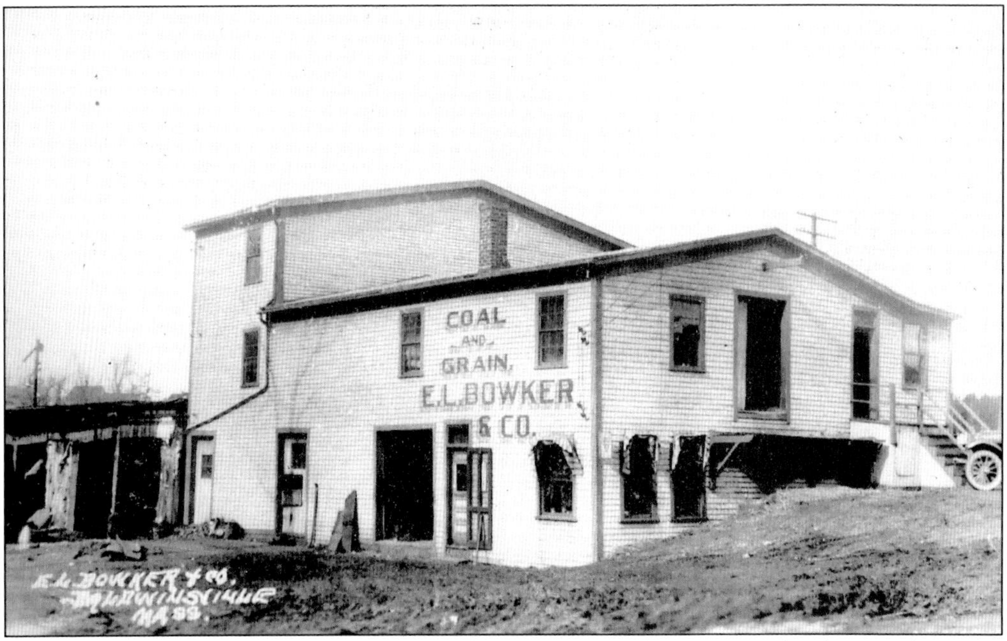

E. L. Bowker and Company was located on Elm Street across from Louis Leland's store (now the Athol Savings Bank). Dealing mainly in coal and grain, the company was also commissioned to clear the timber and brush for the construction of Mason Street in Baldwinville.

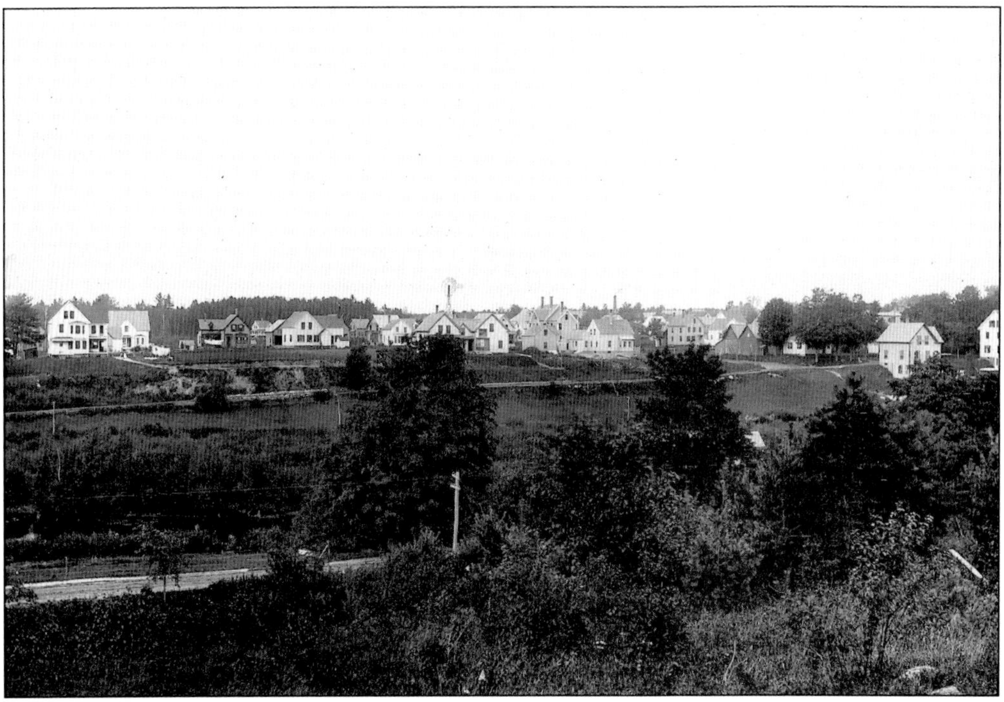

This image was taken standing behind Maple Street and looking across the river at Pine Terrace and Memorial Street when it continued down to the factories on the river. In the distance is Pleasant Street.

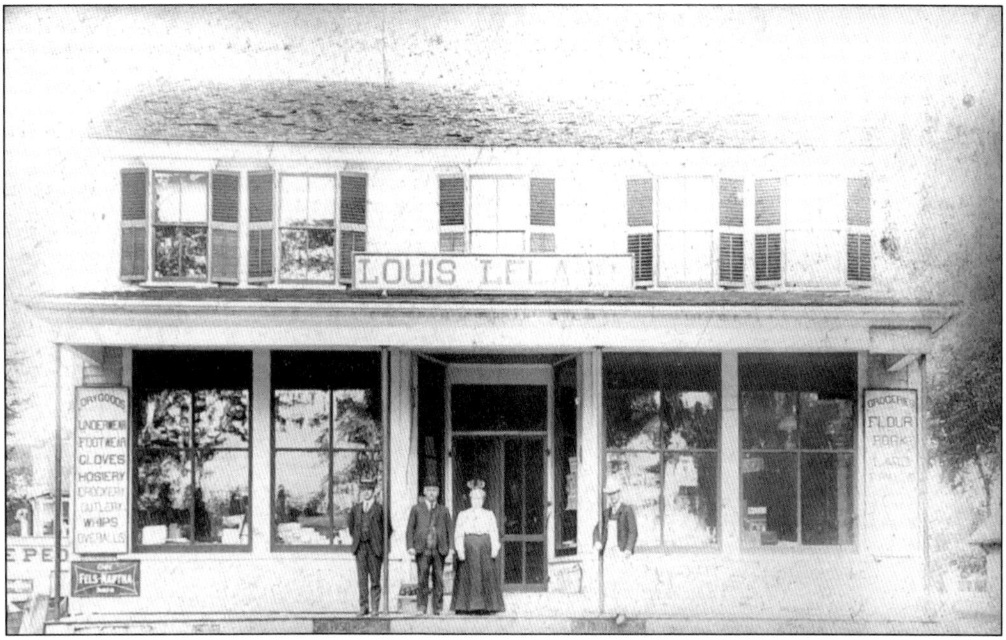

Louis Leland Store was opened in 1870 by brothers Louis and Francis Leland. Pictured are, from left to right, Herbert Leland (son), Louis Leland (father), Anna Leland (mother), and Frank H. Hunt. The Leland family ran the store until 1928. Walter Oliver later converted the building into his photography studio. It was destroyed by fire on January 16, 1950. Cumberland Farms now occupies this location.

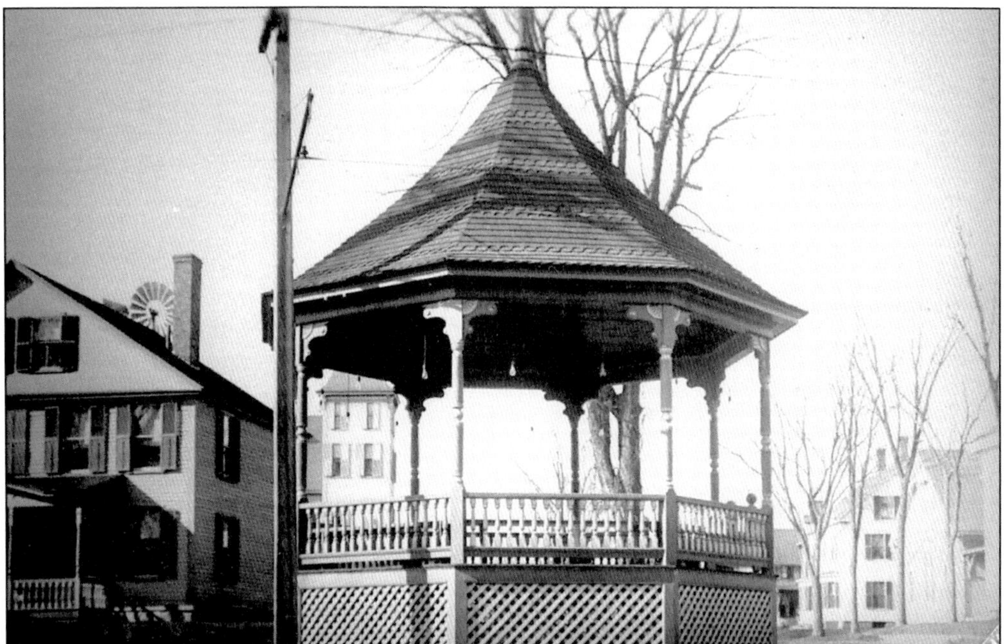

The bandstand was located in front of the Leland Store where many gatherings were held to entertain residents living in and around Baldwinville. Behind the bandstand is Pleasant Street, and S. F. Hildreth's house is on the corner.

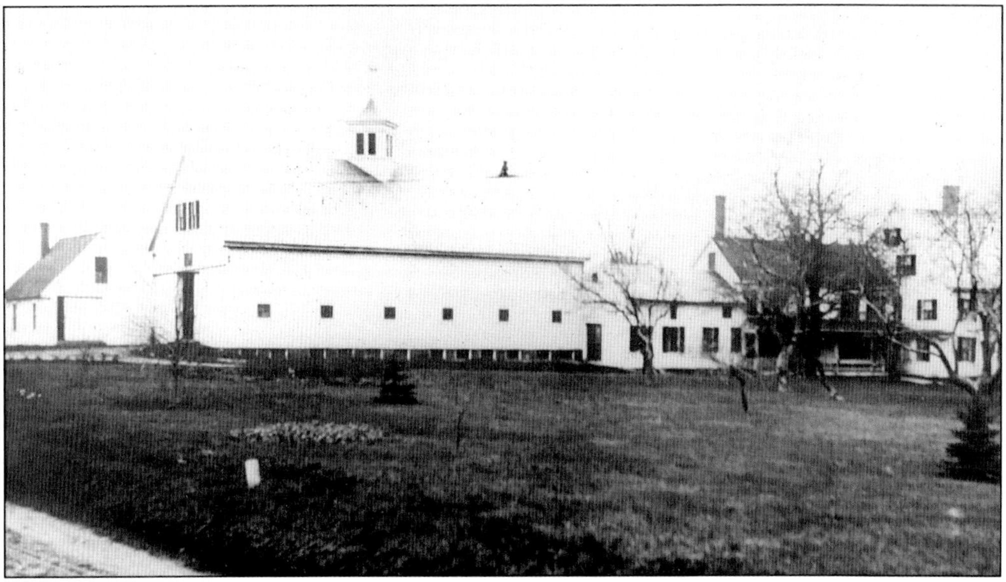

The residence of Gilman Waite is the old homestead of his wife's family. Part of it was one of the earliest houses in the village. Joshua Hosmer, Waite's father-in-law, remodeled it. Besides Waite's advances in business, he is a great admirer of purebred stock, both horses and cattle. He has a fine apartment barn, equipped with all the modern improvements, where his stock are treated like honored guests. The buildings once stood on the opposite side of the railroad track from Lee's Hot Dog Stand. Waite was at one time the sole owner of the Waite Chair Company.

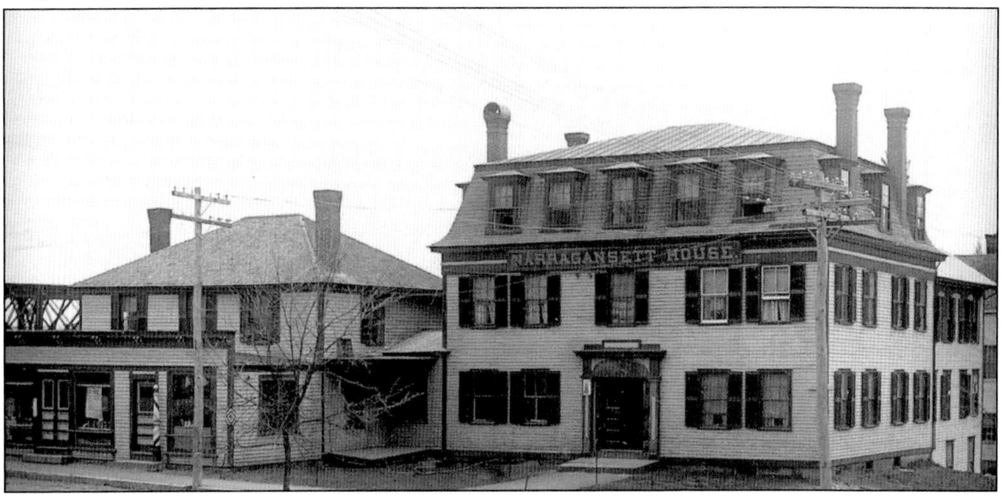

In 1832, Capt. Joseph Davis built the Narragansett Hotel. He was the village's first postmaster. Davis operated the hotel for five years. Frank Ray, his son-in-law, succeeded him. Several different proprietors ran the hotel after Ray until 1870, when George Partridge bought the hotel and ran it successfully for 20 years. In 1871, the hotel was partially destroyed by fire. It was six below zero that day, and the hand engine worked continuously so the water would not freeze in the hose. Firefighter George Grafton froze to the ladder on which he was standing to fight the fire and had to be chopped free. He was taken to the fire room at the Lee and Stearns hat shop, given stimulants, and thawed out. After the fire, the hotel was repaired and rebuilt, and in 1876, Lysander Bronsdon was hired to build the ell that housed the new dining room for the facility.

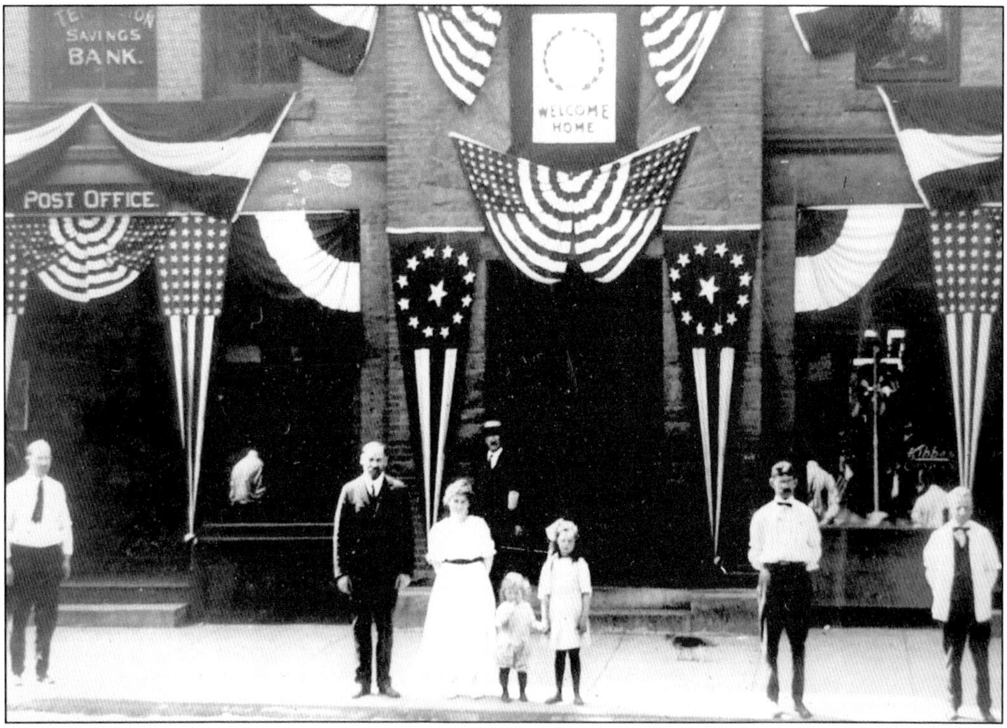

C. A. Fletcher, D.D.S., and his family are shown here in front of the Bank Building on Central Street during the welcome home parade for the soldiers of World War I. Dr. Fletcher was the town clerk from 1908 to 1923. The youngest child in the picture is Louis Fletcher (who became a doctor of dental surgery) at age 4.

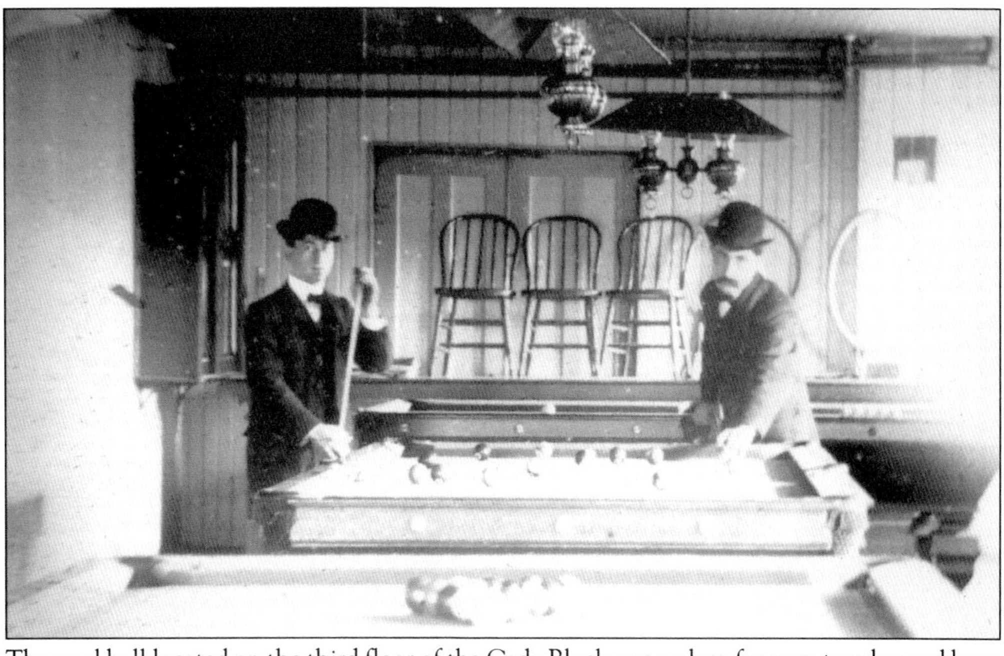

The pool hall located on the third floor of the Cady Block was a place for men to relax and have a cigar.

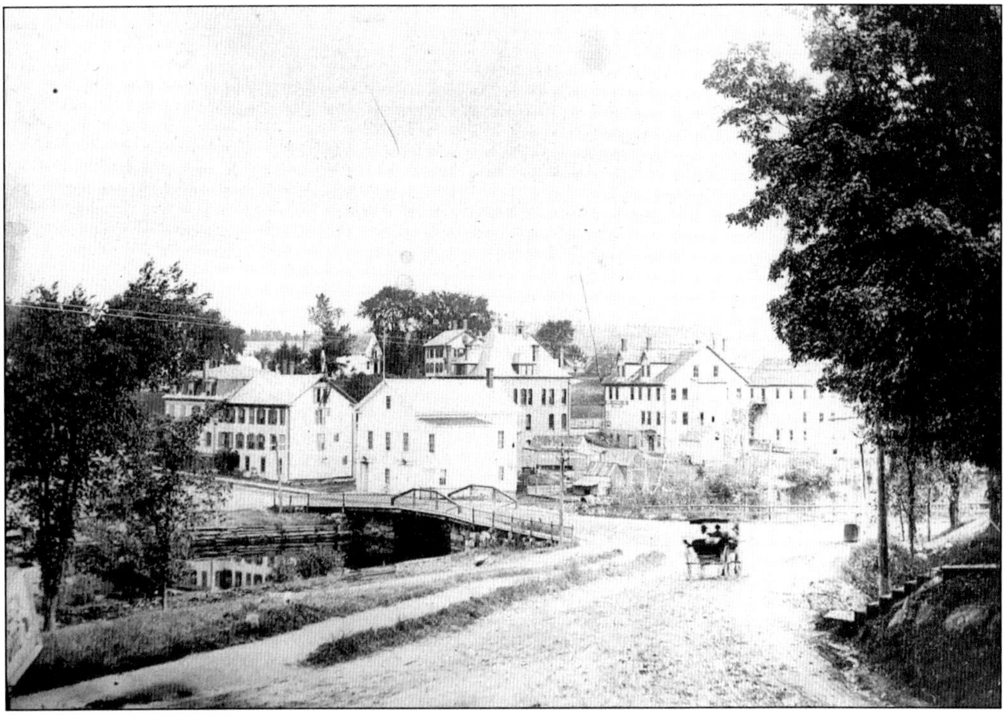

When arriving in Baldwinville from South Main Street, this is the first view turning onto Maple Street. Crossing the bridge, Union Hall and Narragansett Hotel are on the right. Behind Union Hall are the Bank Building, the Cady Block, and the Hammond Block.

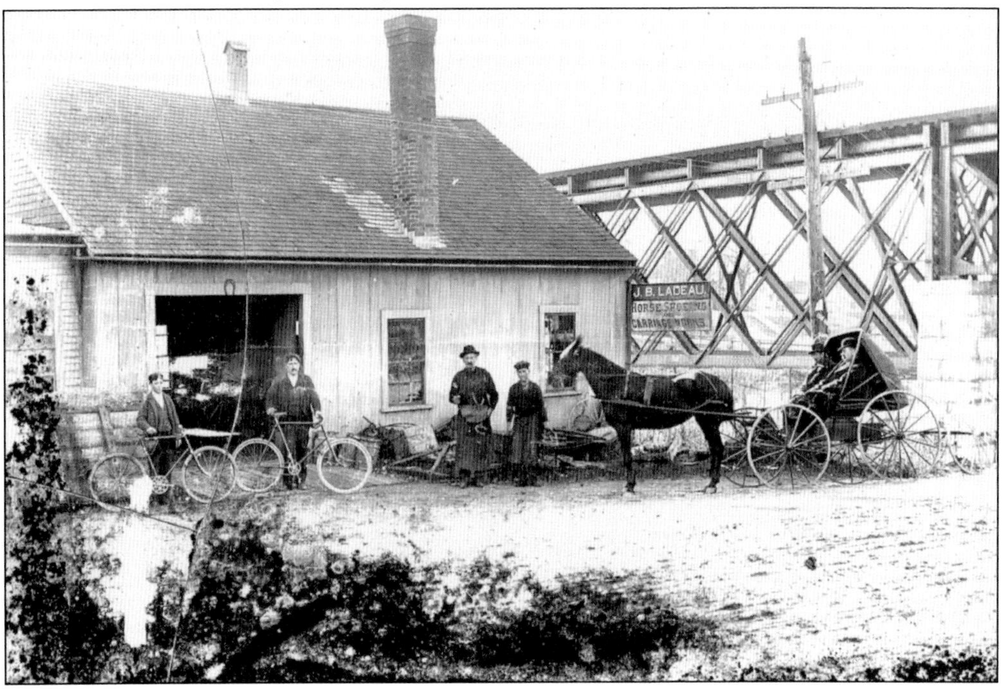

J. B. Ladeau stands outside his blacksmith shop with an apprentice and visitors. This picture was taken on the east side of the trestle on Central Street. The Hammond Block is on the right.

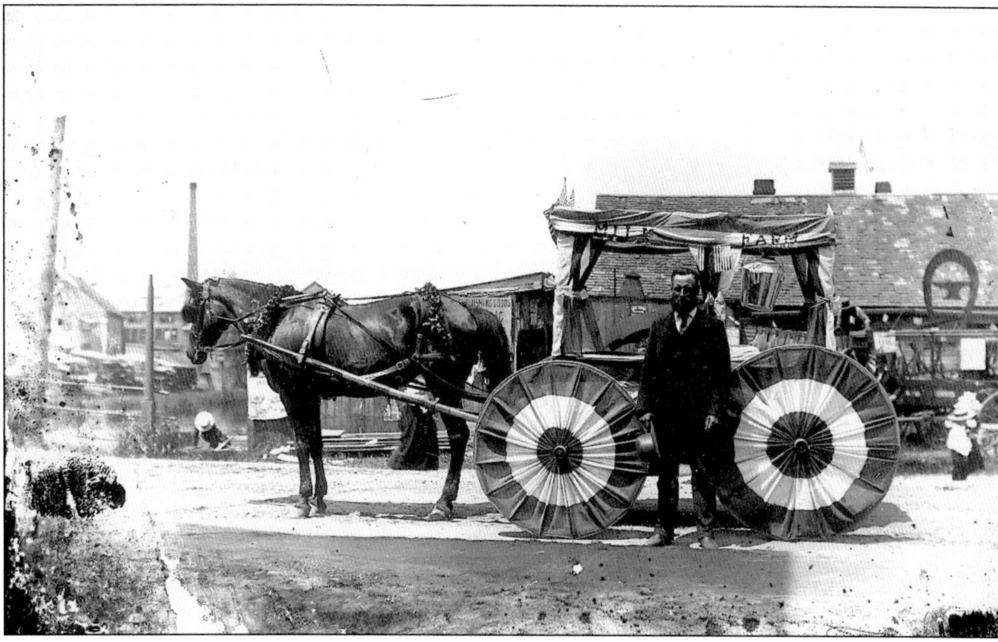

Decorated for the Fourth of July parade in the late 1890s, Genery Stiles shows off his horse and wagon while advertising his milk farm in front of Minot Ellis's blacksmith shop. The farm was located on Baldwinville Road, and the property is now Bill Putnam's. Stiles was born in Gardner on October 21, 1853, and lived until 1936.

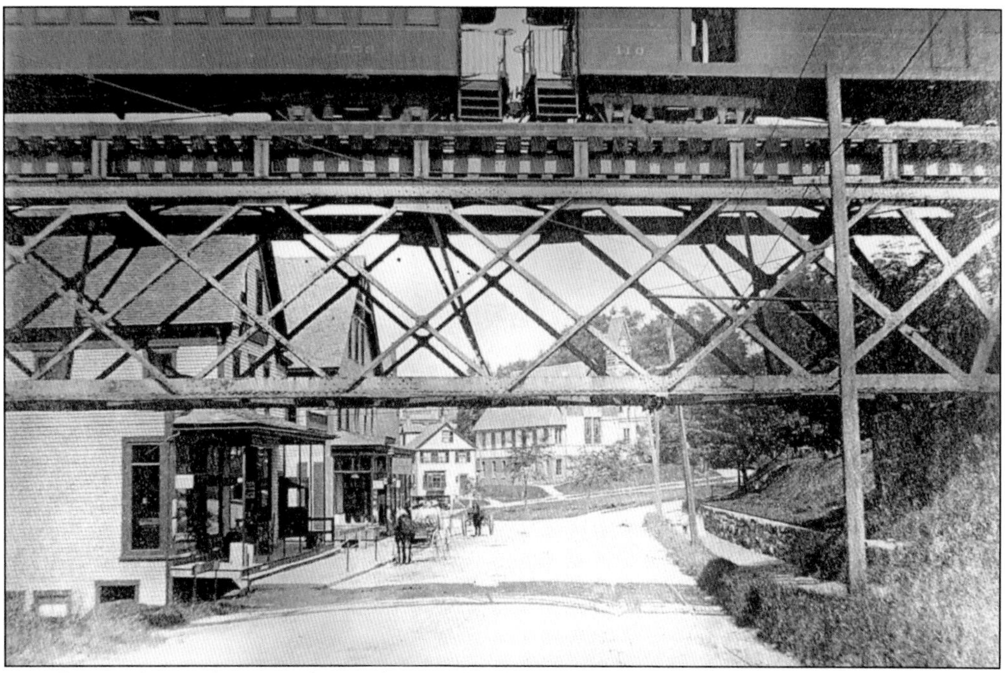

Standing in front of J. B. Ladeau's shop under the trestle one can see downtown Baldwinville. The Hammond and the Cady Blocks are on the left. C. S. Dickinson's general store is located in the Cady Block. Next to the Cady Block is the Bank Building, and straight ahead is the First Congregational Church.

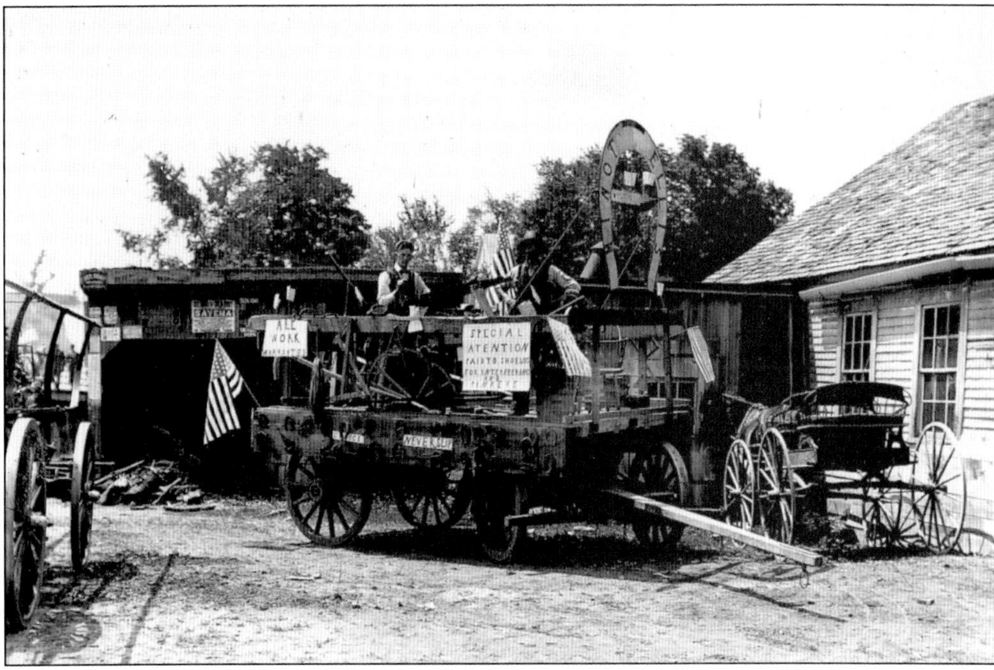

Minot Ellis's blacksmith shop was across from Union Hall in Baldwinville Center (now the site of the town offices). A childhood curiosity, the low, rangy building was grim and bare. Ellis brought the first gasoline engine to the town as a power plant for his workshop.

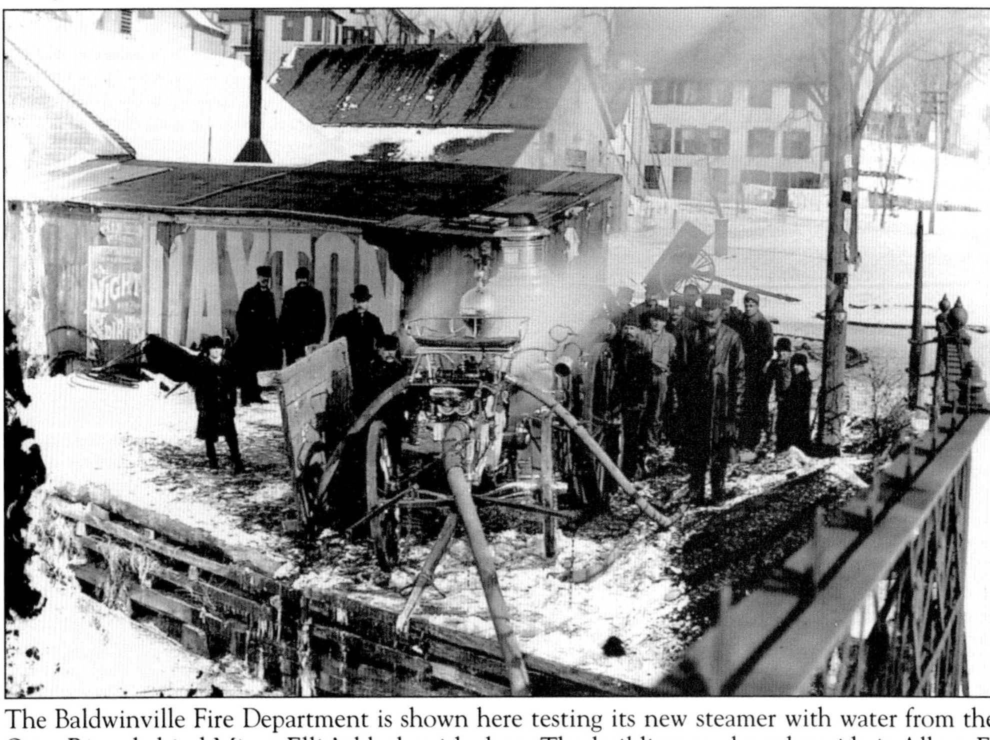

The Baldwinville Fire Department is shown here testing its new steamer with water from the Otter River behind Minot Ellis's blacksmith shop. The building on the other side is Albert E. Sumner's stable. The fire station was located just across the street.

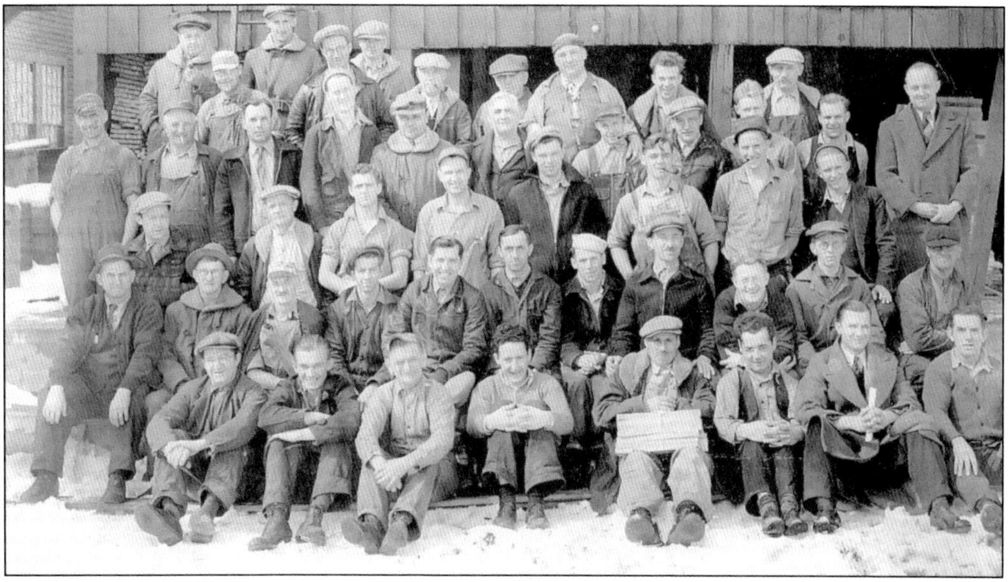

Employees of the Temple Stuart Company pose for a picture in 1930. The company began manufacturing furniture in 1904 and closed 86 years later in 1990. Pictured here are, from left to right, the following: (first row) Frank Graves, Edwin Greenwood, Archie Watson, Frank Quinlisk, Mike Buningshaski, Bucky Quinlisk, Emile Wirkala, and Pete Brehio; (fourth row) Walter Leonard, Frank Yurkus, John Yurkus, Stanley Young, "Lame Tony" Zisk, Herbert Greenwood, Stanley Zablonski, Stanley Nasatka, Bob Whitney, Earl Amidon, and Maurice Miller; (fifth row) ? Duquette, Manuel Carpenter, Waino Silverberg, Stanley Turski, Joe Nasatka, Ovide Cloutier, and "Big Tony" Ziske. The second row includes Guy Squires, ? Dunham, ? Constantino, Wilfred Graves, Tony Naisatka, Pid Mason, Louis Cloutier, Bud Whitney, Carl Harwood, and ? Stone. The third row includes Leon "Bull" Quinlisk, ? Miserek, ? Graves, Mike Danielson, Joe Bullock, and Young Kasper. The three men in the sixth row are unidentified.

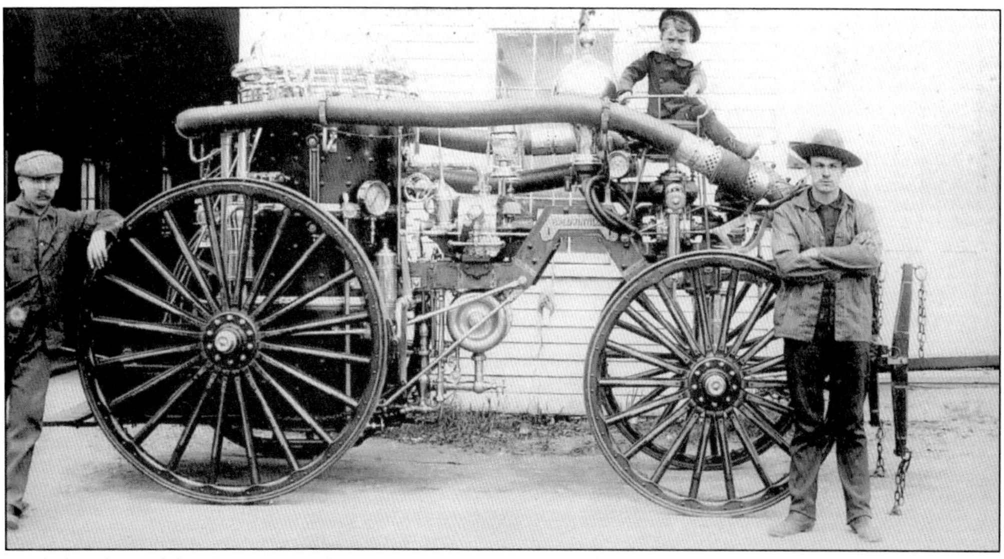

Built by the Silsby Company, Steamer No. 1 was one of two steamers with shiny brass, nickel, and brilliant red paint on its exterior that the village owned. One of the hand tubs is on display in the historical society's building today. Standing on the left of the steamer is Eugene Cushing.

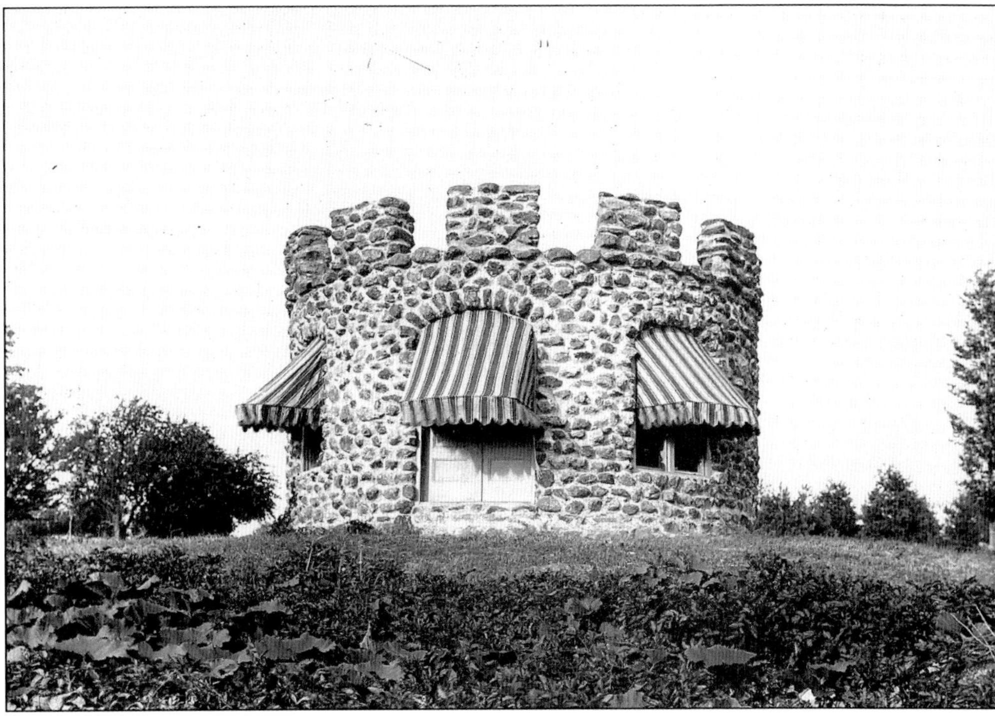

Dr. Baker's Castle was located off North Main Street (Bridge Street) near the Cottages for Children. Dr. Baker built this castle for the children of the hospital and the village to play in. The castle was dismantled *c.* 1950.

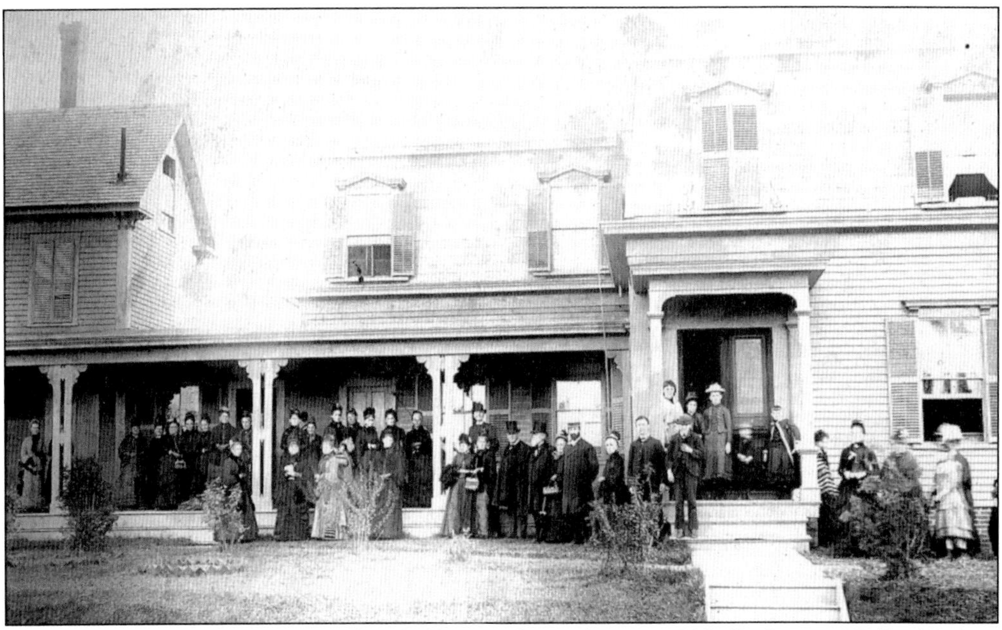

A view of the Hospital Cottages for Children is shown here *c.* 1882. Dr. Lucius Willard Baker, son of Dea. Willard Baker, founded the hospital located on Pleasant Street in 1880. The institute opened with formal exercises on June 17, 1882, and was incorporated in December of that year.

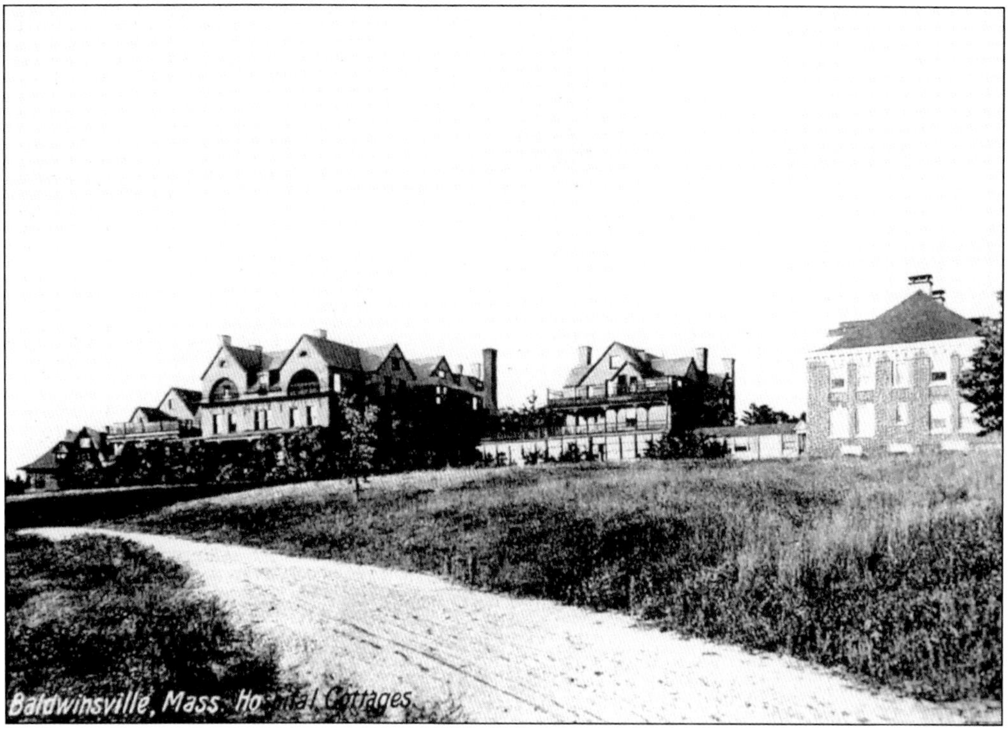

Here is the new location of the Hospital Cottages for Children. A large tract of land was purchased off of North Main Street in 1890, and another new building was added to house the hospital. The hospital eventually discontinued the use of the old location on Pleasant Street. The new home for the hospital grew and acquired over 469 acres of land. It is now dismantled, and the new Cottage Hill Academy is located on this site.

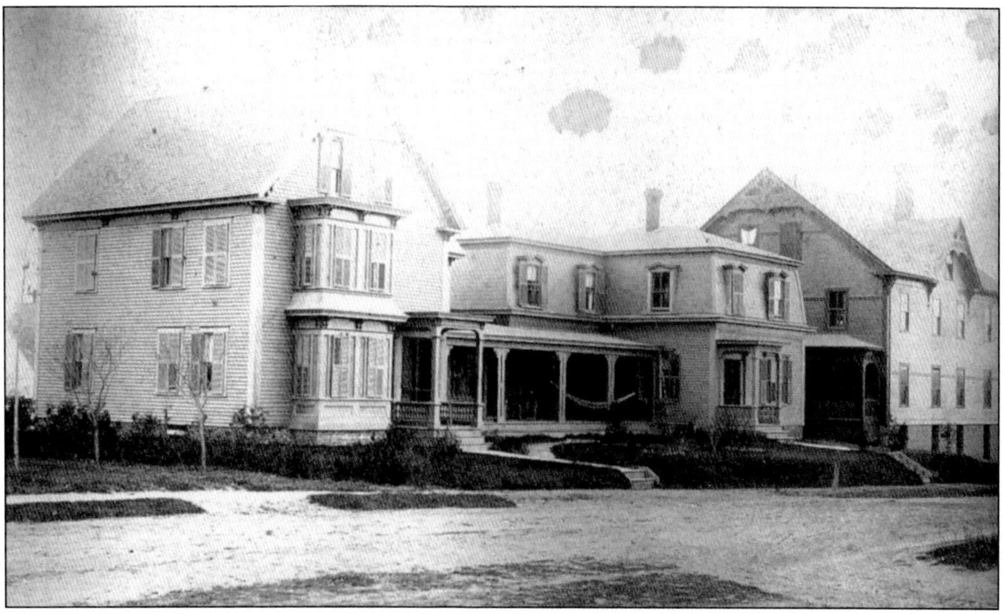

Due to increased applications of the hospital, Dr. Baker added a third building, shown here, in 1887.

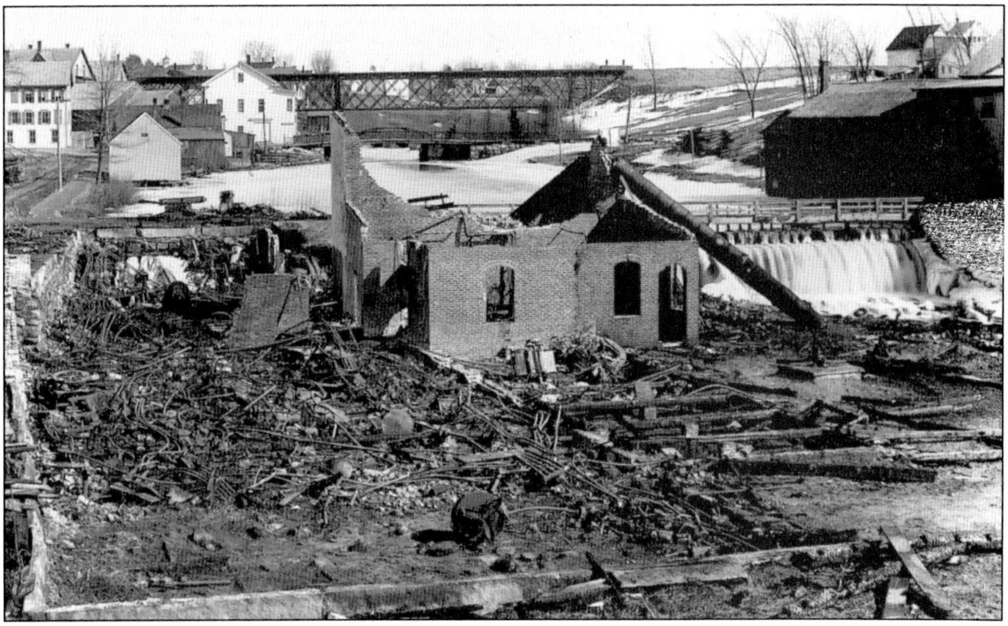

The Thompson, Perley, and Waite Company is shown here in ruins in 1895. By 1904, the Waite Chair Company purchased this land and built a new factory, moving from the south side of the river to the north. Several owners operated the building until the U.S. government took it over after the 1938 hurricane. The building was torn down in 1945.

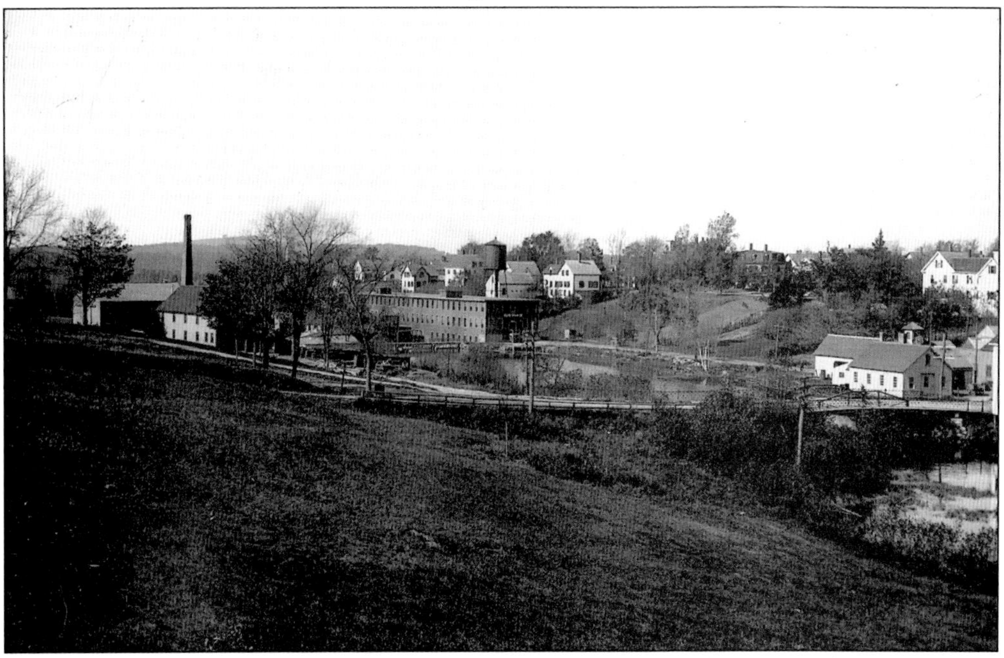

This is a view looking down-river from a field on School Street. The Waite Chair Company's new building can be seen on the north side of the river. Behind the trees are the old buildings of the Waite Chair Company. At the bridge is the new garage built by Minot Ellis to house his blacksmith shop. This image is part one of a panoramic view completed with the image to the right on the bottom of page 63.

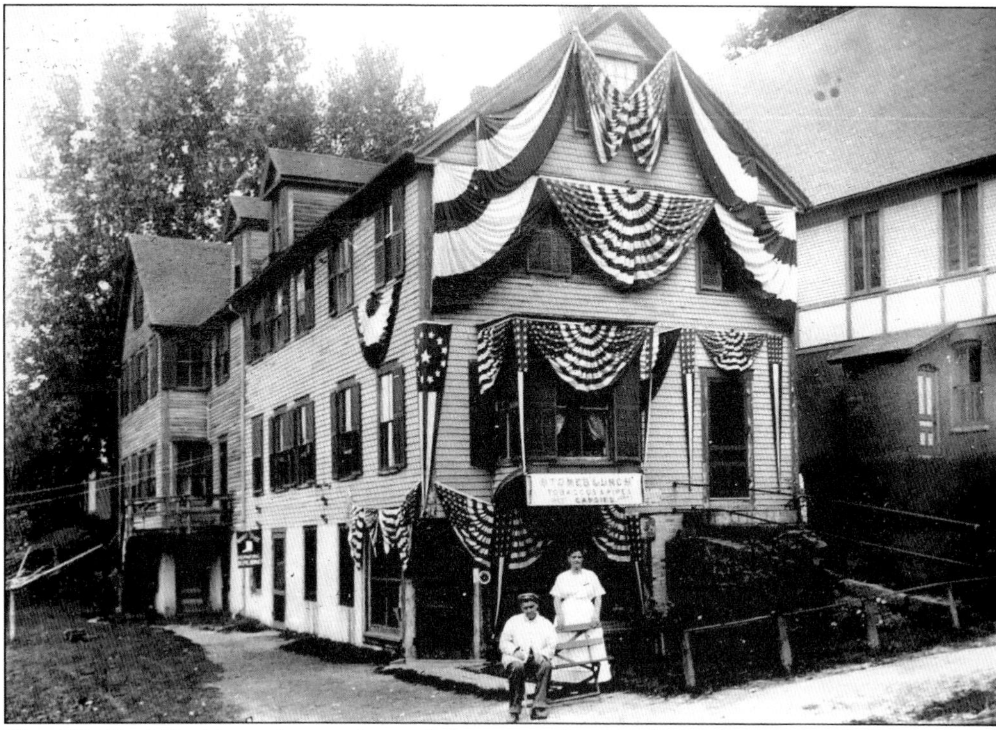

The W. Hird Building, facing Central Street, is decorated for the town celebration. The white sign says, "Stones Lunch tobacco & Pipes, Candies." Over the years, the building was a laundromat and a police station. In the early days, it housed a reading room on the second floor. Today, it is an apartment house and a laundromat.

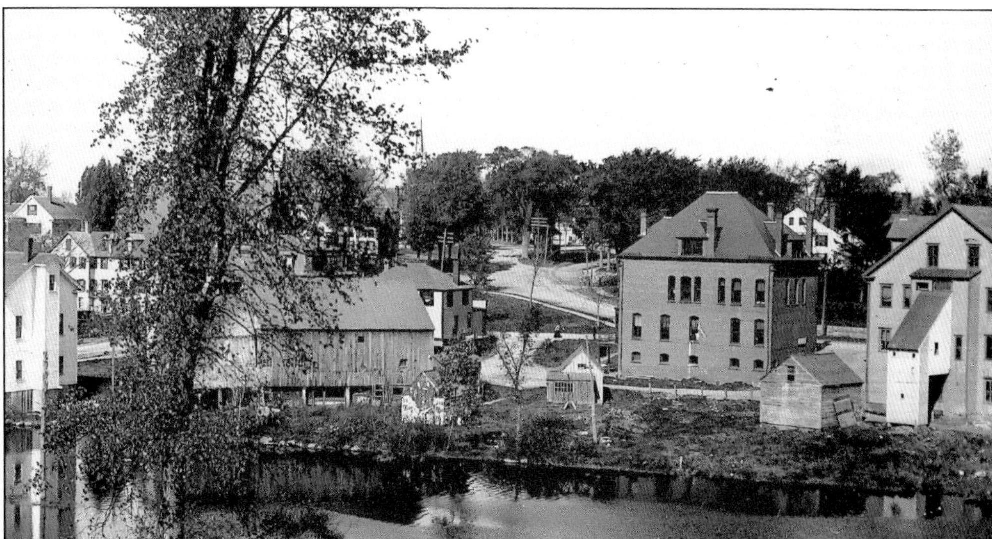

This image was taken behind Baldwinville Center from across the river. The backsides of Tiger No. 1 firehouse, Union Hall, and the Bank Building (the tall dark building) can be seen. To the right of the Bank Building is the Cady Block, which housed a drugstore when this photograph was taken. The barn on the riverbank was a stable for the Narragansett House. This image is part two of the panoramic view matched with the image to the left on page 62.

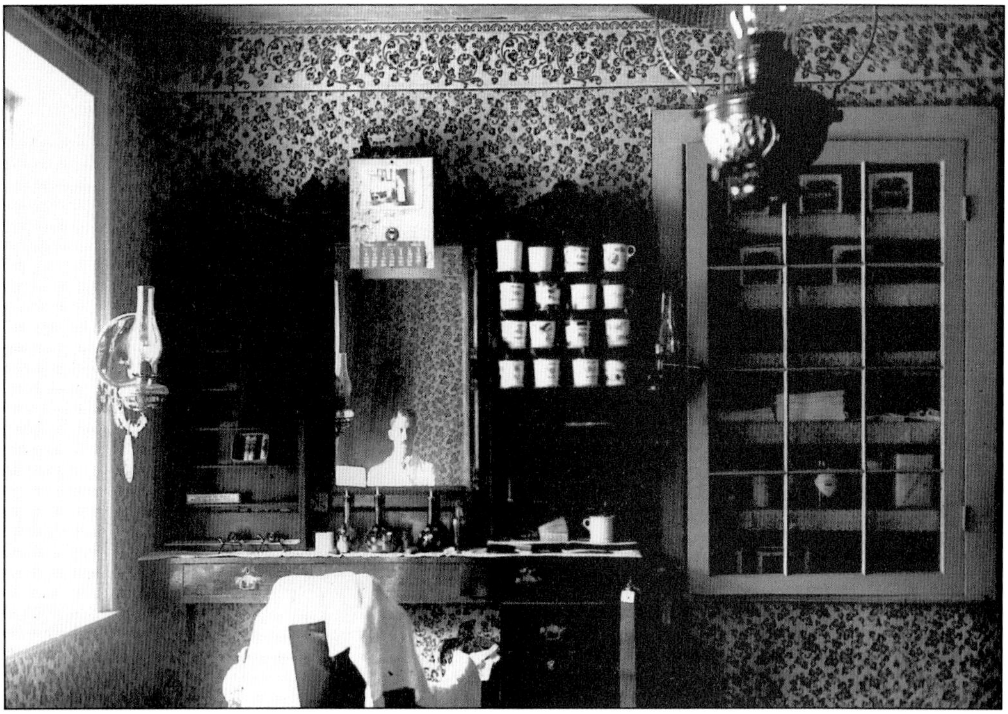

This local barbershop was located on the first floor of the Bank Building. With electricity not yet installed, the barber needs the light from the window on the left. His view overlooks the Narragansett Hotel and Stables.

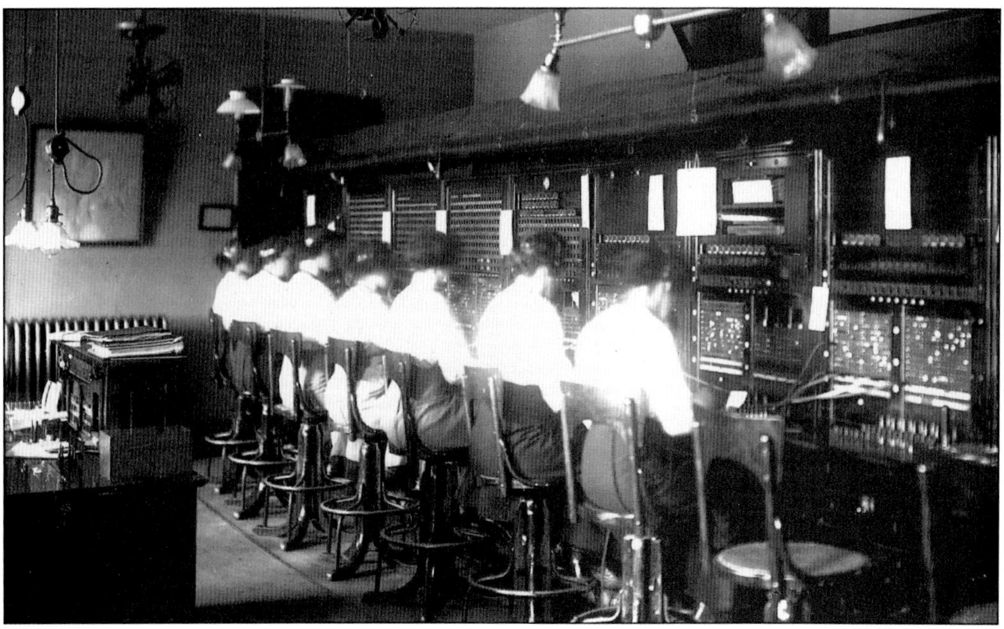

The first switchboard was located in Louis Leland's general store in 1884. Five switchboards were added, moved to the second floor of the store, and operated by Milton Gleason and his wife, Eva. Mill King later purchased a house on Memorial Street and installed several larger switchboards.

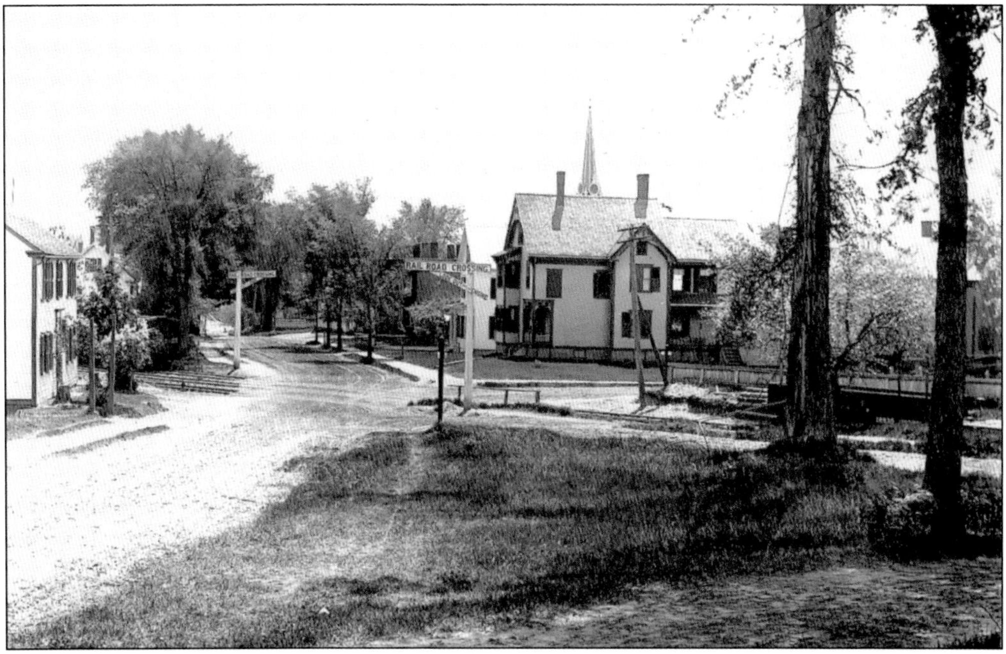

This is a view of North Main Street looking south onto what is now Circle Street. The house on the right lost its top two floors to a fire; the roof was rebuilt over the first floor. On the left is the Merritt House. The photographer was standing on what is now Bridge Street.

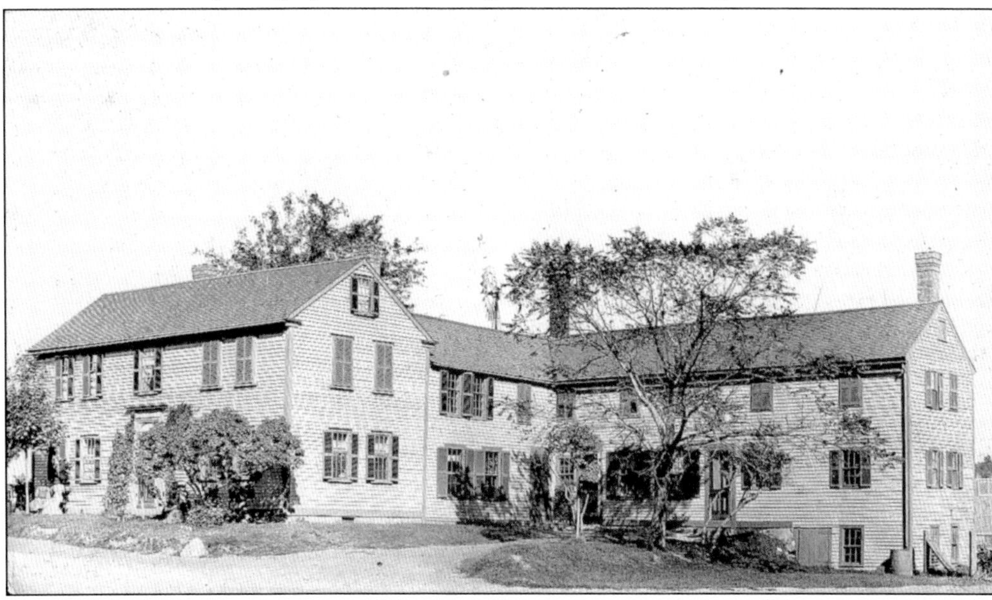

The Merritt house was once owned by Capt. Warren Merritt, father of Emma Merritt, and is located on Pleasant Street. The barn was used as a livery stable. This house was later owned by Nellie Speare and is now located off of Bridge Street. At one time, Circle Street was called North Main Street and it crossed over the railroad tracks right in front of this house. The ell out back was torn down, but the original part of the house is still standing. A greenhouse can be seen behind the building. This photograph is signed, "the Old Homestead September 18, 1897," and was taken from the railroad tracks looking northeast.

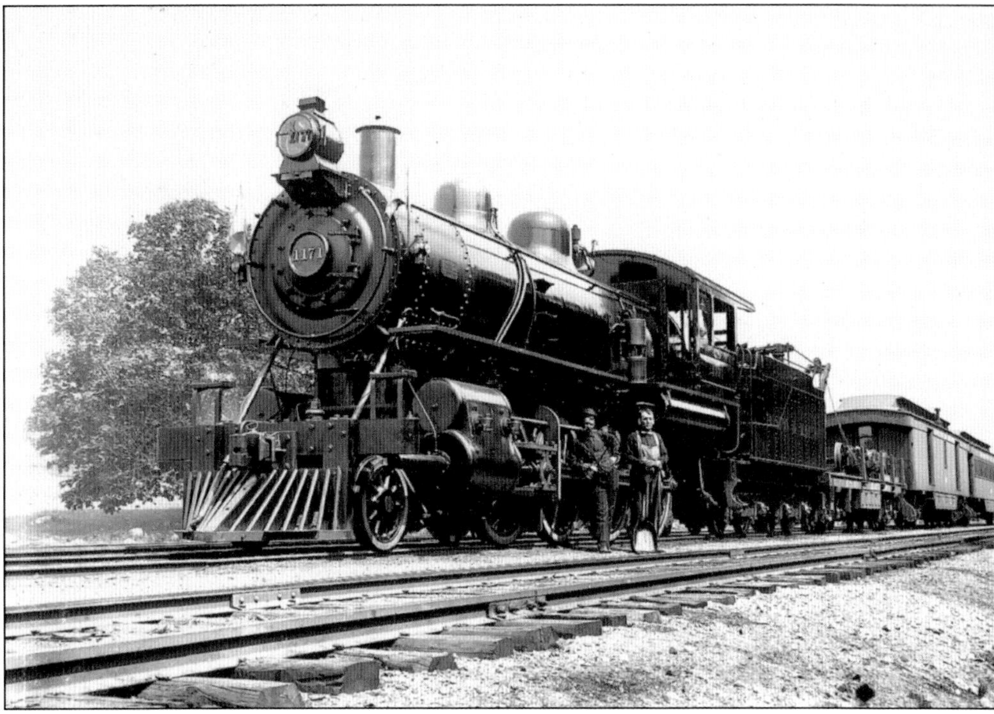

Taking a break at the Baldwinville Depot, these railroad workers proudly stand in front of their steam locomotive No. 1171.

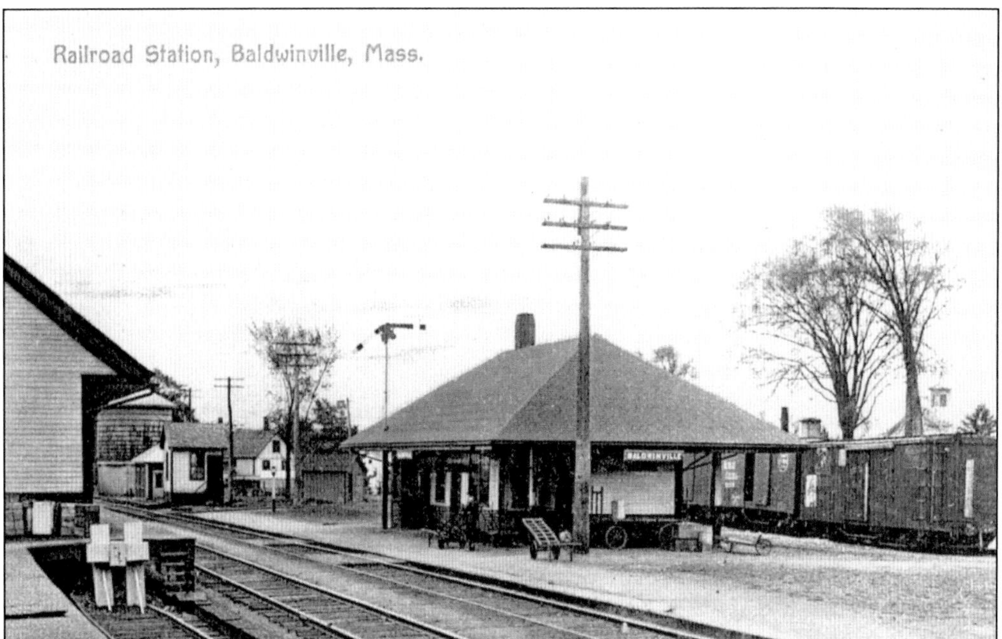

The busiest spot in town in the early 1900s was the Boston and Maine passenger station, which was one of several stations that existed in Baldwinville. The water tower was located behind C. A. Perley's residence. Part of one of the freight stations can be seen on the left side of the picture. South of the station and behind the boxcar, the top of the Baptist church can be seen.

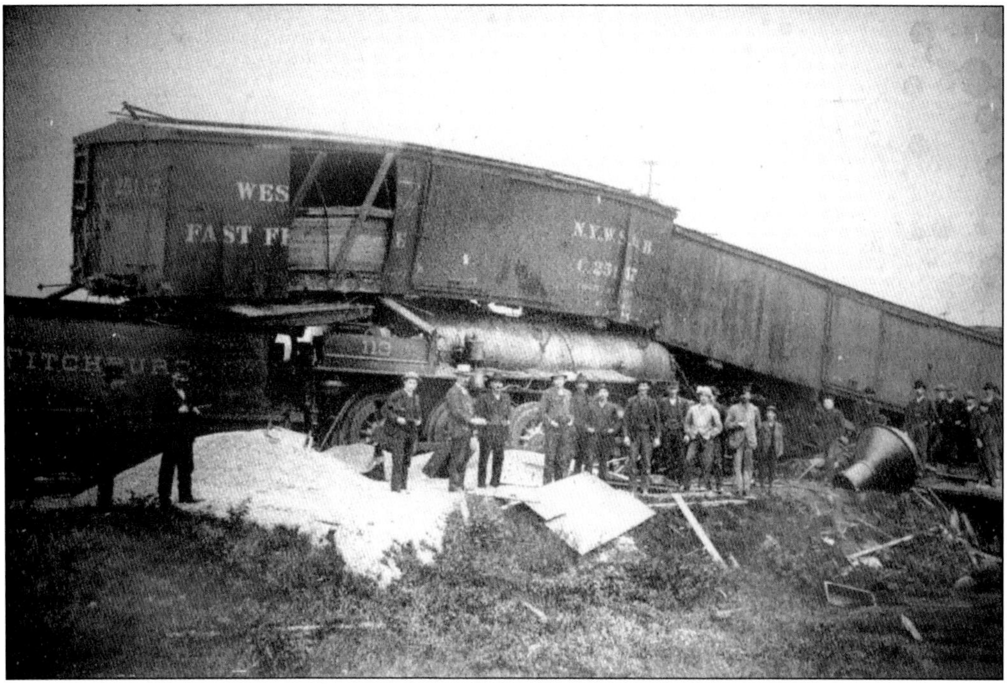

Not all trains made it to the depot on time. This train wreck near the Baldwinville Depot was one of a kind: the locomotive plunged under a waiting boxcar.

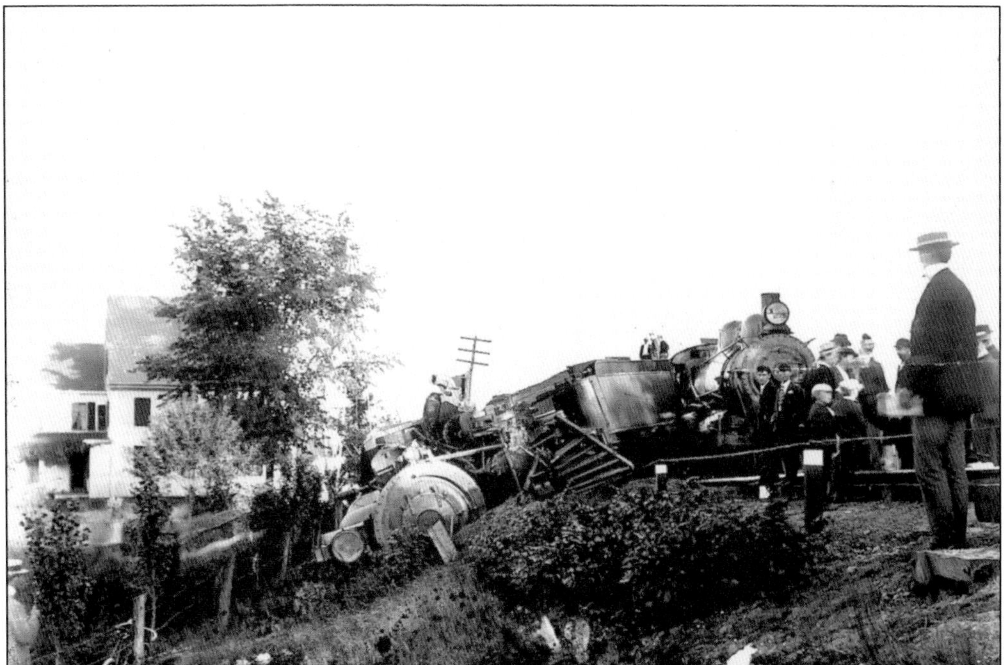

A train wreck in front of Gilman Waite's house is shown here. Behind the photographer and to the right is the bridge to Central Street in Baldwinville Center. Train wrecks were quite common, as timing was a problem for engineers. Wrecks prompted watch companies to produce high-grade pocket watches called "railroad watches."

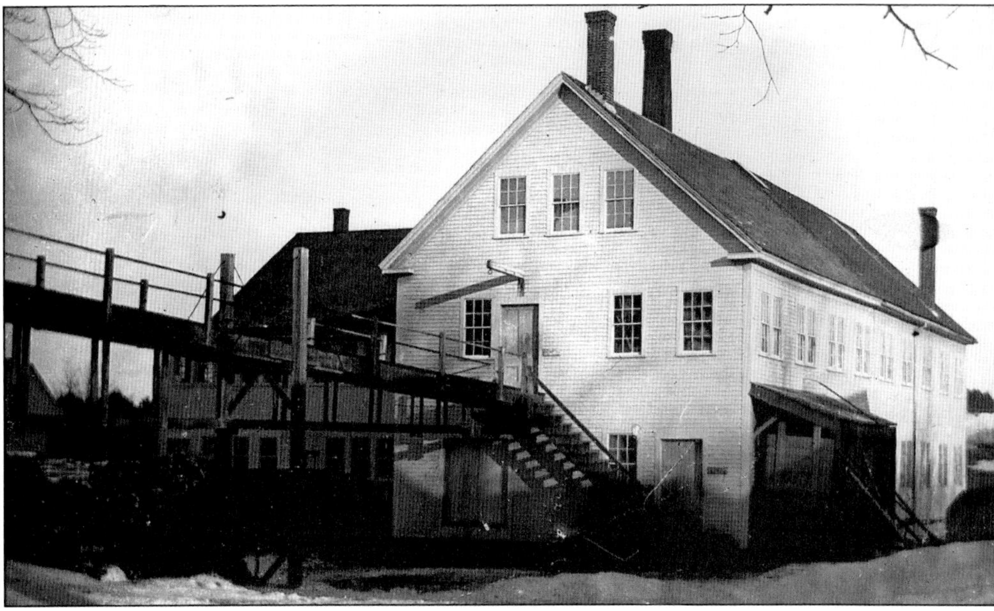

D. L. Thompson and Son was located down the river from the Waite Chair Company on the south side of the dam. On the opposite side of the dam was the Baker and Wilson Company. Cane-seat chairs were manufactured there for a number of years. The seat frames were delivered to private homes to be caned. After the death of D. L. Thompson, his son continued the business as E. L. Thompson and Company until Orange Whitney of Winchendon became a partner. After a few years, Whitney sold his shares back to Thompson, who continued alone until he sold it to Thomas Brazell of Gardner in 1922. After the flood of 1938, a new factory was built on the corner of Prospect and Mechanic Streets. It was renamed the E. L. Thompson Chair Corporation.

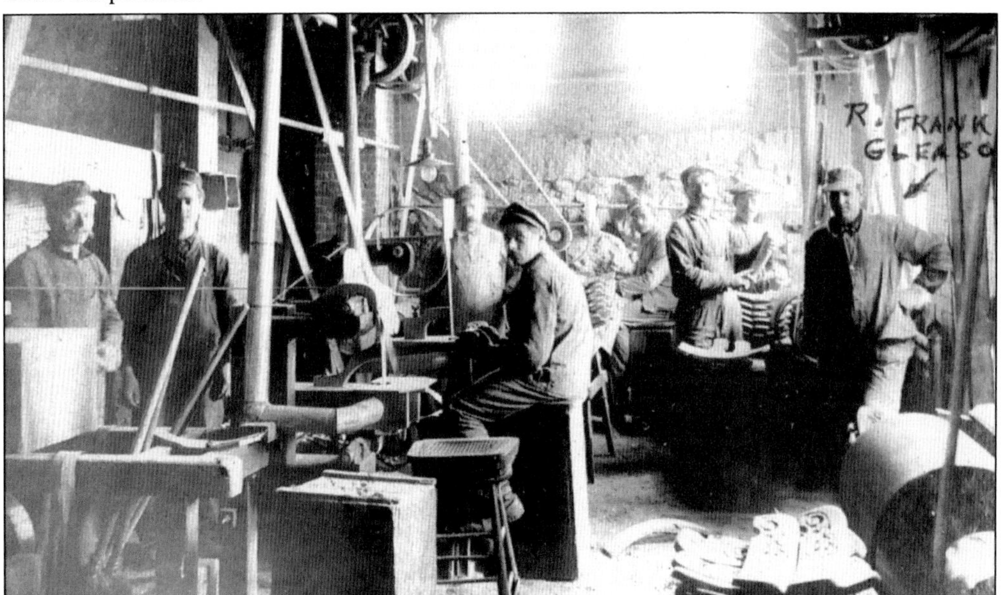

R. Frank Gleason (right) is shown here inside the E. L. Thompson Chair factory, down river from the Waite Chair Company on the south side of the dam.

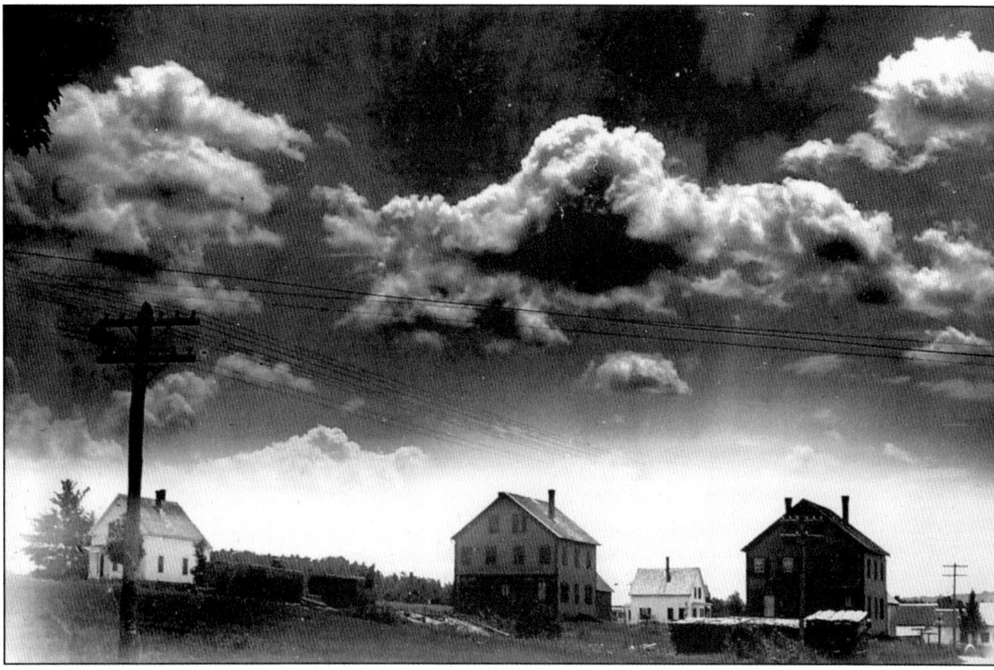

The twin buildings on the corner of Prospect and Mechanic Streets were probably used as offices for the furniture companies. (Eliza Phillips's house is shown on the left.) These buildings, along with all of the others to the right, were torn down to make way for the Birch Hill Dam. Many families in this area had to be relocated.

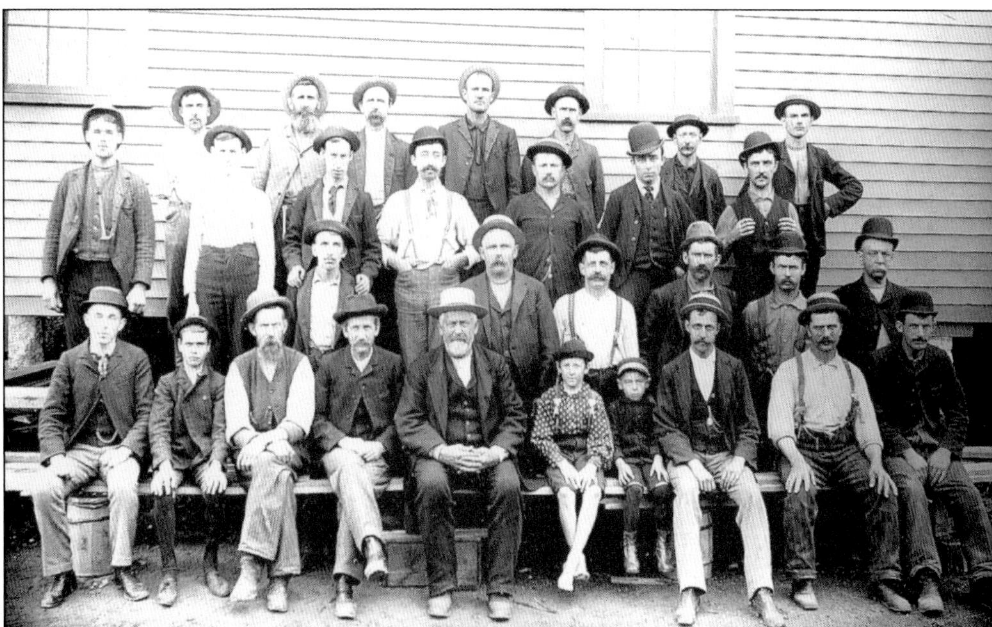

Sitting outside of the E. L. Thompson and Company factory, these men get the opportunity to take a group picture. Standing in the center with the white shirt, suspenders, and hat is Oren Williams. The man to his left is Mr. Paradise, and the man sitting in the center with his hands together is the owner, E. L. Thompson.

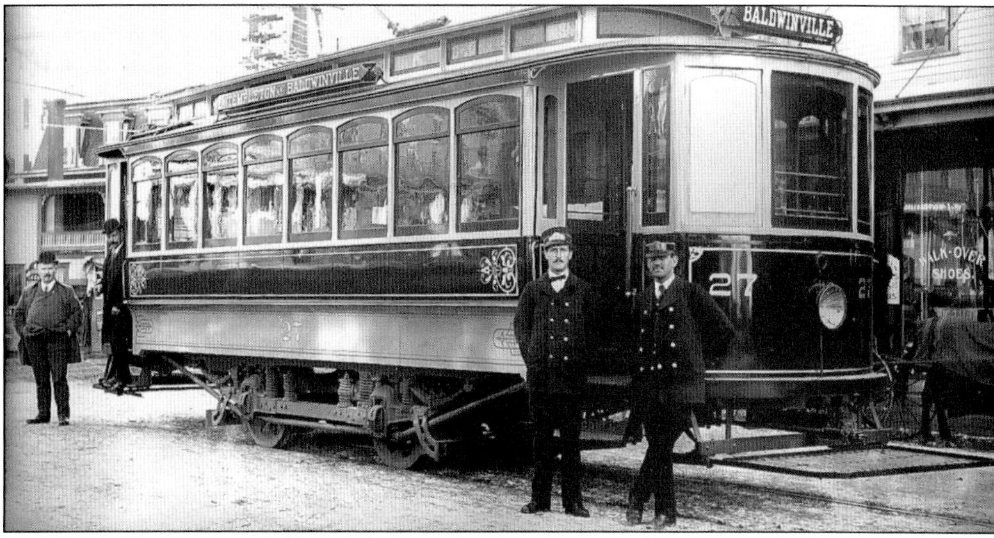

Waiting for passengers, Baldwinville's winter car stands ready to perform its duties. Brooks is standing near the doorway to the trolley posing with his coworker. This picture appears to have been taken on Central Street. A lady can be seen inside the car in the front row ready to head back to East Templeton. Curious passengers are departing from the rear of the trolley, although they have time to observe the photographer and stay in the picture. The passenger on the ground is E. L. Thompson, factory owner. This image was taken *c.* 1905.

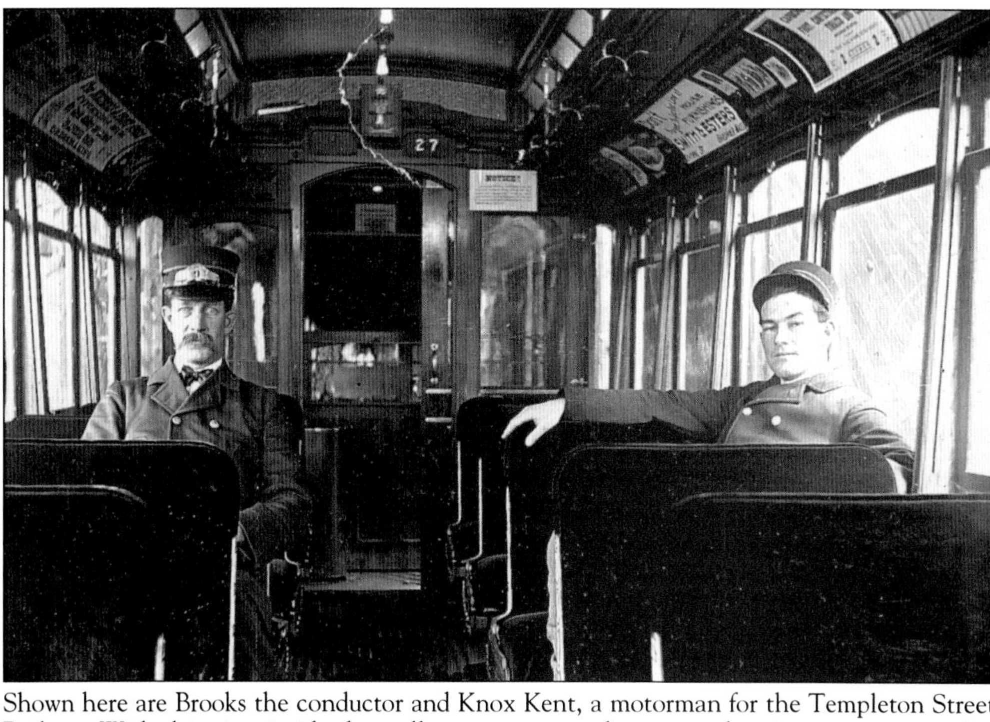

Shown here are Brooks the conductor and Knox Kent, a motorman for the Templeton Street Railway. With this view inside the trolley, one can see the many advertisements on its sides. One advertisement is for Smith and Esters home furnishings in Gardner. This photograph was taken *c.* 1910.

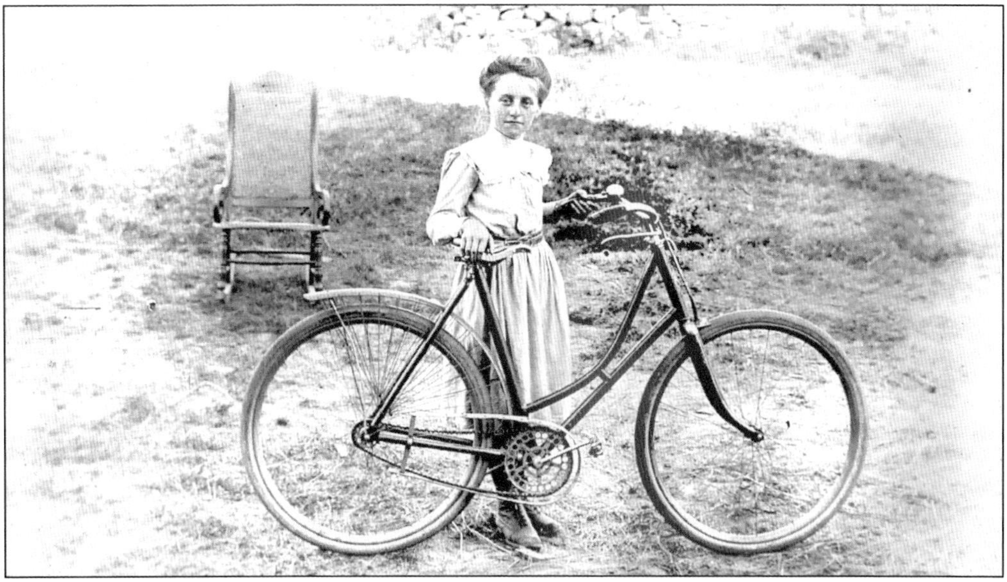

Here, an unidentified young girl shows off her new bicycle. This was the first of 200 glass-plate negatives found in what is now Brian Tanguay's private collection, and it has yet to be identified.

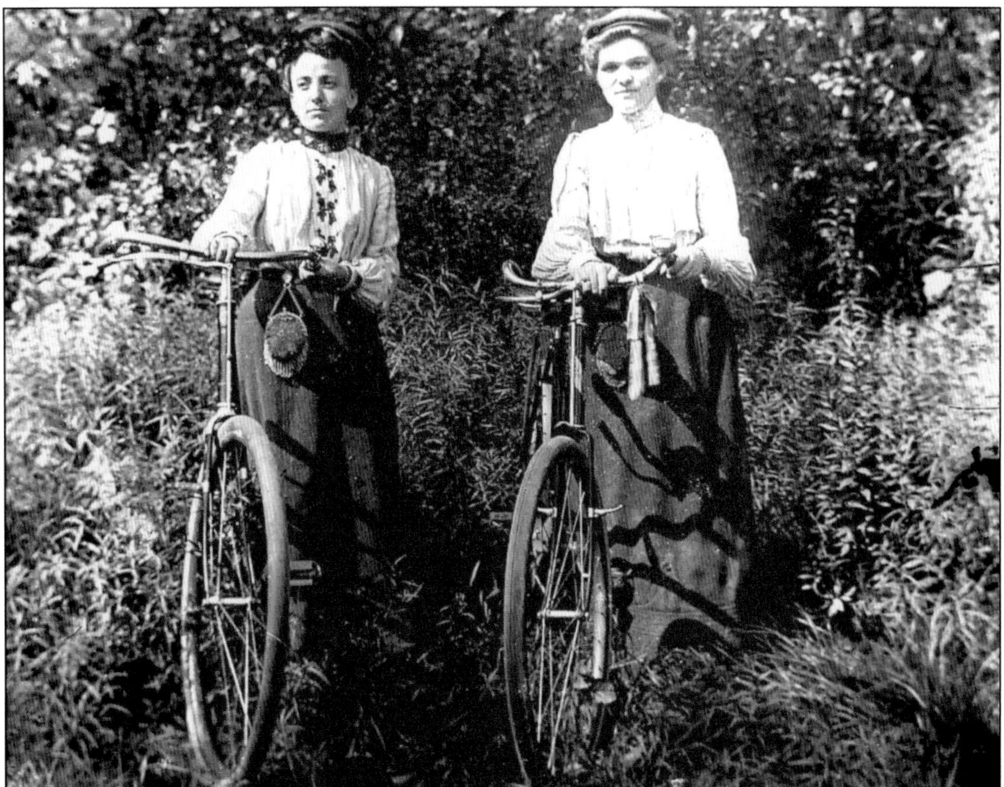

These ladies are adventurous enough to take their bicycles, better than horses or walking, and see the town at their own pace. With the roads in the condition that they were, these two are true daredevils.

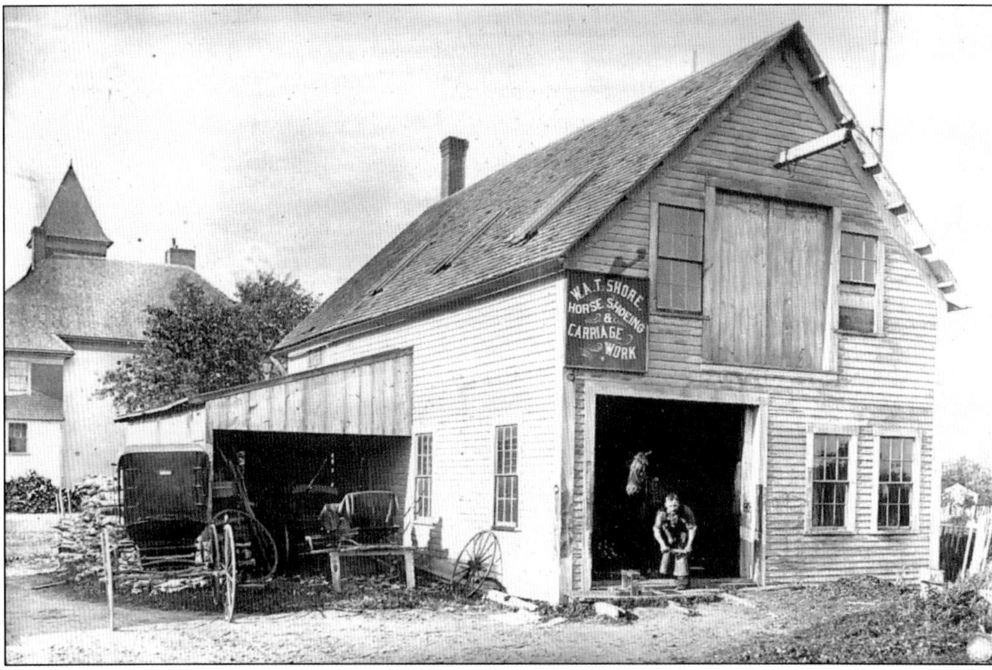

W.A.T. Shore Horseshoeing and Carriage Works was located on Cottage Street. The shop was run by William Shore, son of W. A. Shore, a blacksmith from Nottinghamshire, England. This shop was destroyed by fire in 1900. During the 1800s, they had to create horseshoes entirely by hand and fit them to each horse's hooves. W. A. Shore had an idea for making horseshoes using machinery and jotted it down on paper. A salesman visiting the business stole the plans and soon had the idea patented and marketed. Shore never received credit for the idea. Behind Shore's shop is the old Templeton High School on School Street.

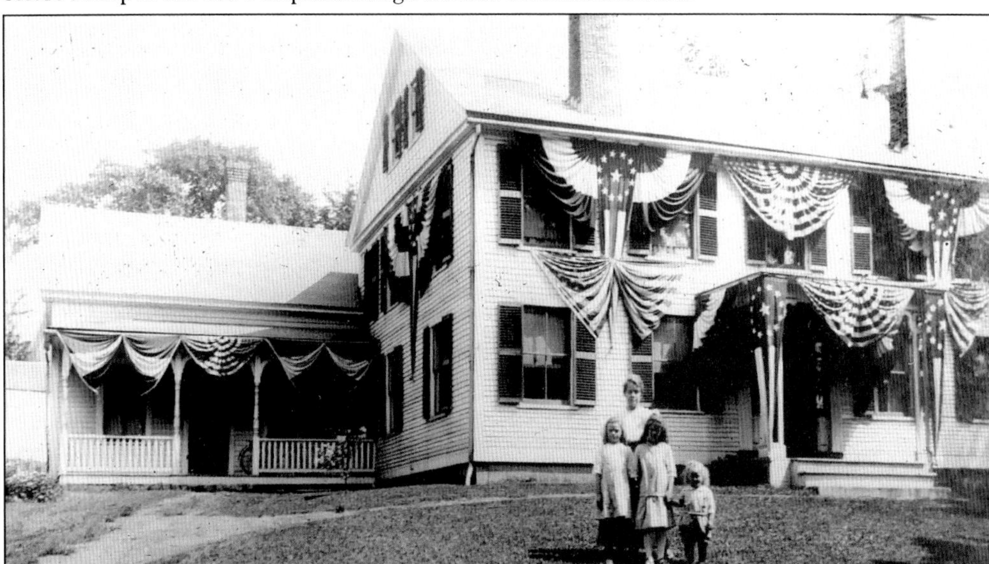

Dr. C. A. Fletcher resided here in 1899. His son Louis, who carried on his father's practice as a dentist, is the small child on the right. The house is shown here decorated for the welcome home parade. Originally, Louis Leland and family occupied this house.

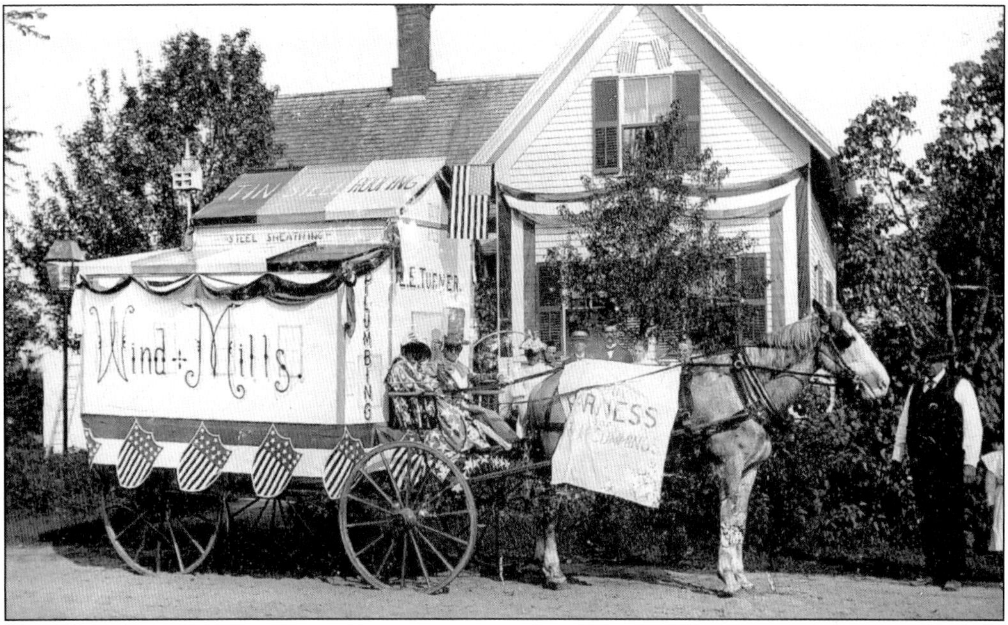

Leonard E. Turner lived on Mechanic Street in the area of the little league ball field. This July 4, 1897, picture shows a float with his family members ready for the parade. On the wagon are Ruth E. Turner and Winfield Washburn. Leonard Turner is at the head of the horse with Eva Cook beside him. In back of the horse are, from left to right, as follows: Mammie Turner, Josie Turner, Leonard Turner Jr., Harry Turner, Carol Turner, and Eva Turner.

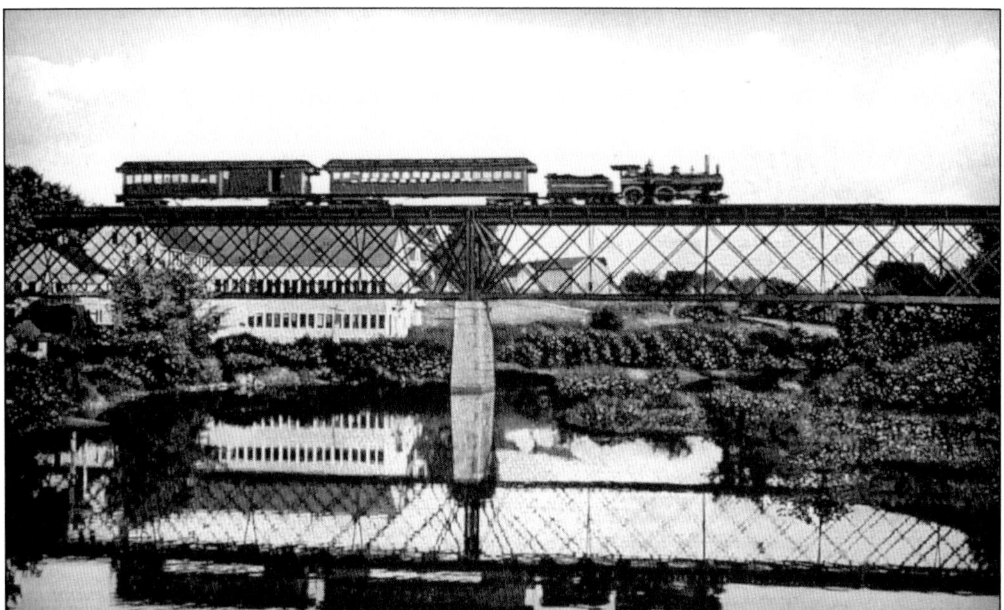

Looking east from the Otter River Bridge next to the fire station is a view of the Ware River Railroad trestle. Redesigned several times, the first trestle was made of wood. The first passenger train passed over this bridge in 1873. The large white building to the left is the Waite, Damon, and Gould Factory.

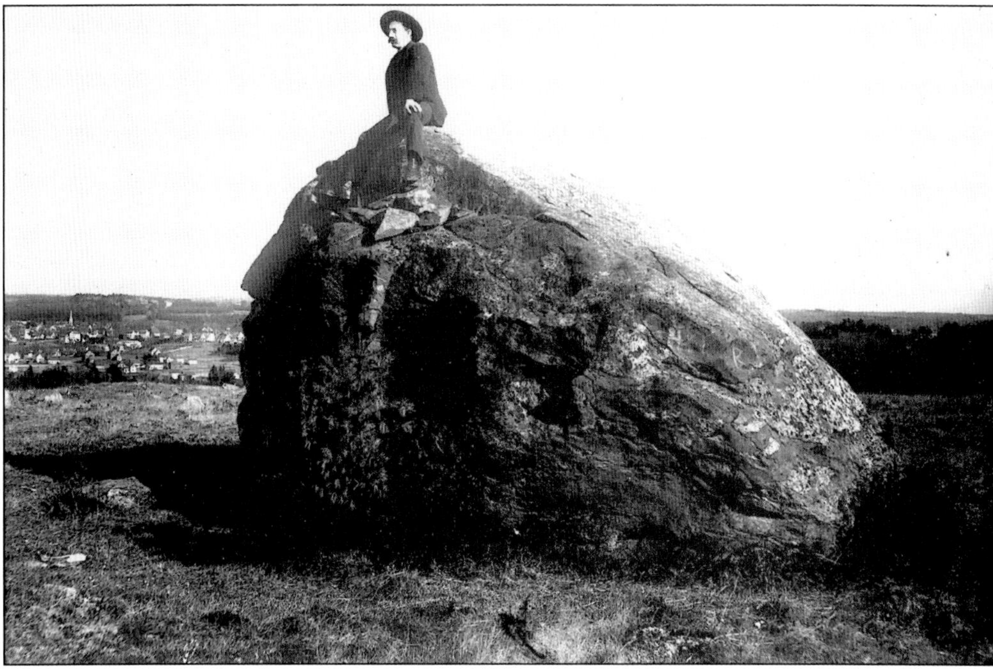

Milton Williams, Oren William's brother, sits on top of Profile Rock, located on Norcross Hill overlooking the town of Baldwinville. The rock's profile is said to resemble that of George Washington. It is now surrounded by trees and located on private property owned by the Tucker Family.

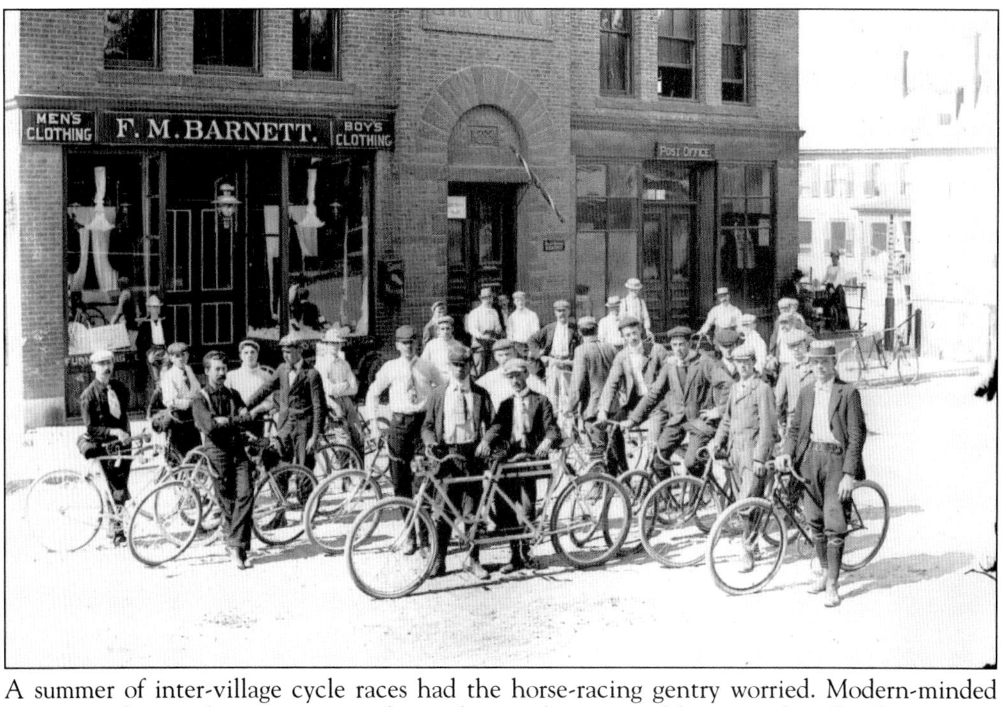

A summer of inter-village cycle races had the horse-racing gentry worried. Modern-minded young people were beginning to prefer tandems to buggies and long, grueling Sunday tours to restful all-day picnics at the end of a short drive.

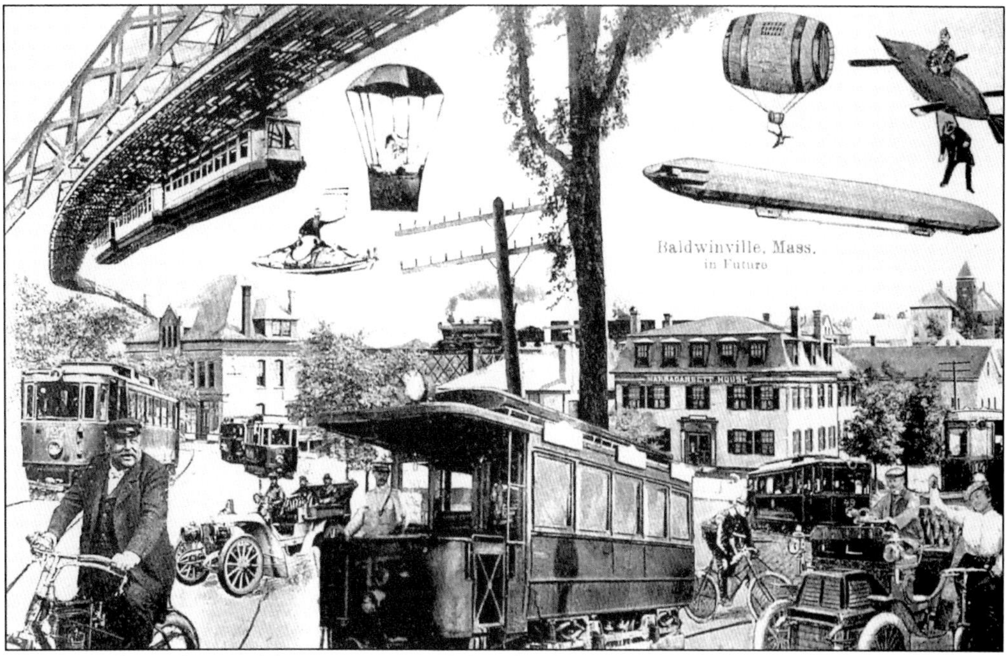

Baldwinville is depicted here as imagined for the future. These postcards were drawn up for many area towns. The artist used his imagination on some of these means of transportation, as the postcard is dated 1909. The aerial tramway was the only means of transportation that never made it to Baldwinville.

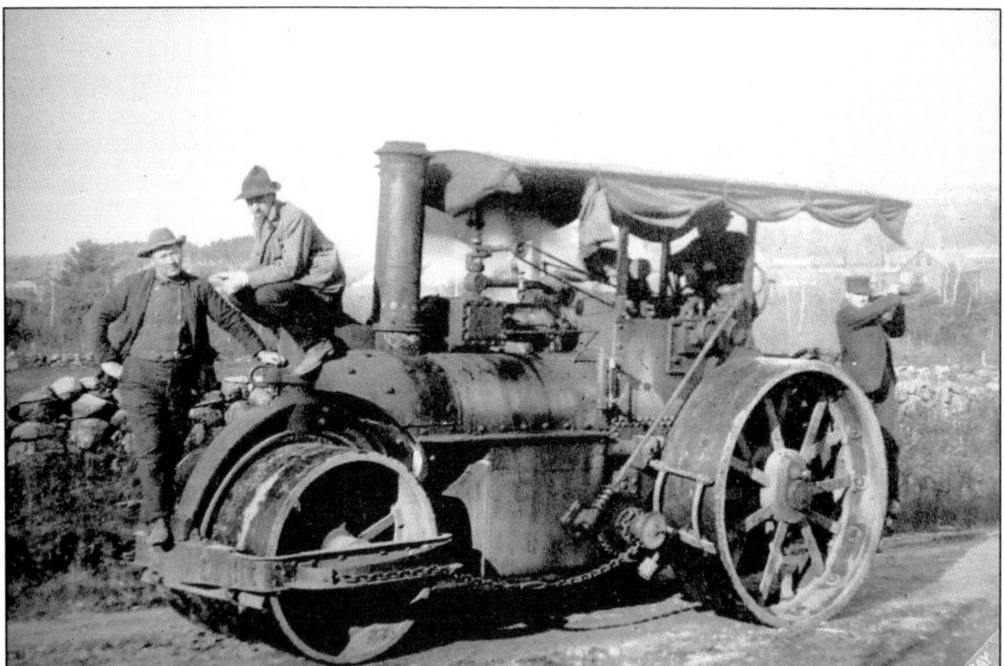

This 1905 image from Reservoir Street shows the new steamroller that helped compact roads and keep them easier to navigate for a longer period of time. Keeping roads somewhat flat was no easy task, as horses and wagons left the dirt roads a mess.

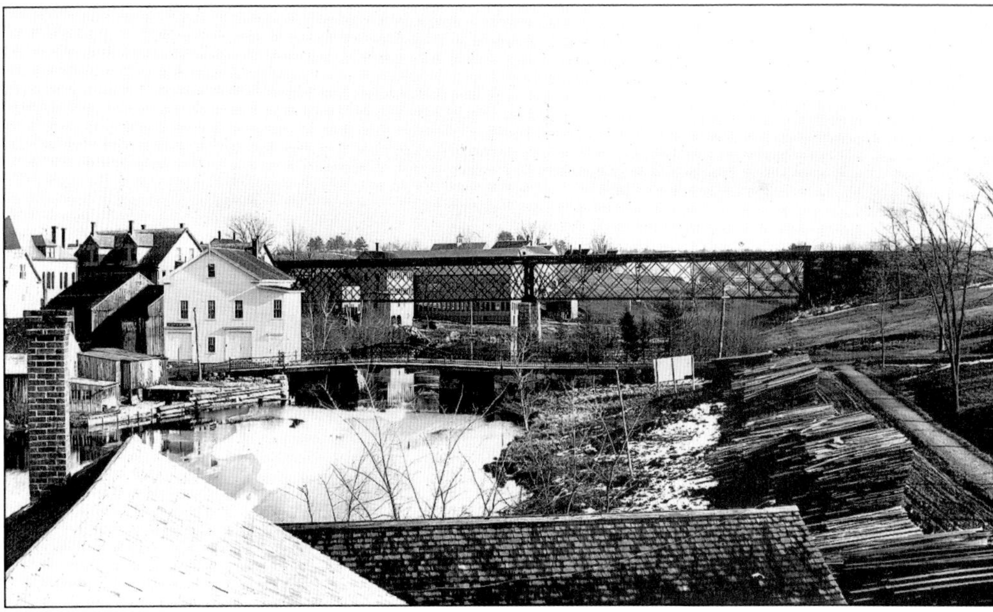

This is a view of the Union Hall and Tiger No. 1 Fire Station from the roof of the old Waite Chair Company on the south side of the Otter River. The stables for the hotel are seen just to the right of the building, and the Narragansett House is shown on the corner. Straight ahead up river is the Ware River Railroad Trestle, which leads to the Baldwinville Depot.

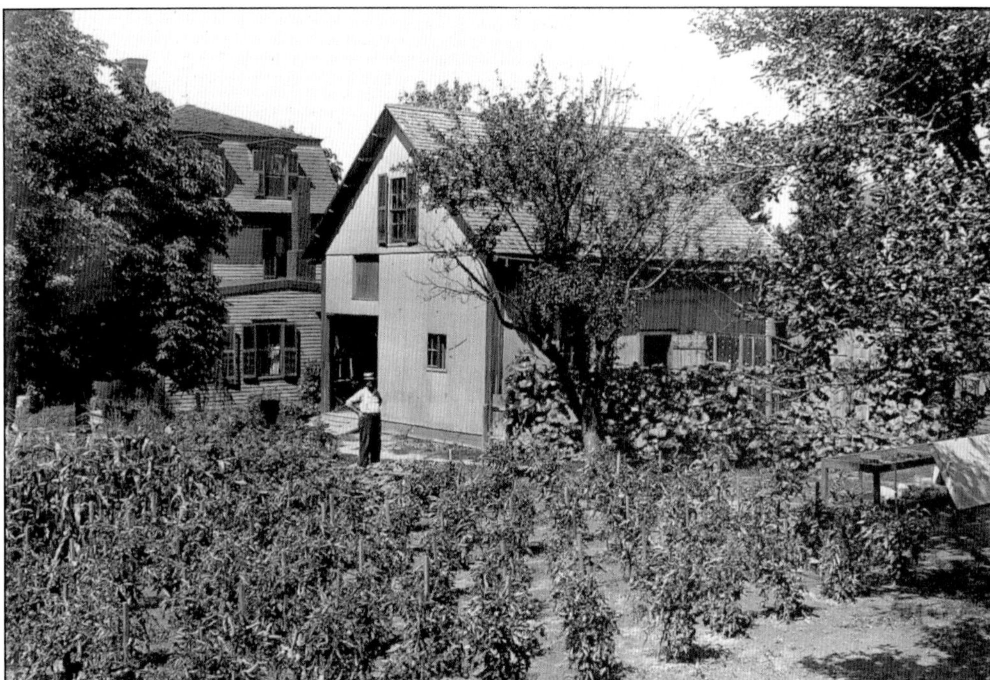

Lysander B. Bronsdon is shown here on the corner of Elm and Bridge Streets. Bronsdon was a builder and carpenter with many homes and additions to his credit in Baldwinville. The tomato plants on the left in this picture had to be removed to make way for Bridge Street. Prior to the Bridge Street construction, one had to cross the tracks on North Main Street (now Circle Street).

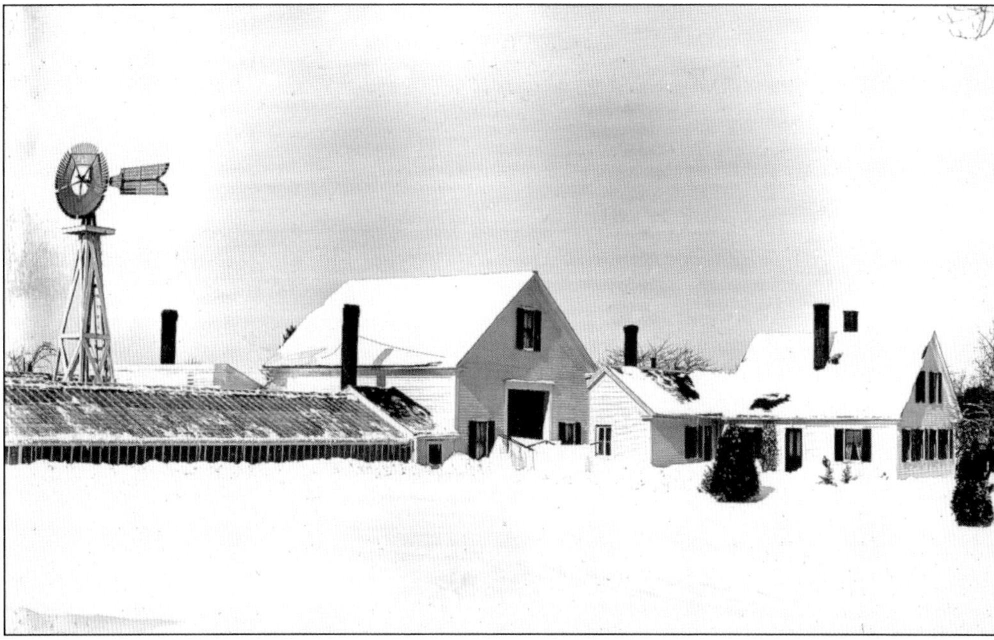

Shown here is F. L. Hosmer's house *c.* 1898 on South Main Street (now Baldwinville Road). His cucumber greenhouses are on the left in this picture. Now the Gingras family lives here.

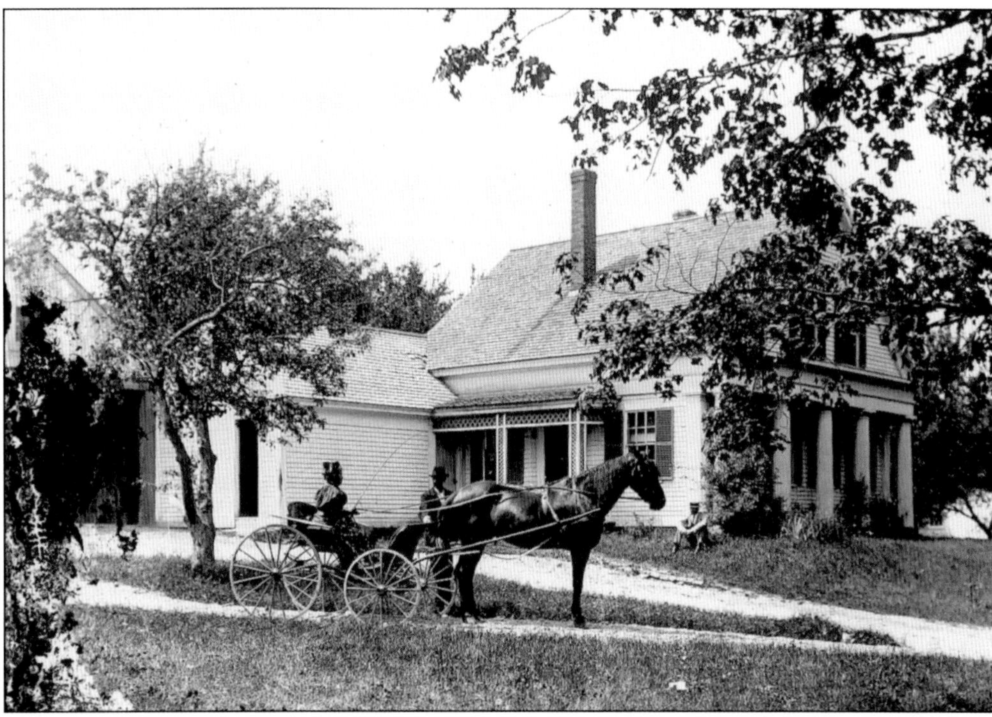

George Bryant built this house in 1850. In 1898, it was the home of L. E. Merrill. The house has been in the Paine family for the last four generations and is owned today by Richard Paine Jr. The people in the photograph are unidentified. The two with the horse and buggy might be Alanson and Cora Paine.

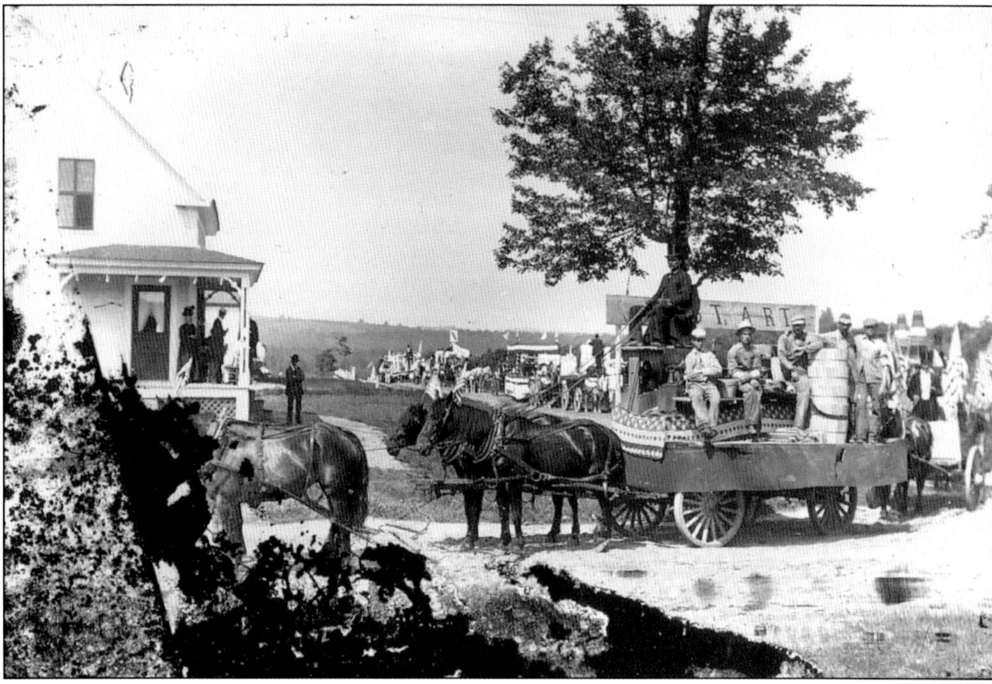

Lined up for the parade, most of the local businesses decorated their wagons to celebrate the Fourth of July in 1897.

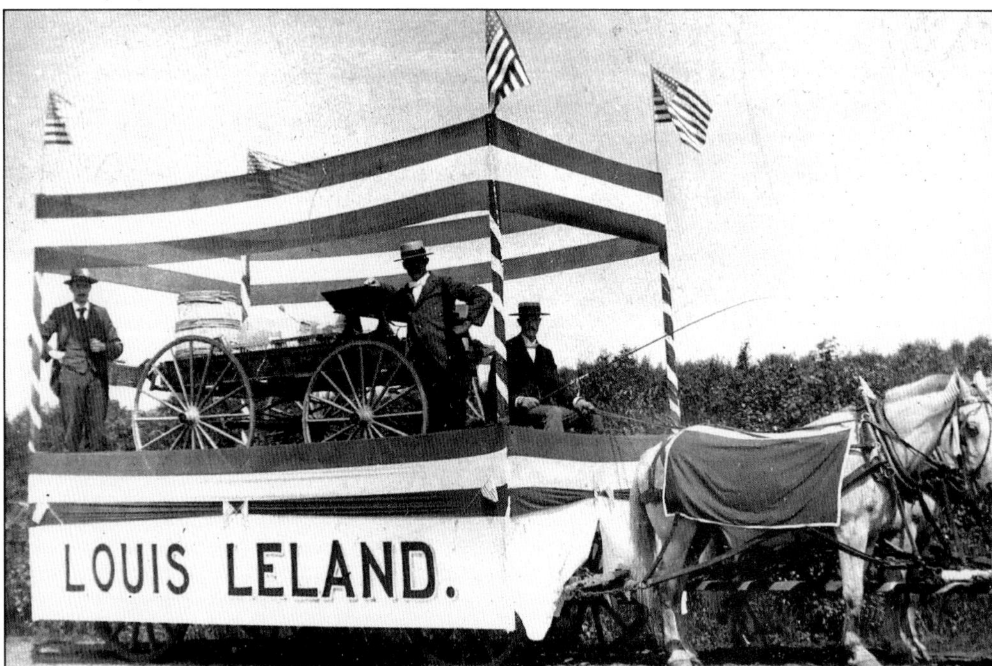

Louis Leland owned the general store in Baldwinville. He decorated his float using one of his delivery wagons, filled with his regular inventory. He and his store workers were probably the most recognized members of the parade.

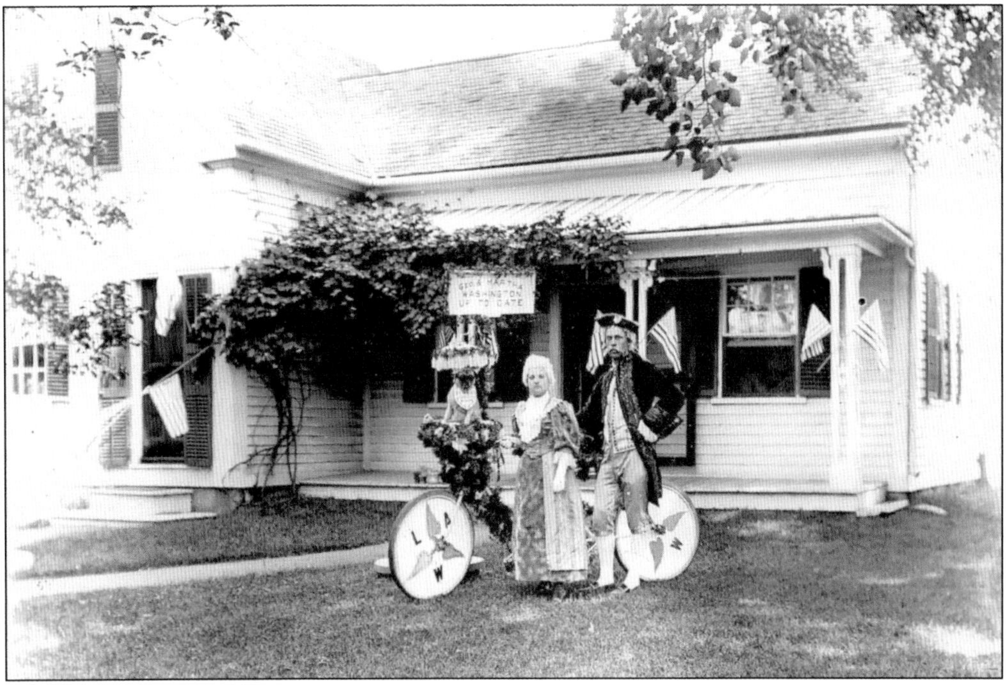

Dressed as George and Martha Washington for the parade, C. W. Coleman and his wife stand in front of their Cross Street home (now Circle Street).

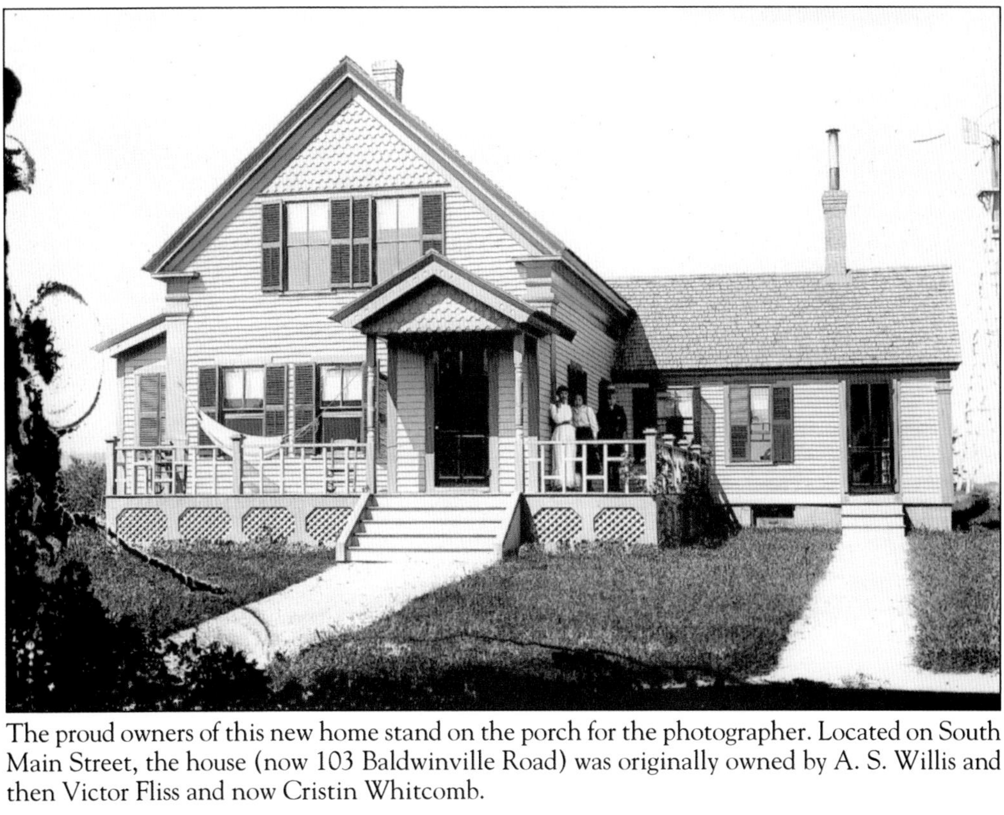

The proud owners of this new home stand on the porch for the photographer. Located on South Main Street, the house (now 103 Baldwinville Road) was originally owned by A. S. Willis and then Victor Fliss and now Cristin Whitcomb.

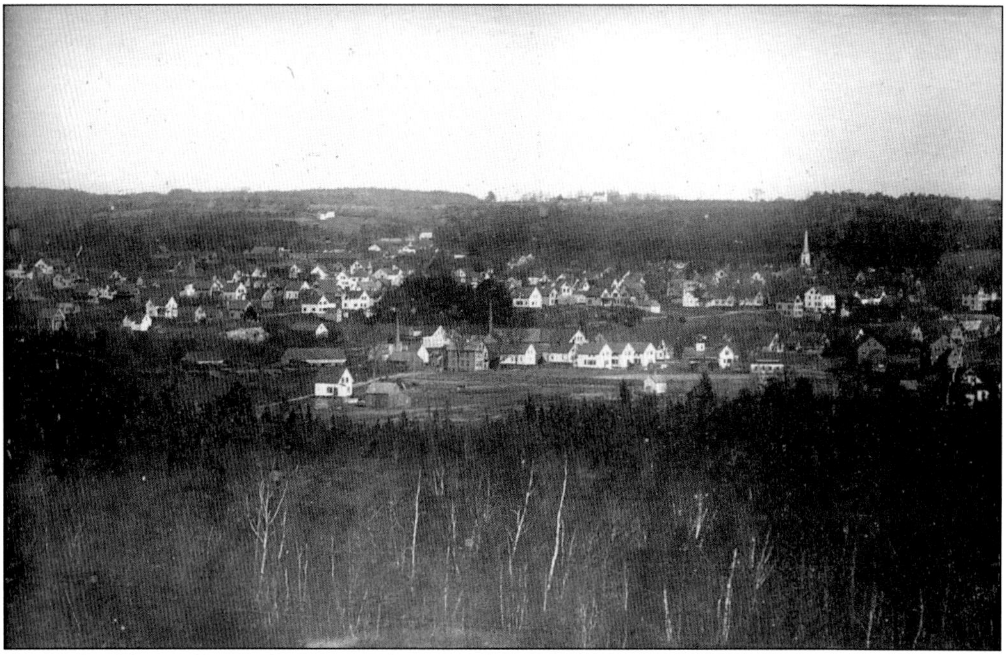

Most of Baldwinville can be seen in this view from Norcross Hill. Notice all of the houses in the lower section. These are all of the buildings that were removed to make way for the Birch Hill Dam project. The photographer was probably standing on Profile Rock.

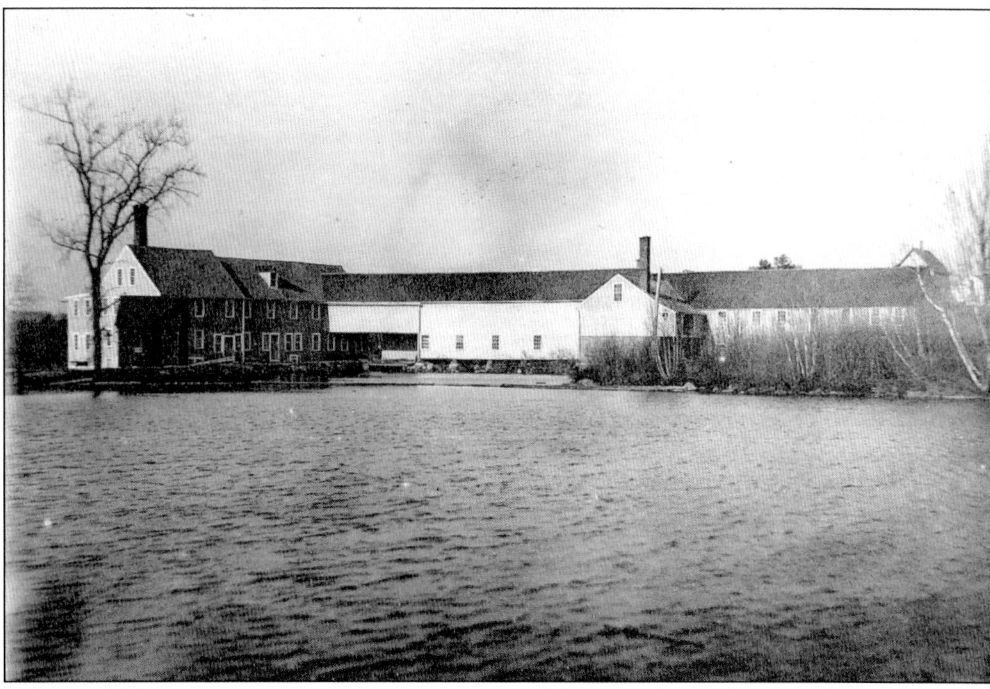

Baker and Wilson Company was started by Rev. Willard Baker, who later helped form the Hospital Cottages with his son Dr. Lucius Willard Baker. The Bishop and Streeter Chair Manufacturing Company bought the property after Baker's death. This factory was located on the lower section of the Otter River across from the E. L. Thompson Chair Company.

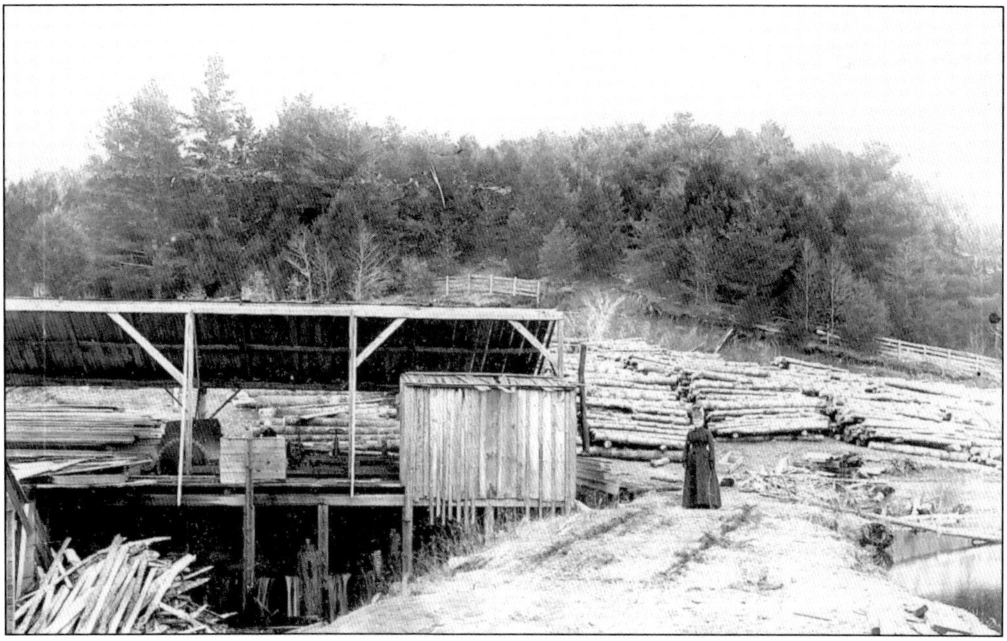

This sawmill was in operation in the late 1800s. It was owned and operated by Gilman Day, which is how it got the name of Day Mill. The water from Trout Brook powered the mill, and a dam was built to create Day Mill Pond.

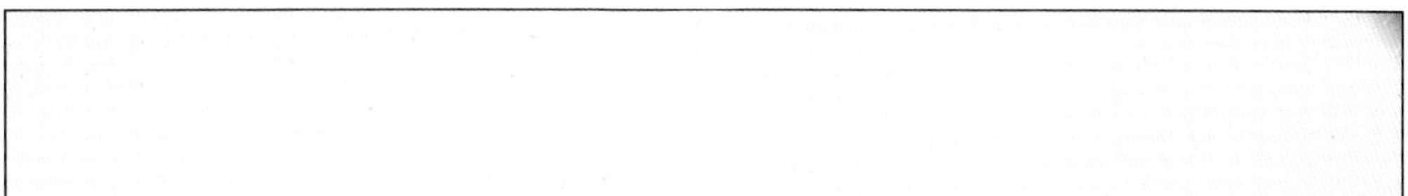

Five buildings of the H. M. Small Paper and Asbestos Works, located on the upper part of the Otter River on the corner of Mill and Reservoir Streets, are shown here. On the right of the picture, the largest building with the smoke stack is the Smith and Day Chair Factory. On the left of the picture is a large white house and barn, which belonged to Gilman Waite. To the left of Waite's house is H. K. Wright's house. On the right is George Brooks's house and barn.

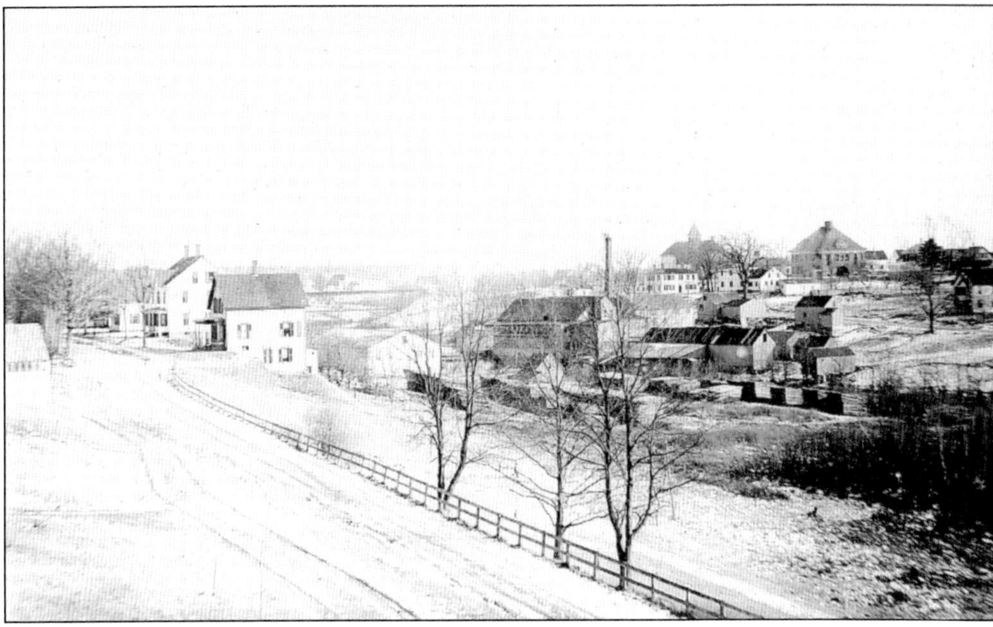

In the background on the hill, the two schools are in plain view. Taken from the end of Memorial Street, this picture shows the old Thompson, Perley, and Waite Company prior to the fire of 1895. Over the river are the buildings for the Waite Chair Company before they built their new factory. Notice the water building up downstream caused by the E. L. Thompson Dam.

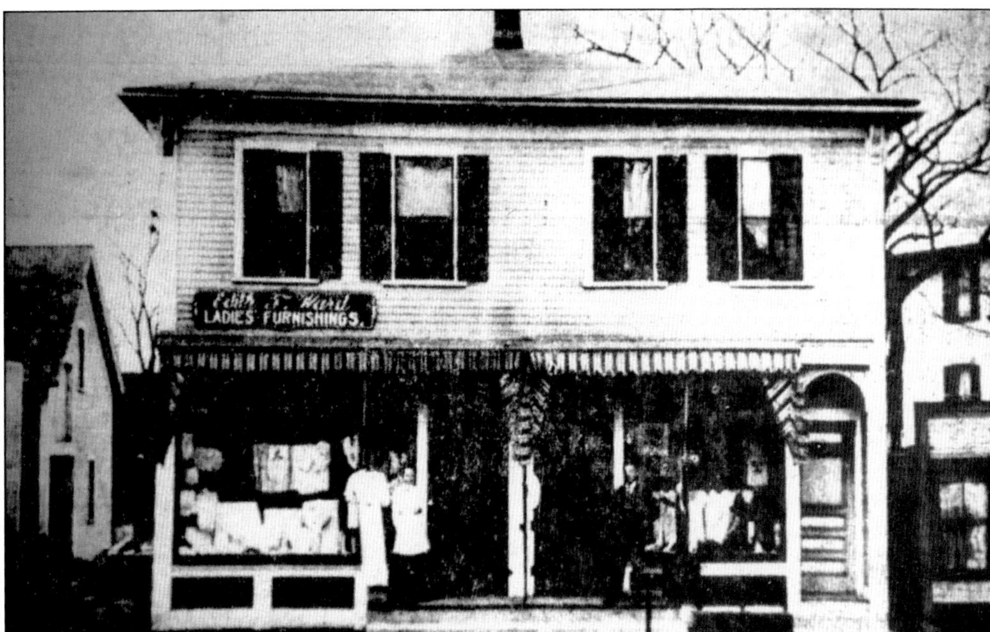

Edith "Ward" Peabody operated this woman's clothing store on North Main Street, now Circle Street. She was the mother of Bayard Peabody. On the right side of the store was a millinery shop operated by Nellie Tourtellot.

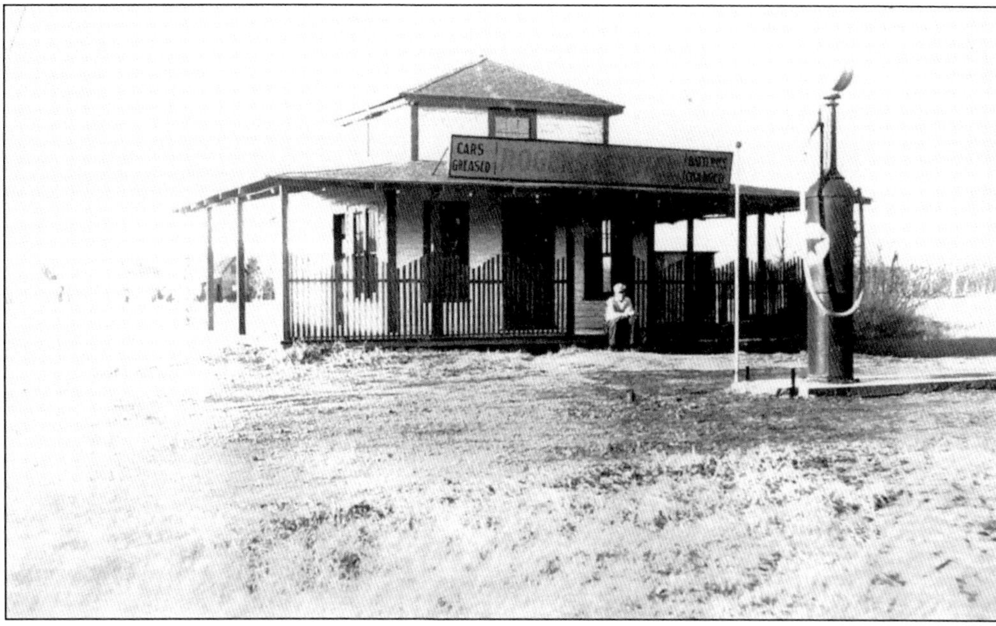

Shown here is Roger's Service Station on Maple Street in Baldwinville. By 1920, cars were just starting to show up around here, and this attendant has to wait quite a while between customers filling up with gas.

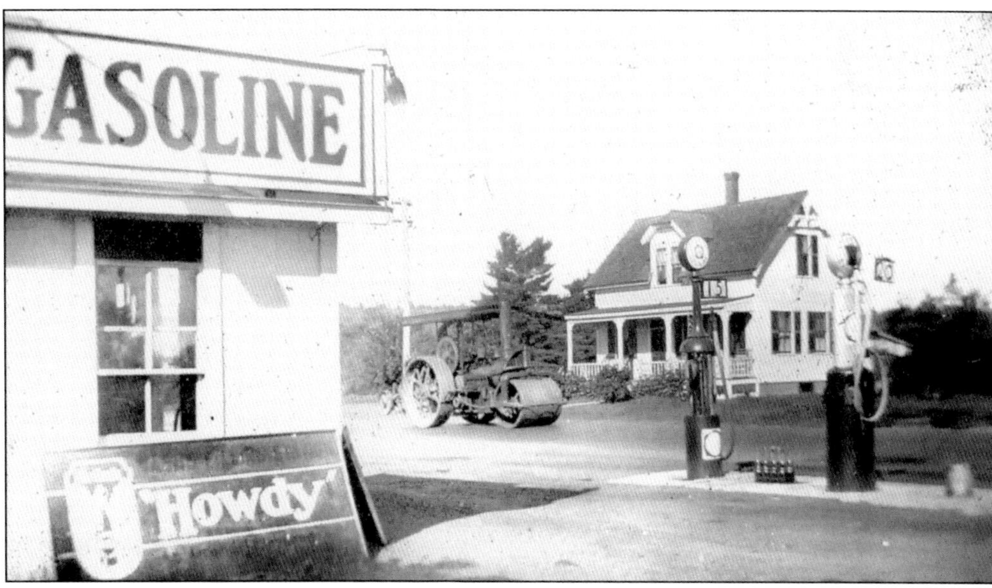

Harry Nash owned this gas station on Mechanic Street. Part of the Birch Hill Dam project, this entire area was flooded.

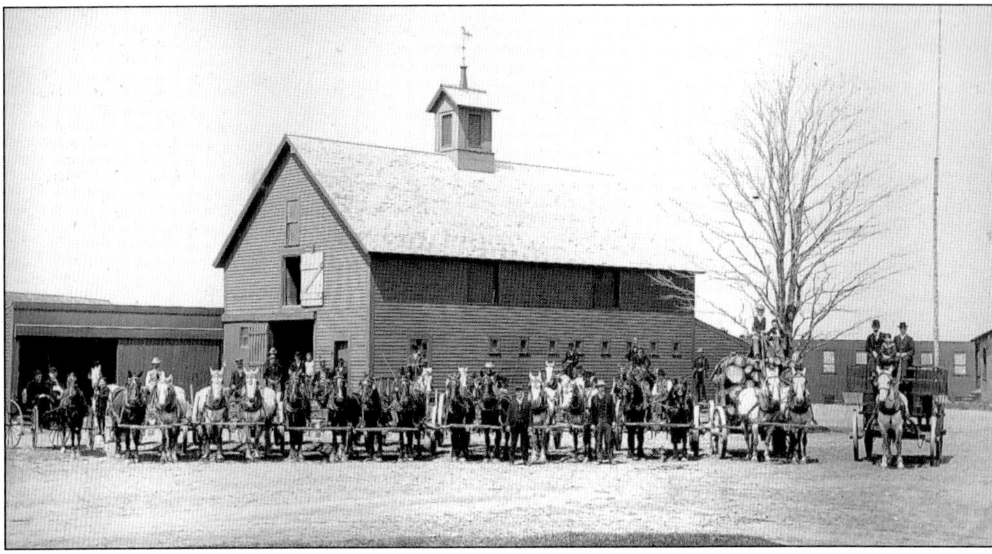

In 1900, the Harris and Murphy Company manufactured pails and buckets. Owners John P. Murphy, in the buggy on the far left, and Arthur T. Harris, on the far right in the wagon, show off their team of horses and wagons with their factory workers. Before Harris and Murphy, the company was called Holman and Harris. The company continued until 1909, when both owners retired. In 1910, J. A. Temple and Arthur L. Stuart purchased the vacated buildings and manufactured kitchen and dining chairs under the name of the Temple Stuart Company.

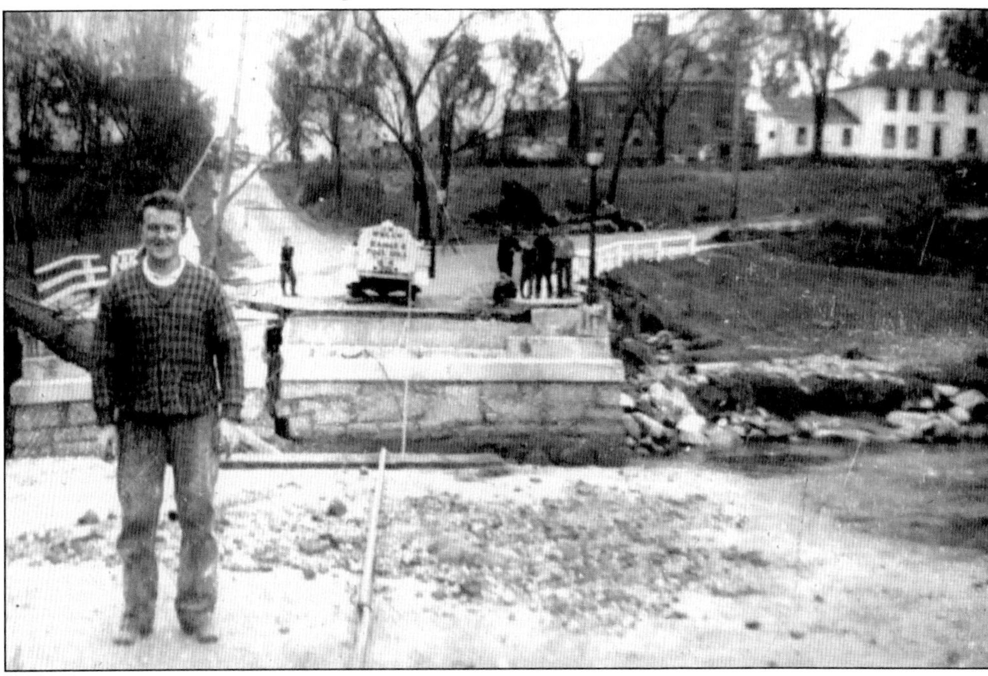

Russell Adams stands where the bridge crossing the Otter River use to be. The 1938 hurricane flooded the river and washed out all the bridges that crossed the river dividing Baldwinville. The only way to cross the river was to walk across the railroad trestle, which was over 70 feet above the river. Boards were placed across the railroad ties to make walking over the trestle as safe as possible.

Three

East Templeton

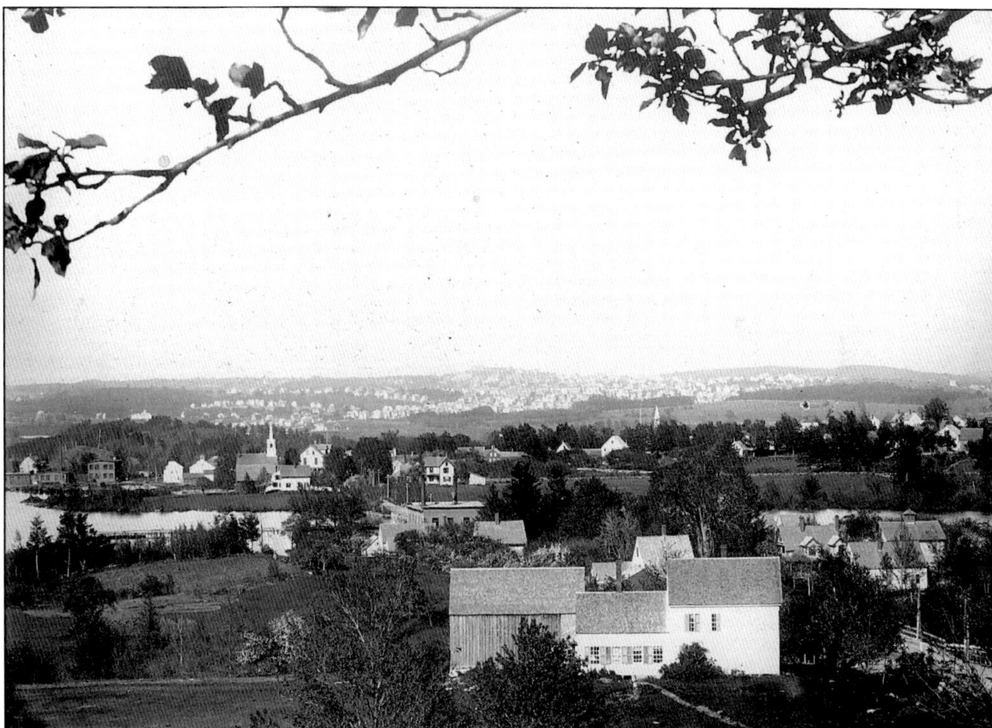

This is a view looking east from Ladder Hill on Patriots Road into the village, formerly named Southeast Plantation, Simondville, Falesville, and finally East Templeton. In the center of the photograph is the Methodist church. The smoke stacks in the center of the photograph define the power plant of the Templeton Street Railway. To the left of the church are some of the factories that prospered before the flood. The large white building was the farm of John Potter, which was torn down c. 1965 to make room for the Route 2 highway. Retired highway superintendent Walter Smith was the farm's last owner. Gardner can be seen in the background.

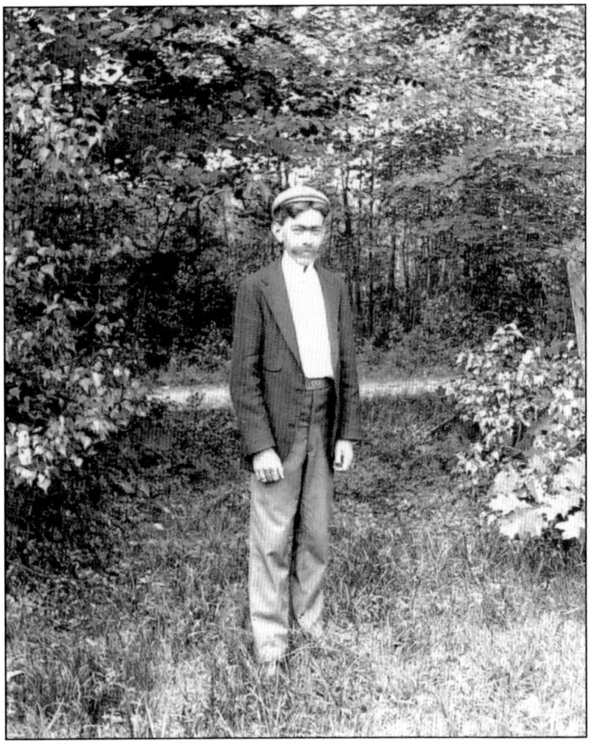

Wallace Underwood was a painter and photographer who lived on Lord Road in East Templeton. Wallace was born on August 1, 1867. His parents were Walter and Eliza Ann (Rugg). Wallace had a passion for photography. His collection covered a great part of East Templeton and is showcased in this chapter.

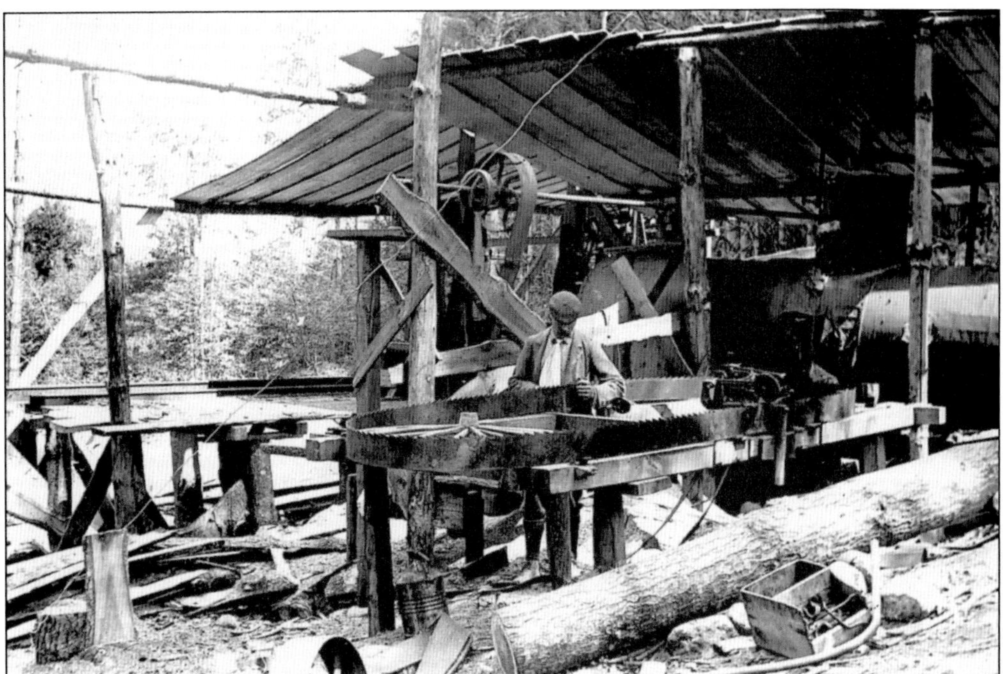

This is possibly the sawmill that was operated by the Underwood family on what was known as Underwood Road. The mill sat below the dam at what is now the Ridgely Club. The pond was then known as Underwood Pond, and the road went from Otter River Road to North Main Street.

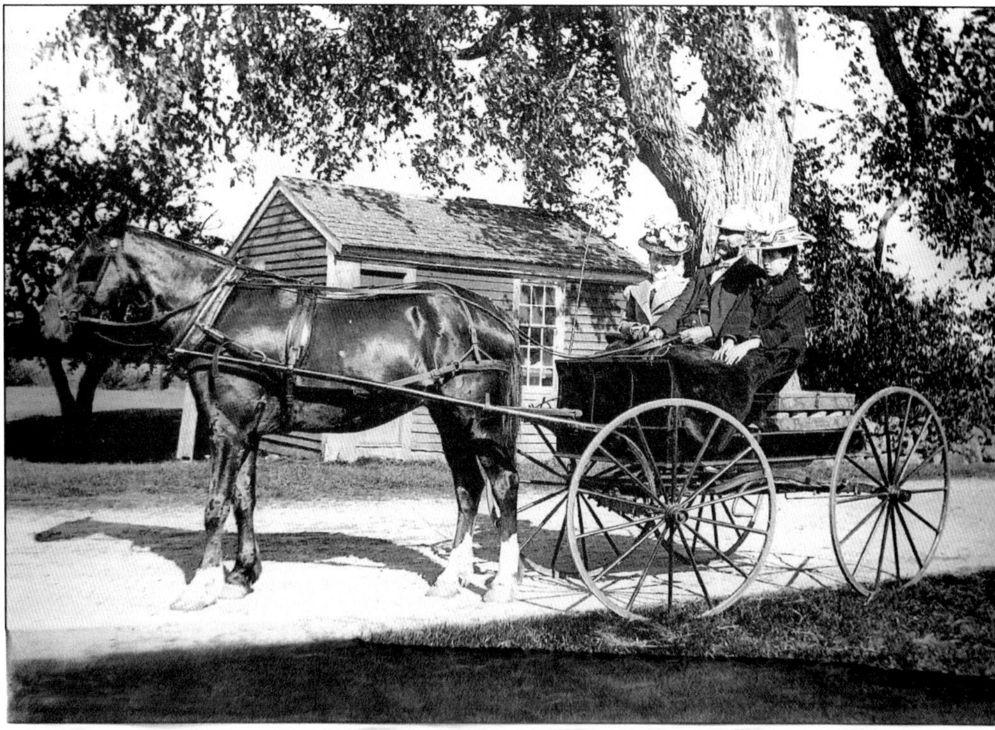

This image was taken at the Wallace Underwood farm c. 1900. A family is shown all dressed up and driving to the village or perhaps church. Underwood's grandfather used this small building as a clock repair shop.

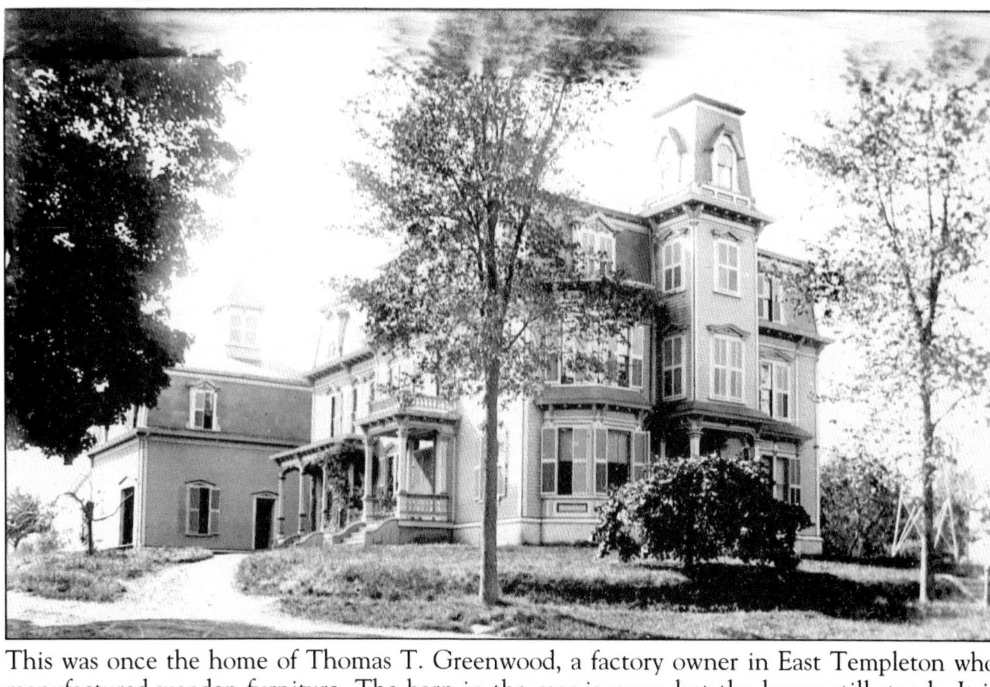

This was once the home of Thomas T. Greenwood, a factory owner in East Templeton who manufactured wooden furniture. The barn in the rear is gone, but the house still stands. It is owned today by Rudolph Sundstrom and used as an apartment house.

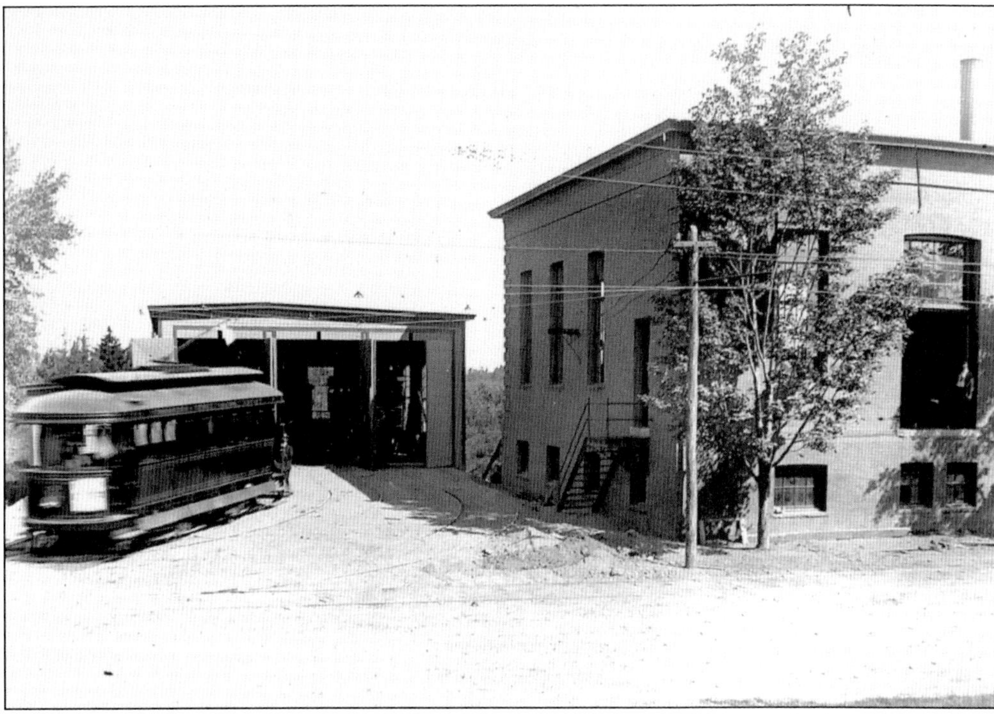

The power plant and trolley barn are shown here. They were once located where Wilson Bus Lines is today. A worker standing in the doorway takes a break or poses for the photographer.

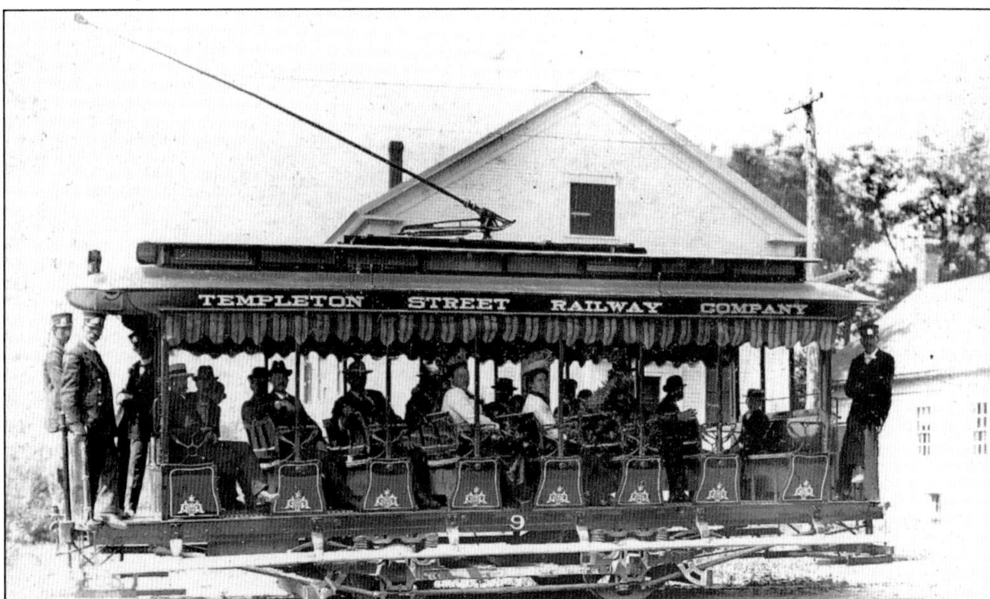

Work began on the Templeton Street Railway on October 6, 1899. The first motormen were Knox Kent, W. E. Snow, Thomas Shaw, and Merrick Blanchard. The conductors were Coleman from East Templeton, Brooks from Baldwinville, and Doherty and Hawkes from Templeton. The trolley shown here in front of the East Templeton Methodist Church from July 1900 was the first on the road.

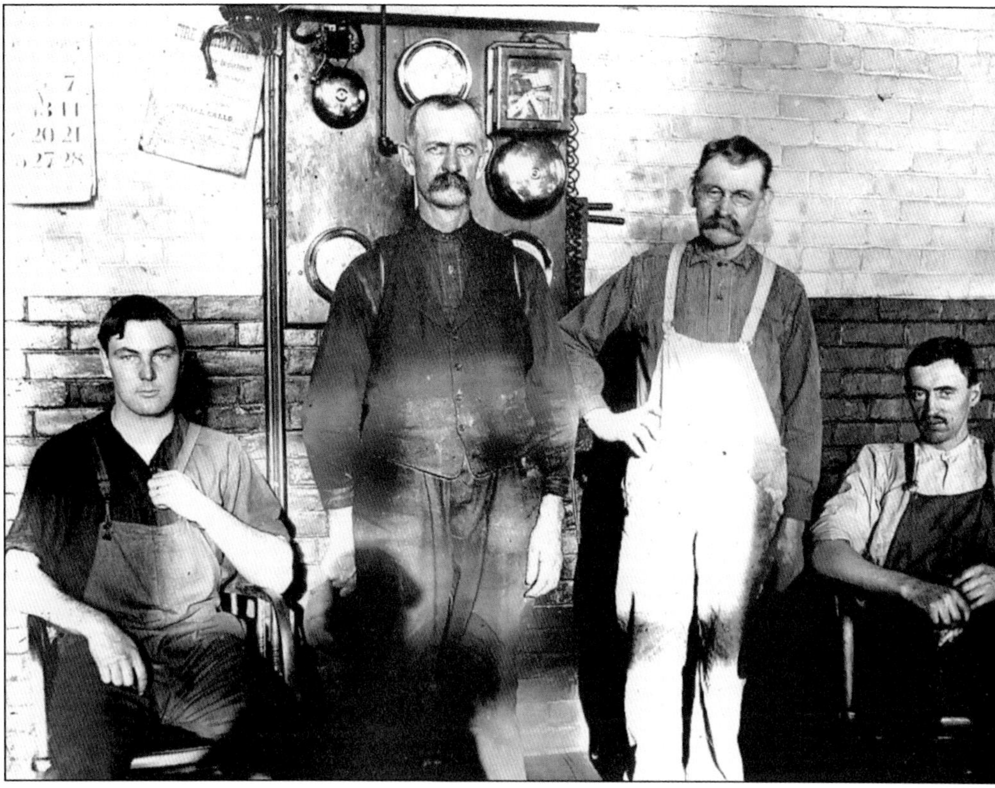

Four men of the Templeton Street Railway Power Station are shown in this photograph. The calendar is dated 1905. On the left is Stuart Winch.

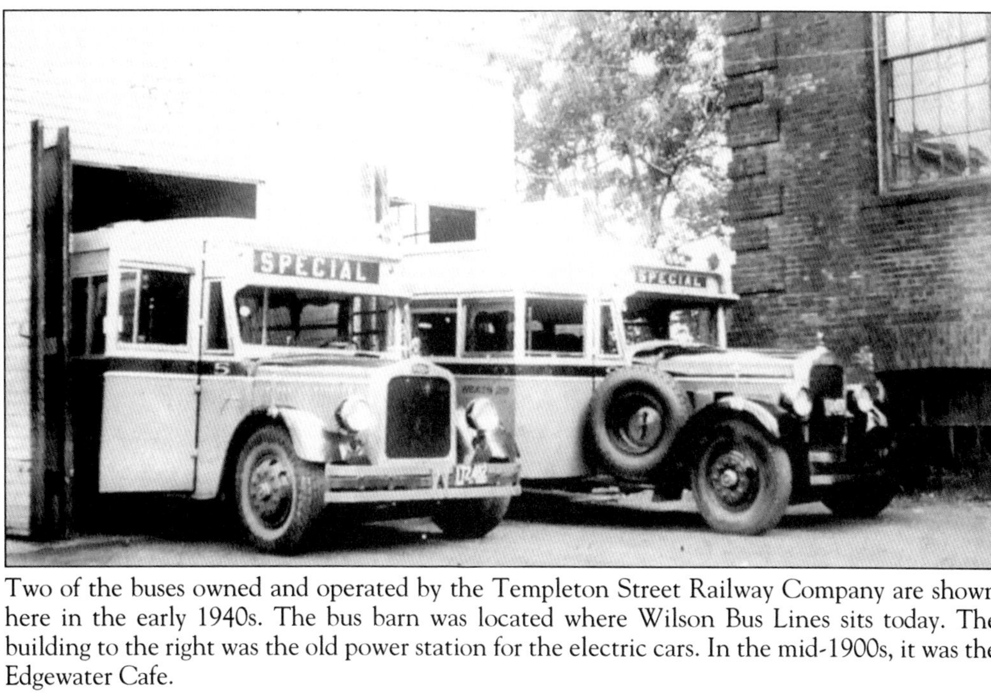

Two of the buses owned and operated by the Templeton Street Railway Company are shown here in the early 1940s. The bus barn was located where Wilson Bus Lines sits today. The building to the right was the old power station for the electric cars. In the mid-1900s, it was the Edgewater Cafe.

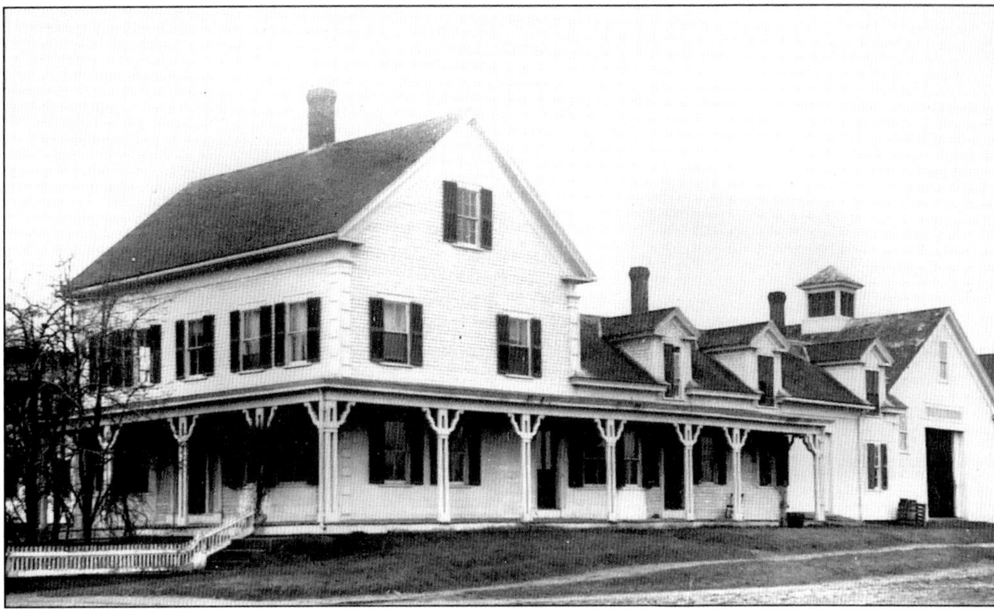

In East Templeton on the corner of North Main and Patriots Road stands the A. S. Hodge house, built during the late 1800s. Amasa S. Hodge, born in 1831, bought the old gristmill on North Main Street in 1863 and made chairs for 23 years until 1886, when the factory was burned.

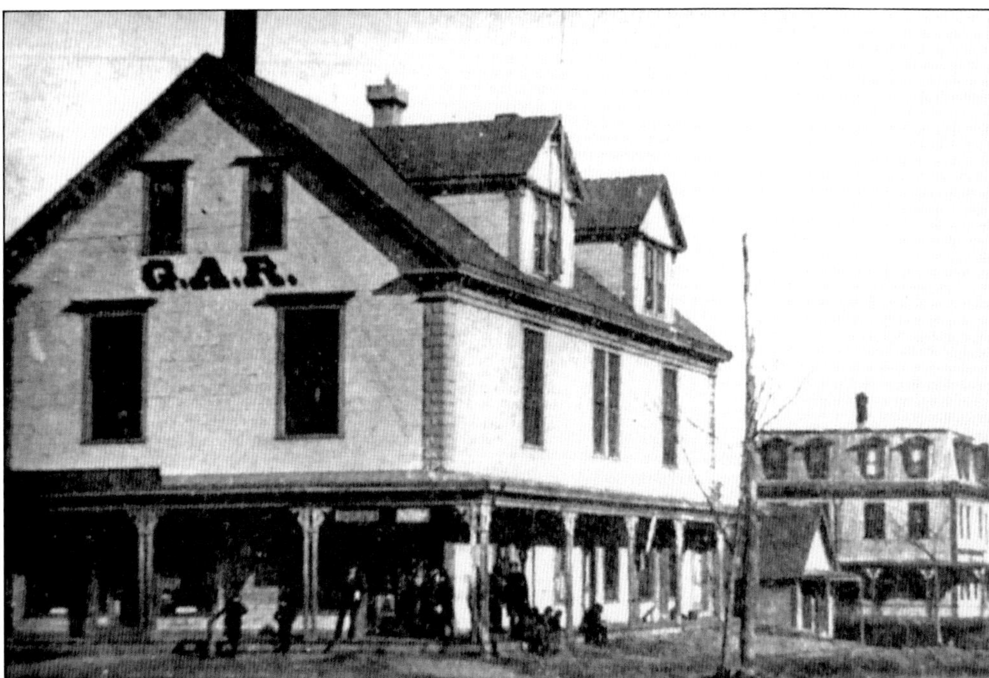

Shown is the Grand Army of the Republic (GAR) Hall in East Templeton with the Robert McGowan Building standing in the back. It was later known as the Monette Block and was destroyed by a fire in the 1950s. The little building was Monette's Barber Shop.

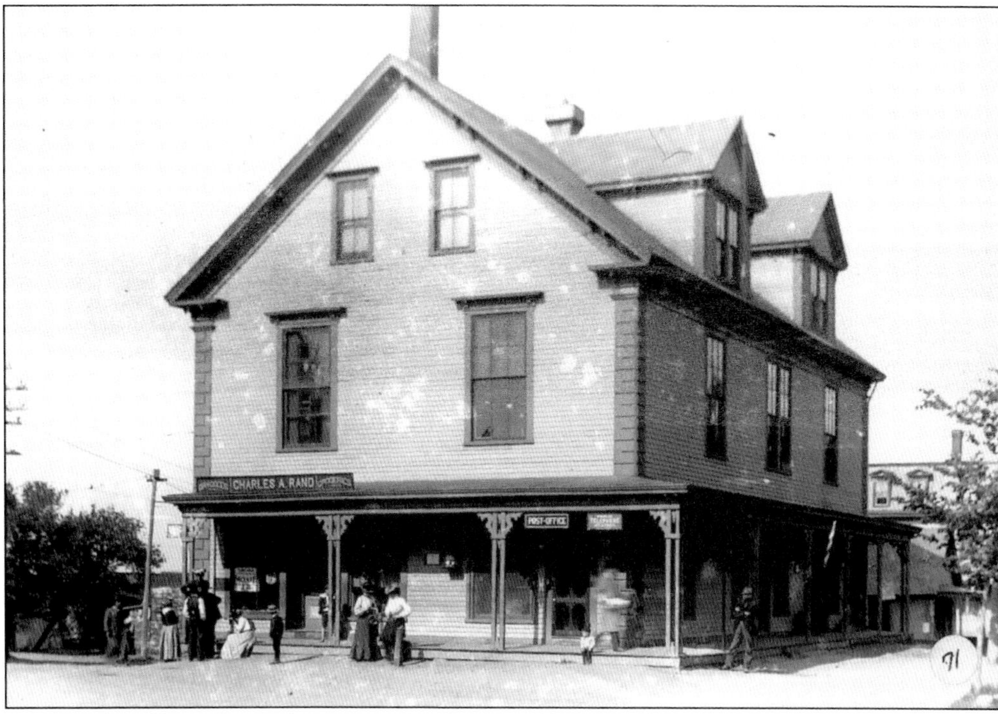

Memorial Hall was better known as the GAR Hall. It stood in East Templeton center at the point where Gardner Road and Main Street met. The building was taken down in August 1980. Over the years, the building was used as a store, post office, library, and an upholstery shop. V. P. Parkhurst erected it, and later it became the property of the Ericson Post No. 109.

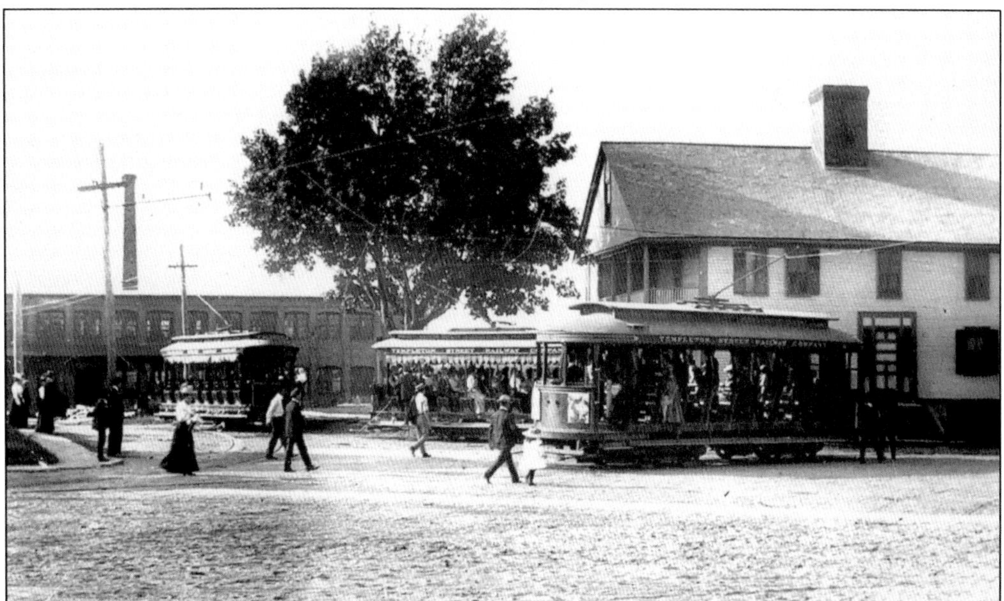

Traffic was heavy in East Templeton Center at the intersection of North Main Street and Gardner Road. The Bay State Wheel Company can be seen behind the trolley cars. To the right was Wright's Tavern, now Kameloht.

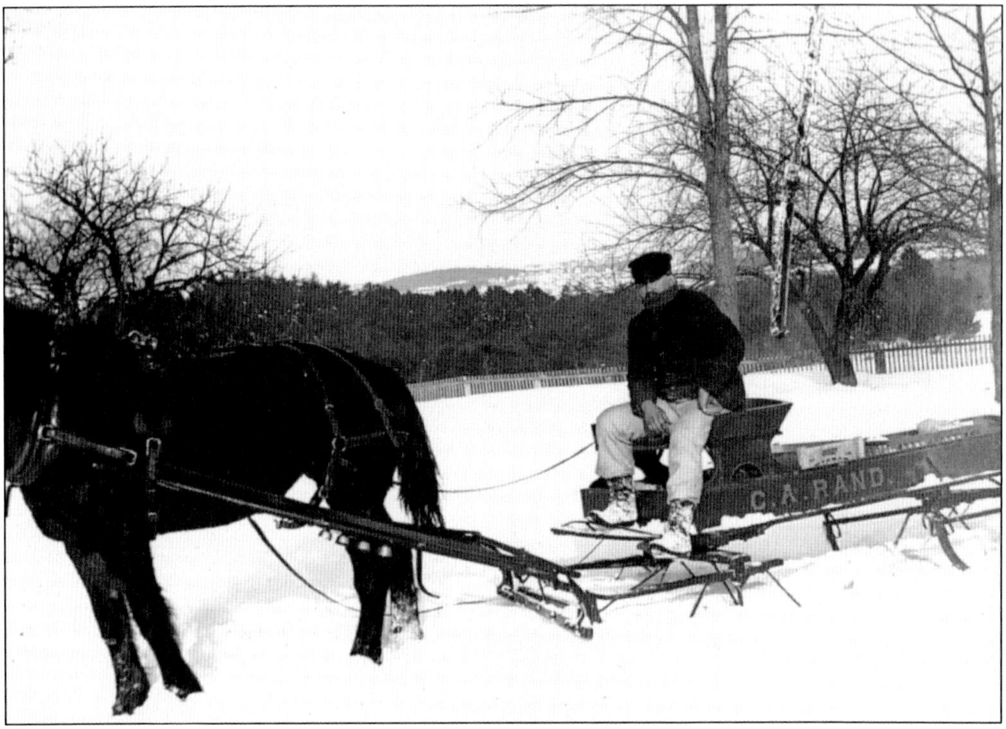

Charles A. Rand operated a store on the ground floor of Memorial Hall (the GAR Hall). Pictured is Cliff Wood making a delivery with a horse-drawn sleigh for Rand *c.* 1915.

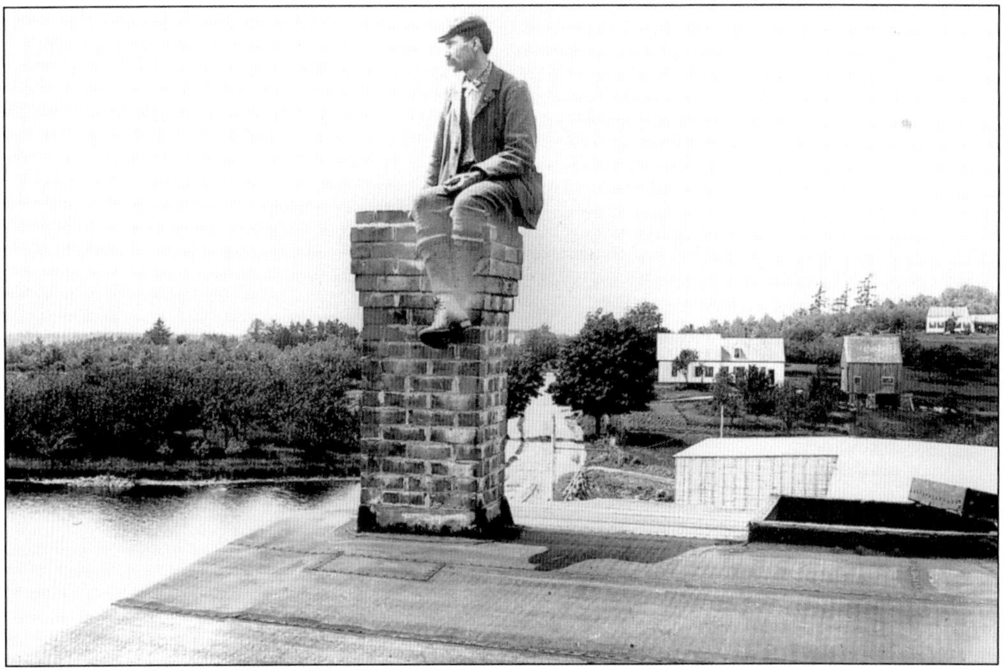

Harry Kay, superintendent, sits on the chimney of the Bay State Wheel Company, looking up North Main Street. The house and barn in the rear belonged to the Gerzadowicz family. Dr. Stevens owned the house on the hill in the late 1900s.

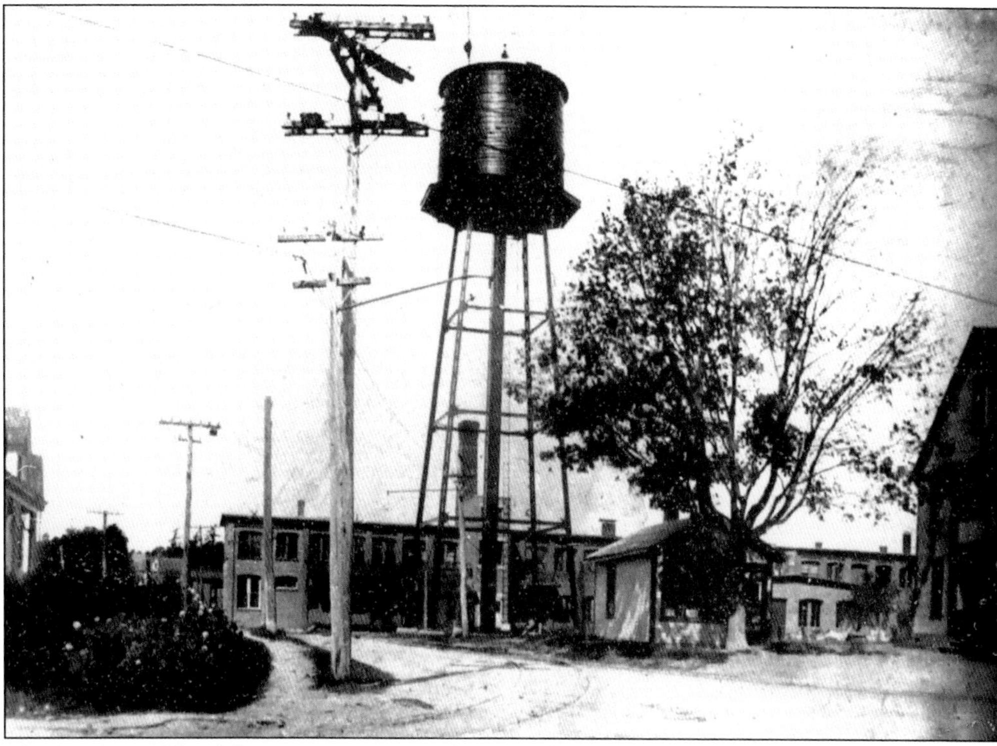

The Bay State Wheel Company was a manufacturer of pedal cars and other children's vehicles. The factory can be seen in the background. The water tower was a landmark in East Templeton.

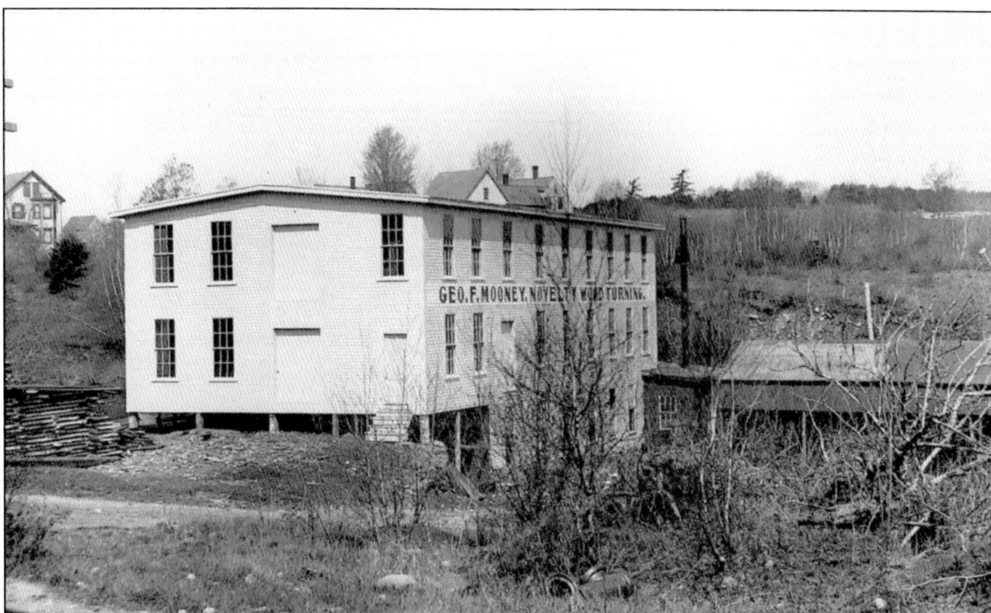

The George F. Mooney Company produced woodturnings and reed furniture. The company started c. 1903 and was located off Mechanic Street. The factory was eventually destroyed by fire.

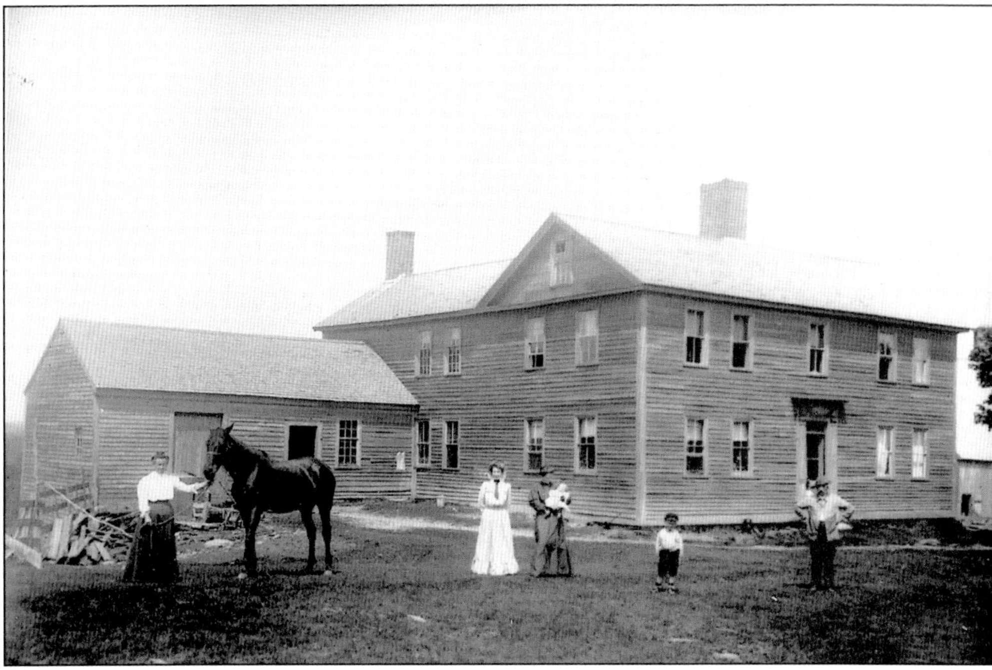

George Hayes's farm is shown here *c*. 1918 and was located on Cottage Lane in East Templeton. The farm was purchased by the state to make way for Route 2. In the mid-1960s, it was being dismantled when it was set on fire by vandals and destroyed.

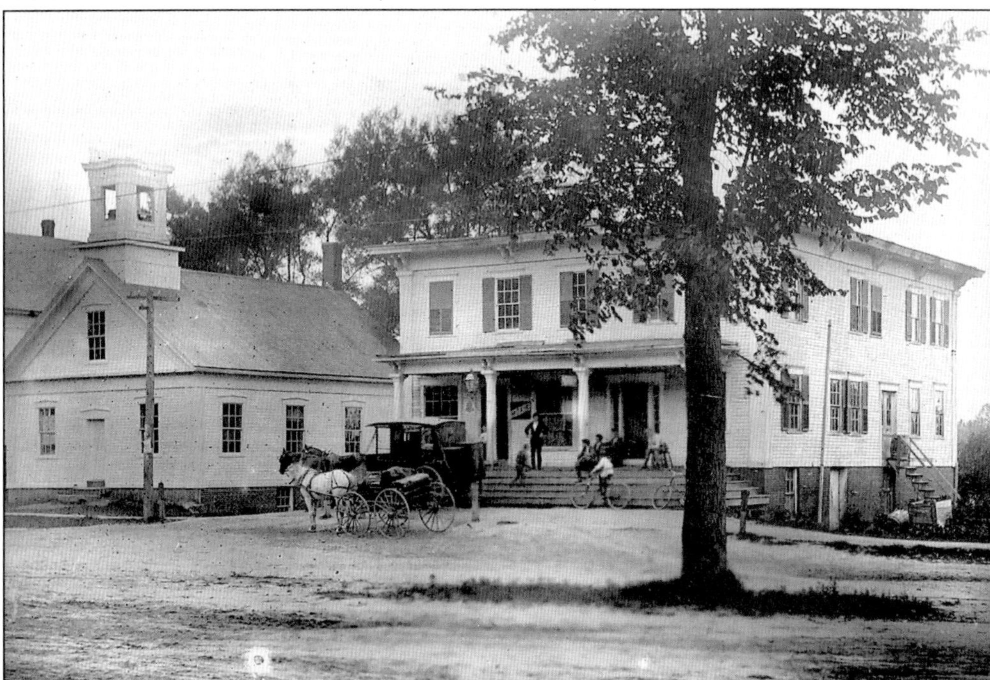

Fitch Sargeant owned this building, where he ran a store. It also served as the first post office in East Templeton and was established as such in 1866, when Sargeant was appointed the first postmaster. The building to the left was the school. Both buildings stand today.

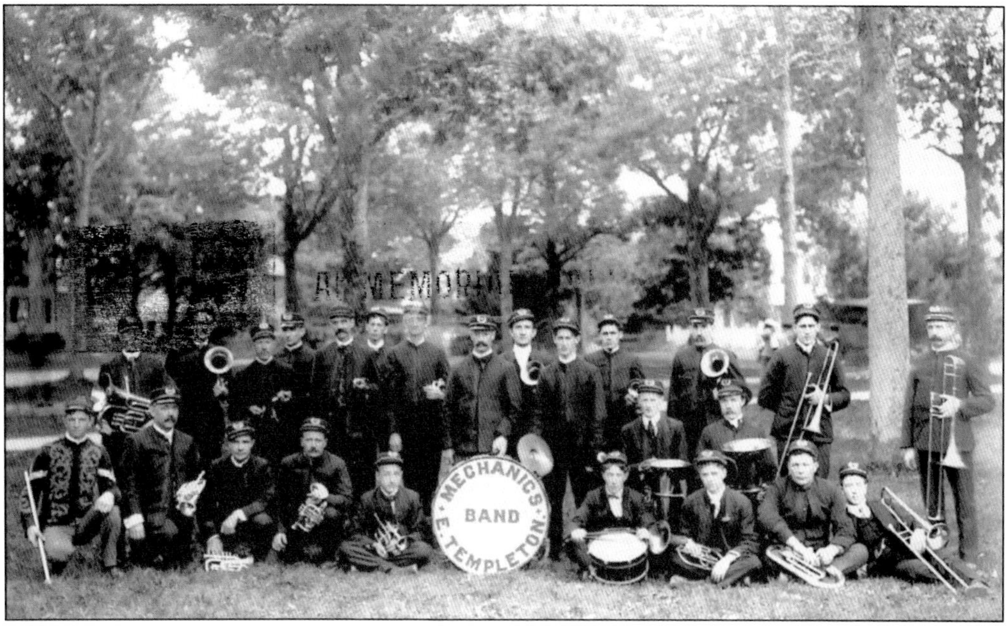

The Mechanics Band was a group in East Templeton that performed at concerts in the village and marched in local parades.

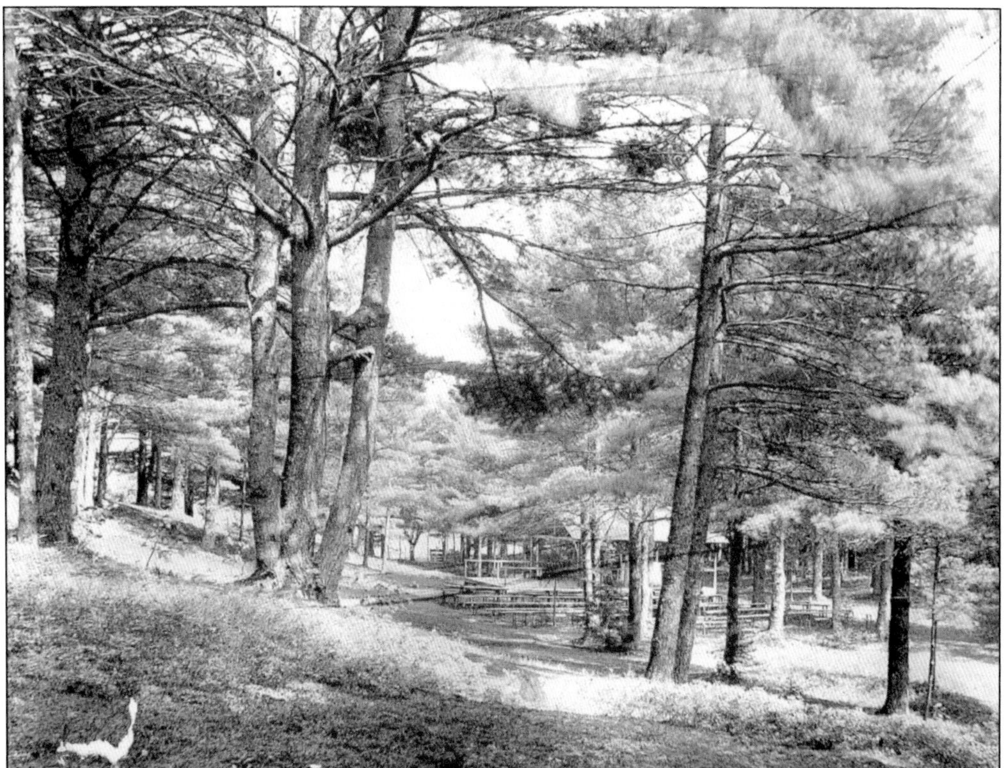
Located off Main Street behind Baker's Grove in East Templeton, the Pines was a very popular dance spot in the early 1900s. Warren Eames now owns the land.

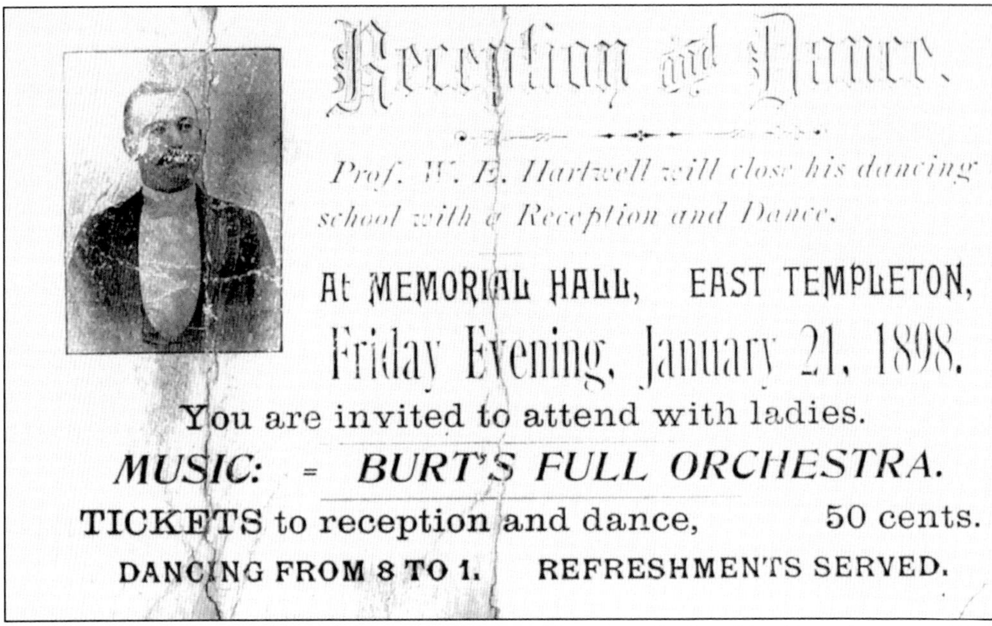

This is an advertisement for a dance to be held at Memorial Hall in East Templeton in 1898. This type of entertainment was very popular on Saturday nights.

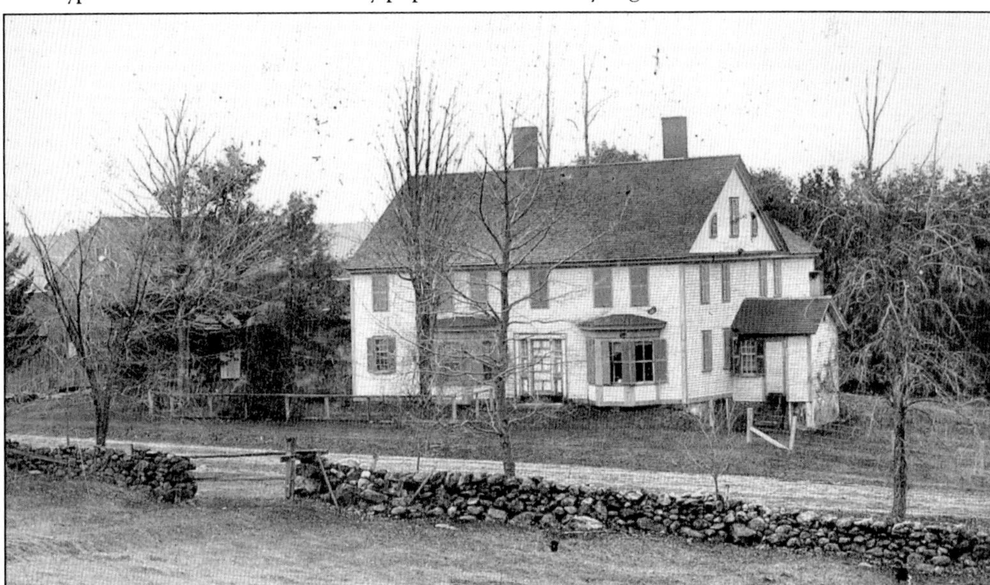

Tucker's Tavern was the largest tavern anywhere along the route from Boston to Brattleboro, Vermont. In 1805, Seras Cook owned and operated the tavern and later deeded it to Joshua Tucker, who made it famous. The tavern had three barns, built to house 200 horses at a time. Above the covered driveway was a bowling alley. Jonathan Greenwood purchased the property on March 16, 1812, and sold it fours years later to William Whitney, who renamed it Whitney Tavern. In 1830, the tavern was remodeled. Half of the old building was moved a quarter of a mile up the road. The remaining part of the tavern was made into a house and was occupied by Lucas Baker and family. Now owned by Warren Eames, the old tavern is listed in the National Register of Historic Places.

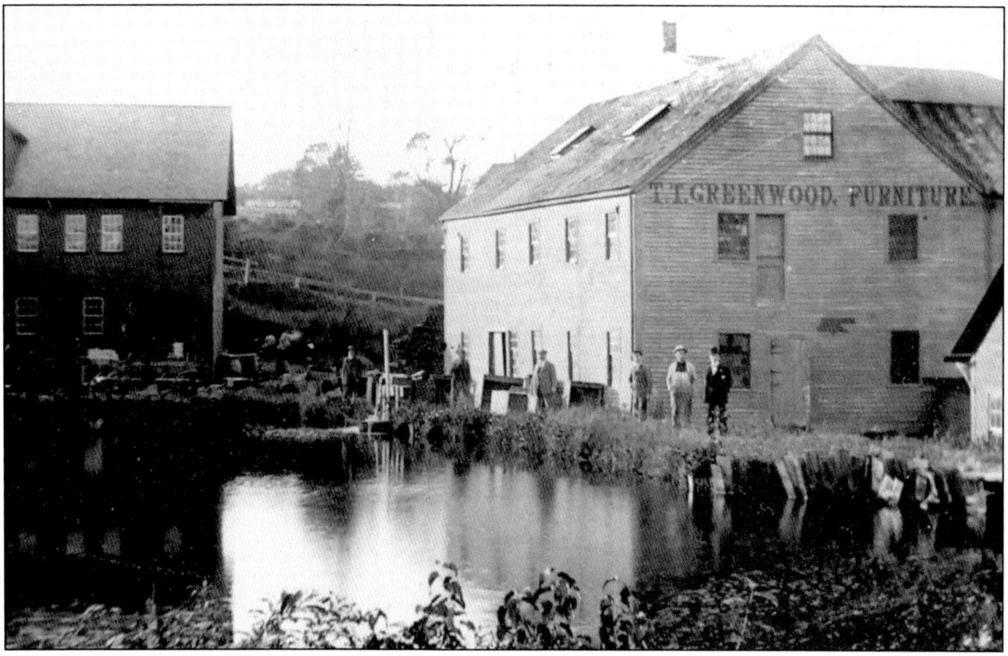

The T. T. Greenwood Company was located on Mill Street in an area now known as Floodwoods. The company made furniture, tubs, pails, and other wooden items. Thomas T. Greenwood can be seen in front of his factory wearing a black suit, a hat, and a gray beard. The factory was lost in the flood of 1938.

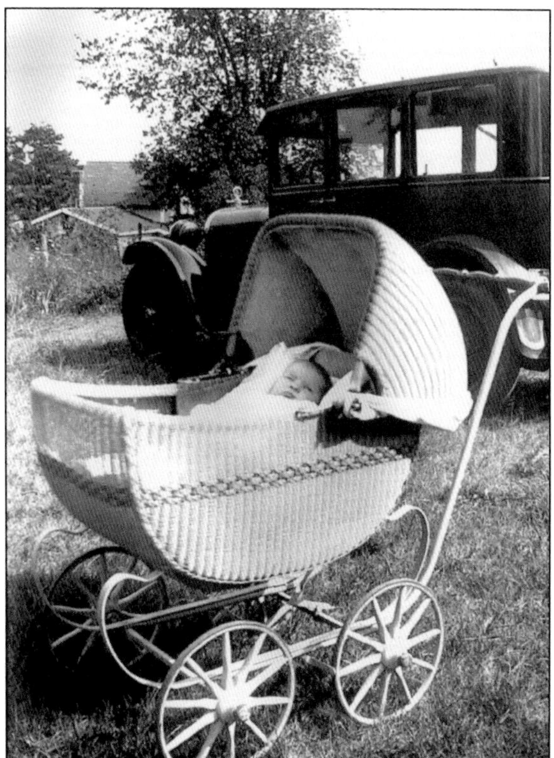

This wicker stroller was manufactured by the Children's Vehicle Corporation of East Templeton. The company started business *c.* 1910 and was destroyed by a fire in 1926. The company rebuilt and was destroyed again in the 1938 flood. The baby in the photograph is not identified.

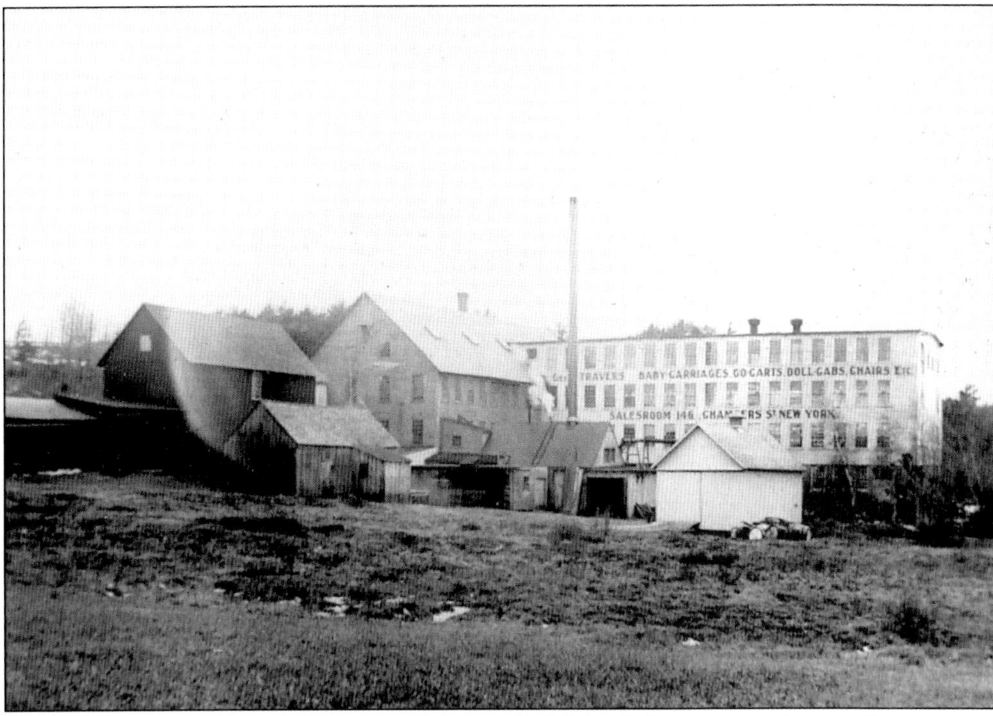

George Travers Company was a manufacturer of children's furniture and toys. The company was destroyed by fire in 1925, and the remains were washed out in the flood of 1938.

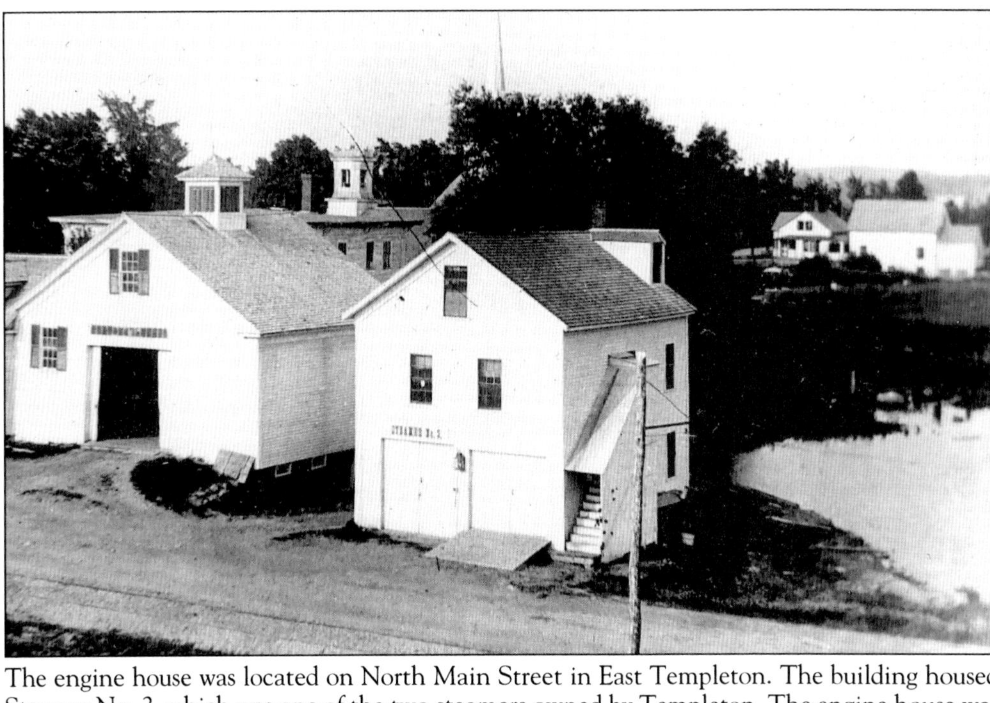

The engine house was located on North Main Street in East Templeton. The building housed Steamer No. 2, which was one of the two steamers owned by Templeton. The engine house was destroyed by a fire on February 19, 1919, and all the equipment was lost.

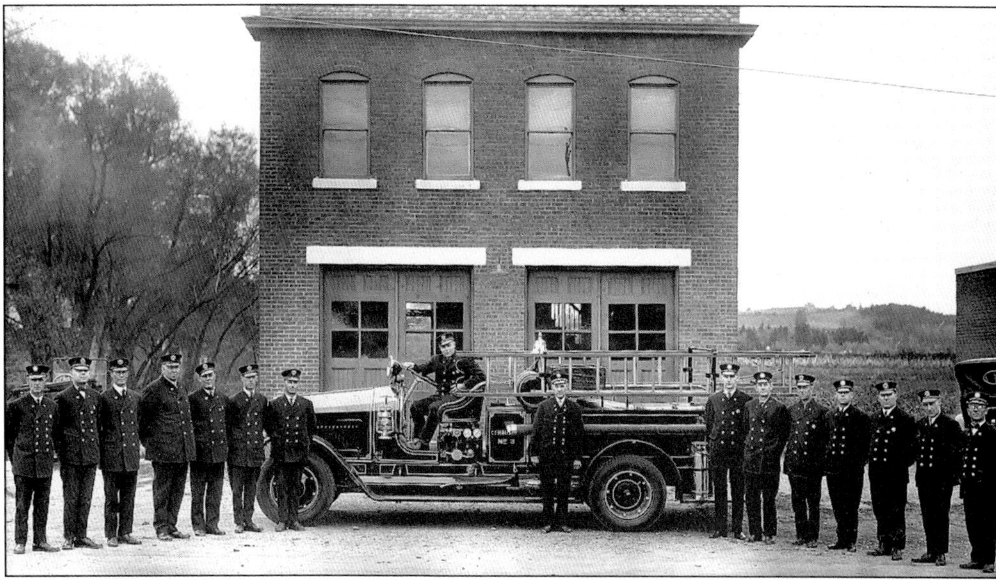

This picture shows the East Templeton firefighters proudly posing in uniform with their new engine. The new engine is believed to be a 1926 Maxim combination pumper, purchased in 1926 at a cost of $6,500. These trucks were called combination pumpers because they served as a hose wagon as well. They carried a load of hose, a tank of water, and could pump from a water source. Prior to this engine, a hose reel was pulled to the fire scene.

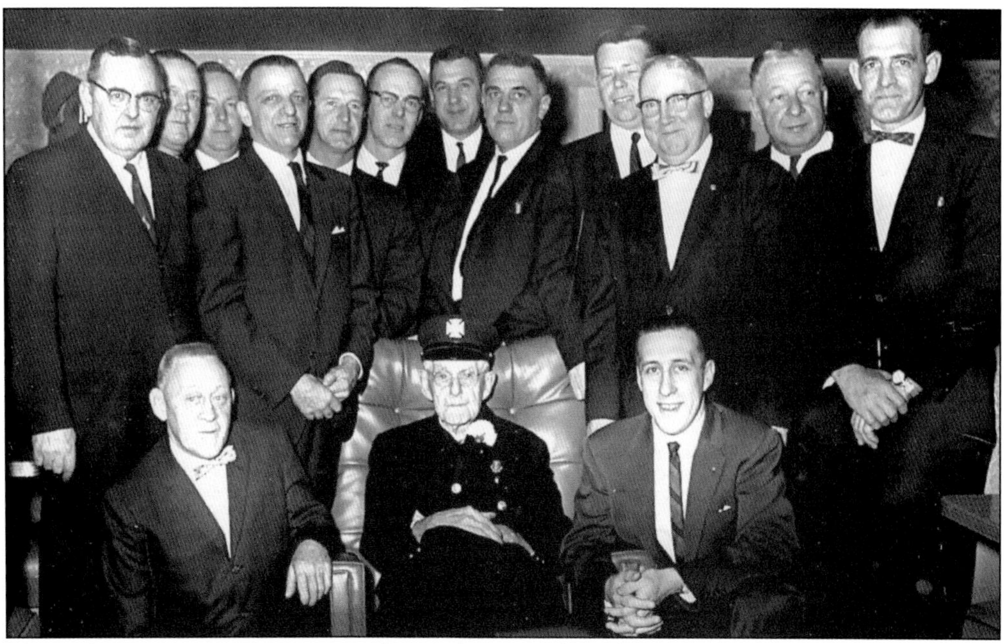

Shown here is a retirement party for Herbert Smith, a firefighter from the East Templeton engine house. Smith became a firefighter as a member of the crew on Steamer Company No. 2 in the early 1900s. Shown in this photograph are, from left to right, the following: (first row) Fred Pierce, Herbert Smith, and Gordon Brown (Smith's grandson); (second row) Doug Farr, Oiva Wick, Allen Newton, Elliott Mann, Bob Sweeney, Jimmy Peterson, Bob Conti, Eddie Lajoie, Dick Swenson, Kermit Coleman, Toivo Huhtala, and Fred Lucier.

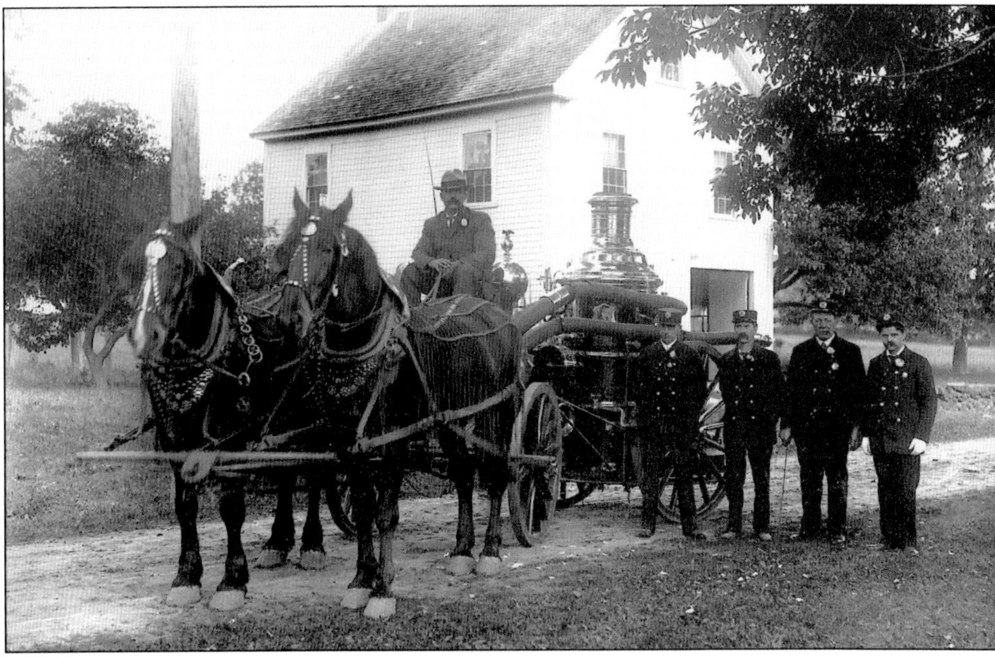

Here, the crew of Steamer No. 2 proudly poses with their engine. The building in the background is the engine house in Templeton Center located on Wellington Road. A school was built behind this building on South Road, and a driveway now runs through where this firehouse once was.

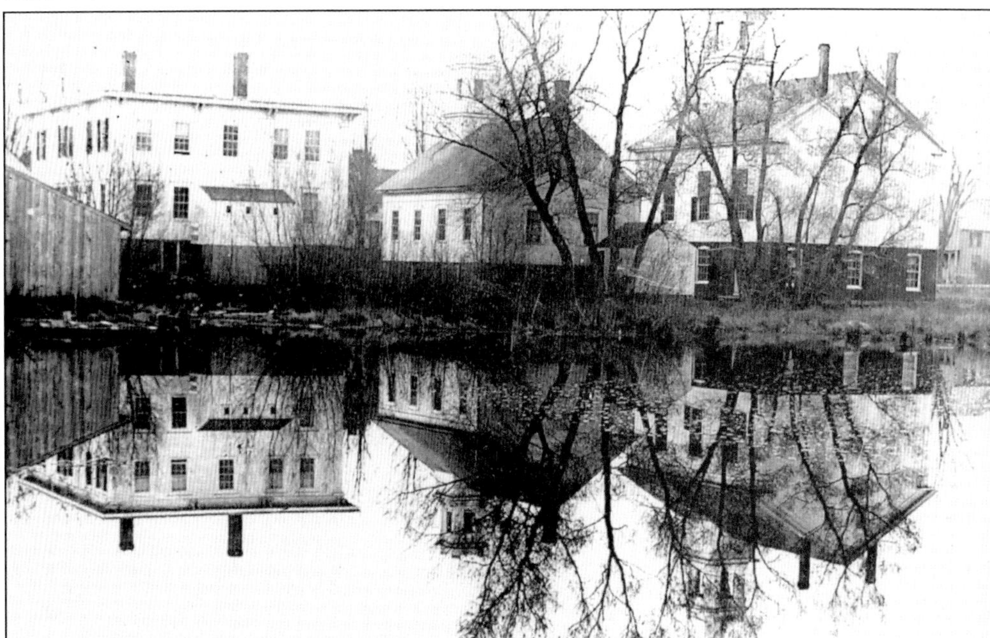

In the beginning of the 1900s, this pond existed in back of the Methodist church and the old schoolhouse, now Scout Hall. The pond supplied water power for the Bay State Wheel Company and other factories in the area east toward Gardner. If not for the leaves floating on the water, the surface would have created a perfect reflection. Flip the picture upside down.

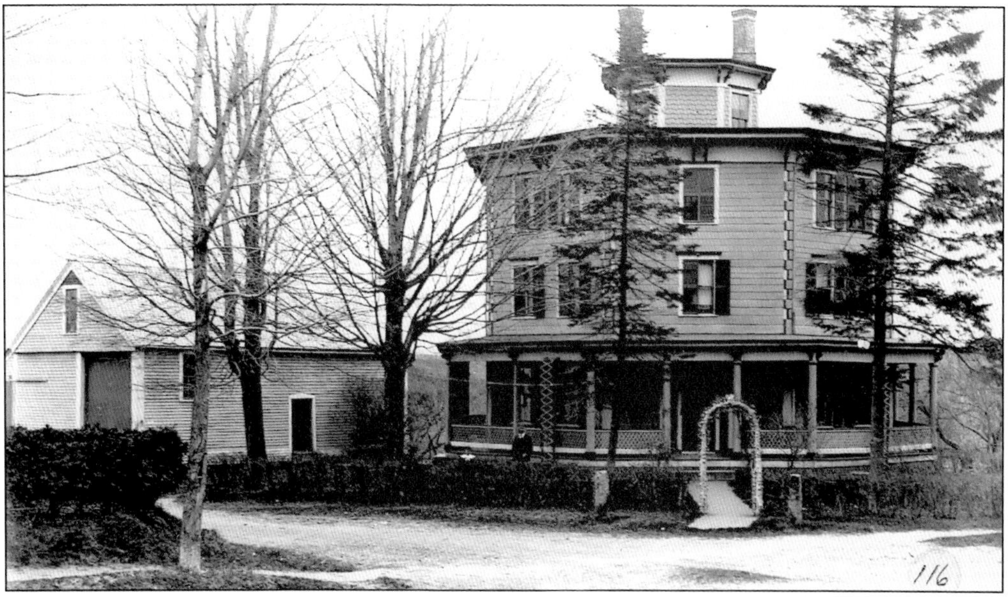

The first of two octagon-shaped houses is shown here with an iron gate. According to present-day owner Karin Orre, T. T. Greenwood began construction on the homes in East Templeton c. 1849. Each floor has four rectangular rooms, the octagonal corners have been made into closets. The iron gate was sold during hard times. A widow's walk was built so Greenwood could check on his factory while he was home. T. T. Greenwood died on July 10, 1885.

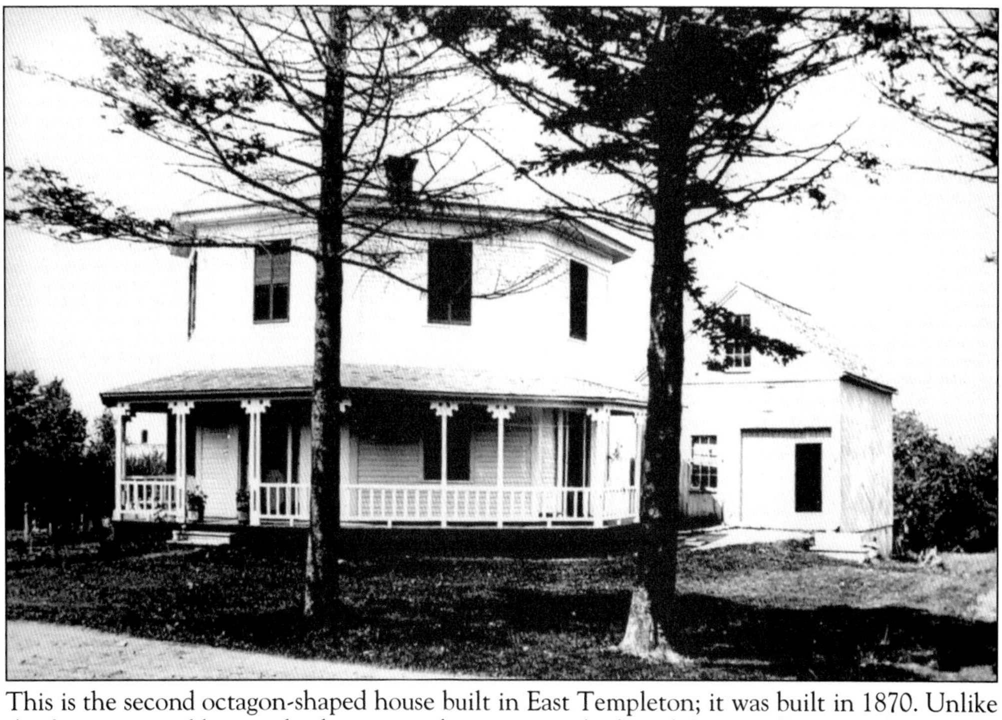

This is the second octagon-shaped house built in East Templeton; it was built in 1870. Unlike the first octagonal house, this house is only two stories high and does not have a widow's walk. In 1870, it was the home of Thomas Glasheen. Sometime later, John R. Buntin purchased it, and today the Ballou family owns the house.

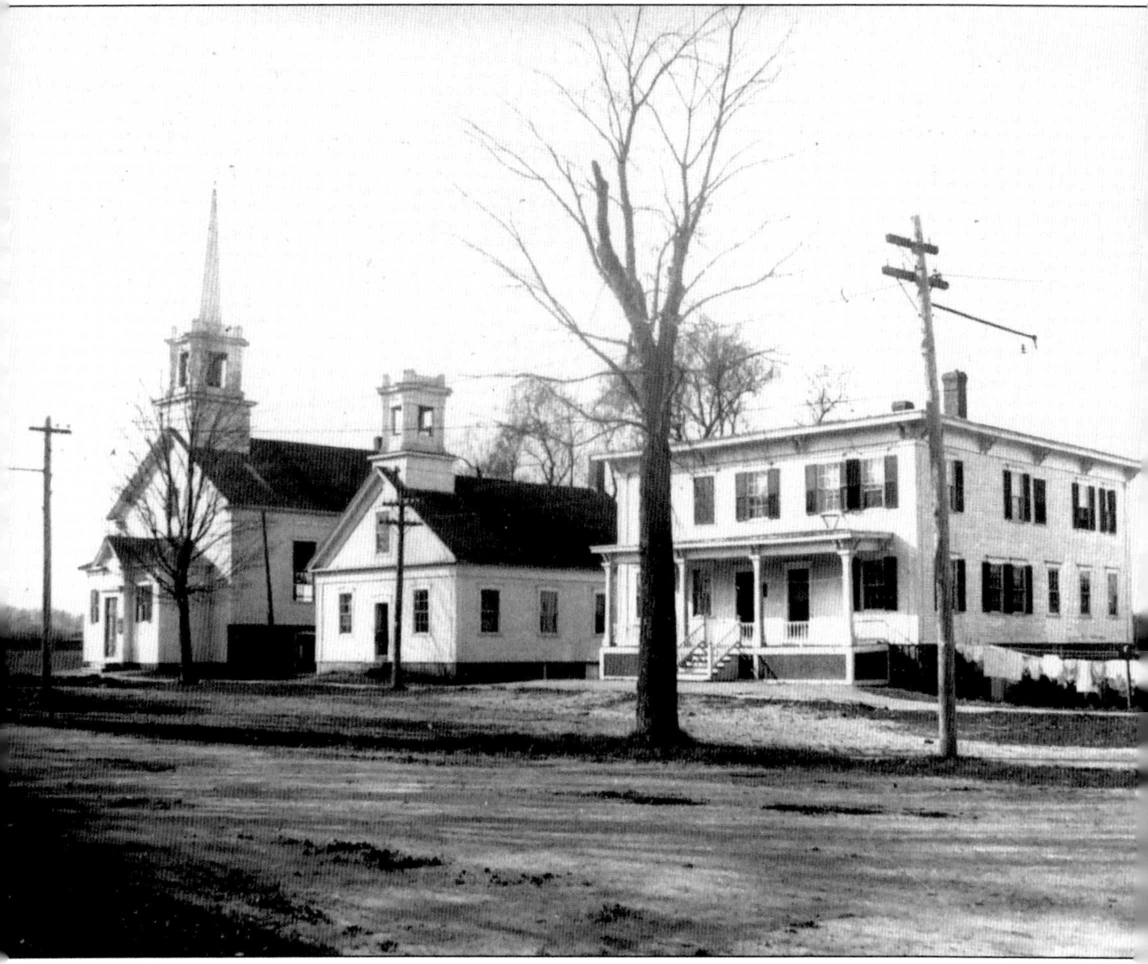

Riding into town from Gardner, this is what one would have seen upon entering the center: the Methodist church, the schoolhouse, and, on the right, a store and post office owned by Fitch L. Sargeant. Sargeant was the first postmaster and served in that position until 1892. Aside from the tar roads and parking lots, not much has changed for these buildings.

Four

Otter River

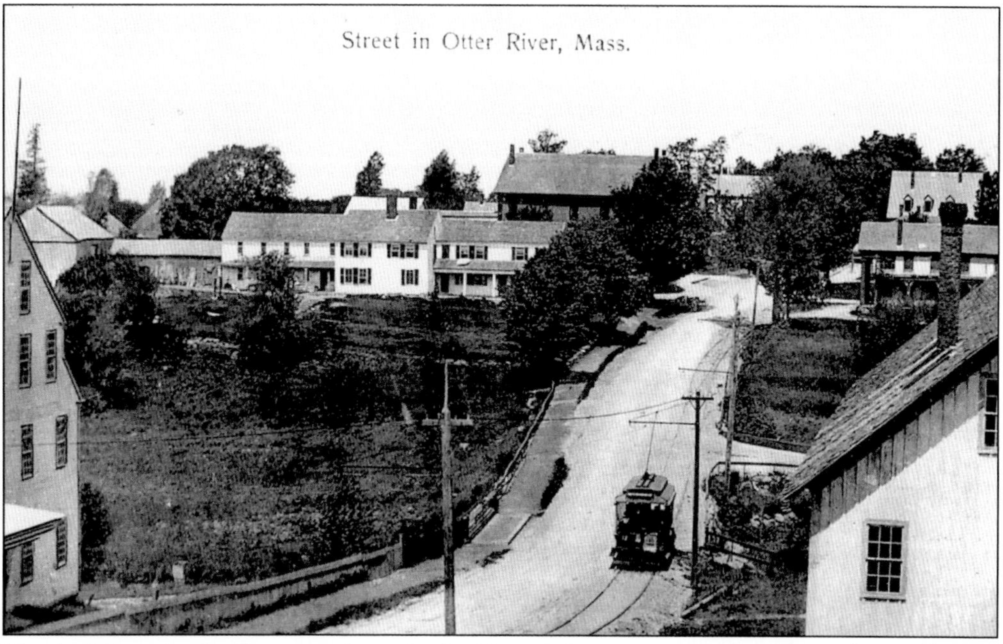

The buildings in the foreground, on both sides of the street, are the old woolen mills that sat where Seaman Paper Company is located today. The C. B. Snyder family, who eventually operated the woolen mill, owned the long white building in the background. The building across the street was the Otter River Hotel, owned by J. F. Campbell.

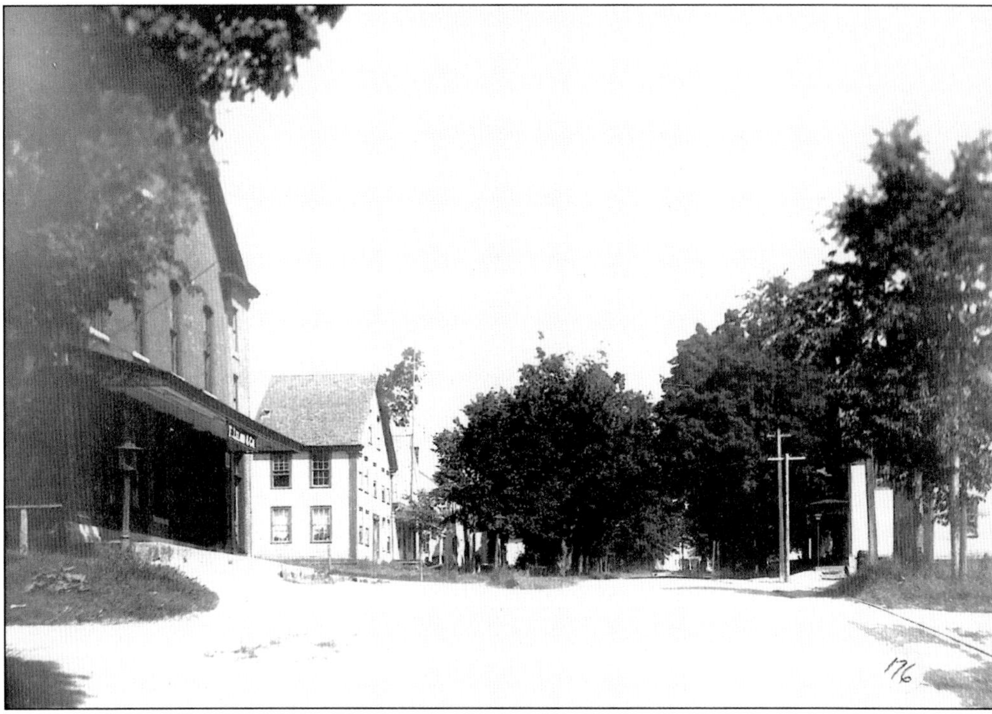

This is a view looking up Main Street in Otter River from the intersection of Main Street and Liberty Street. The building on the left was Francis Leland's store. The post office was in this building also. Leland built the store *c.* 1881.

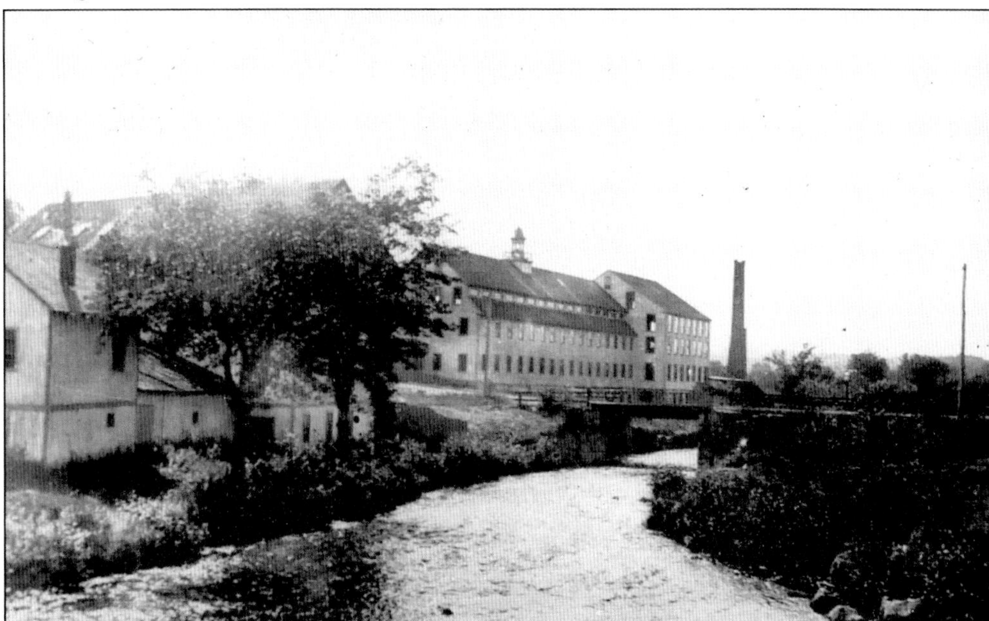

This is the old woolen mill that was located near where Seaman Paper now operates. Two gentlemen from Rutland, Samuel Dadmun and William Graham, built the mill in 1823. This picture was taken from the old abandoned road that went from Main Street to Crotty Avenue.

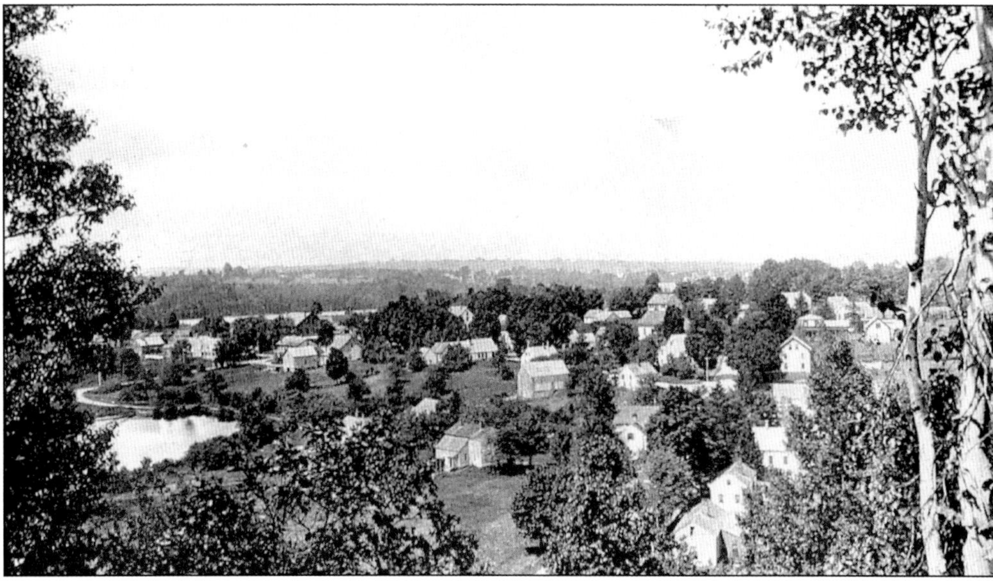

This is an early view of Otter River from the top of Bell's Hill. Bell's Hill is the large hill across from the intersection of State Road and Hamlet Mill Road. The name's origin is unidentified.

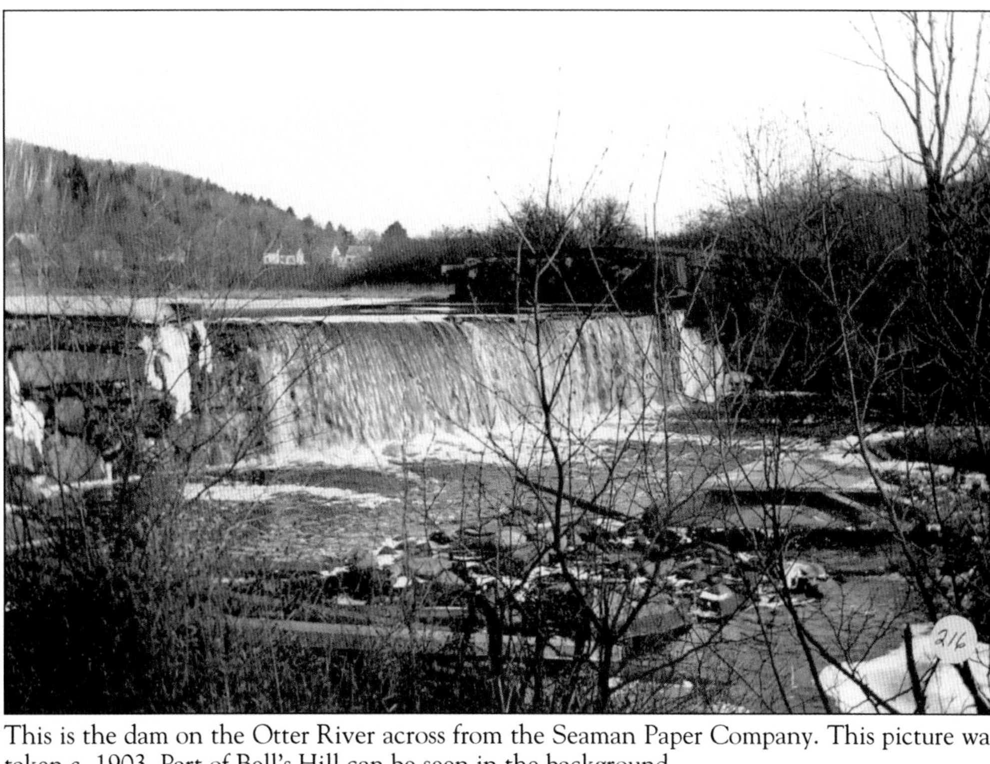

This is the dam on the Otter River across from the Seaman Paper Company. This picture was taken *c.* 1903. Part of Bell's Hill can be seen in the background.

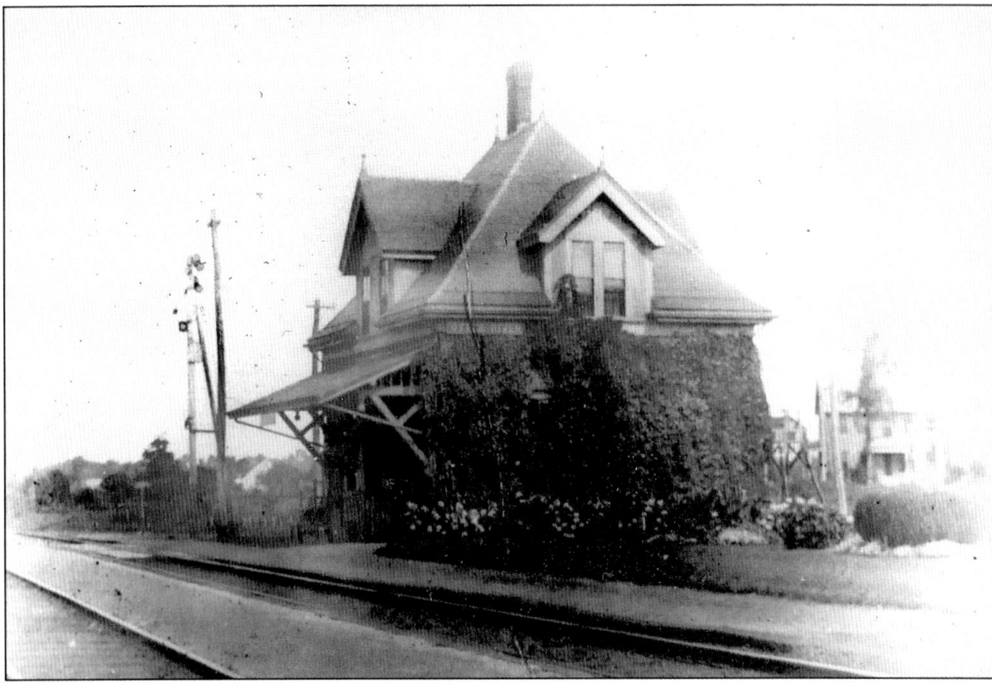

This is a picture of the railroad station in Otter River, which operated at one time by the Fitchburg Railroad. This stop was discontinued since the Baldwinville Depot was so close. Approximately 200 local men were sent to fight in the Civil War, all of whom departed from this station.

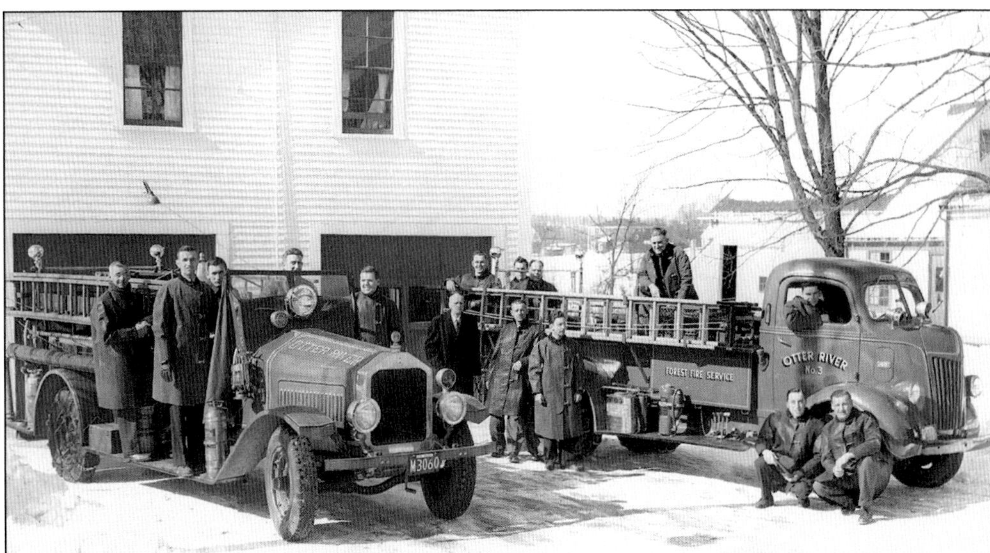

Here, the firefighters from Otter River pose in front of their station, which was rebuilt in 1906 after a fire destroyed the original station. The hand tub Oregon, which was saved from the fire, was housed in this station until 1918. The station was taken out of service and closed in 2003.

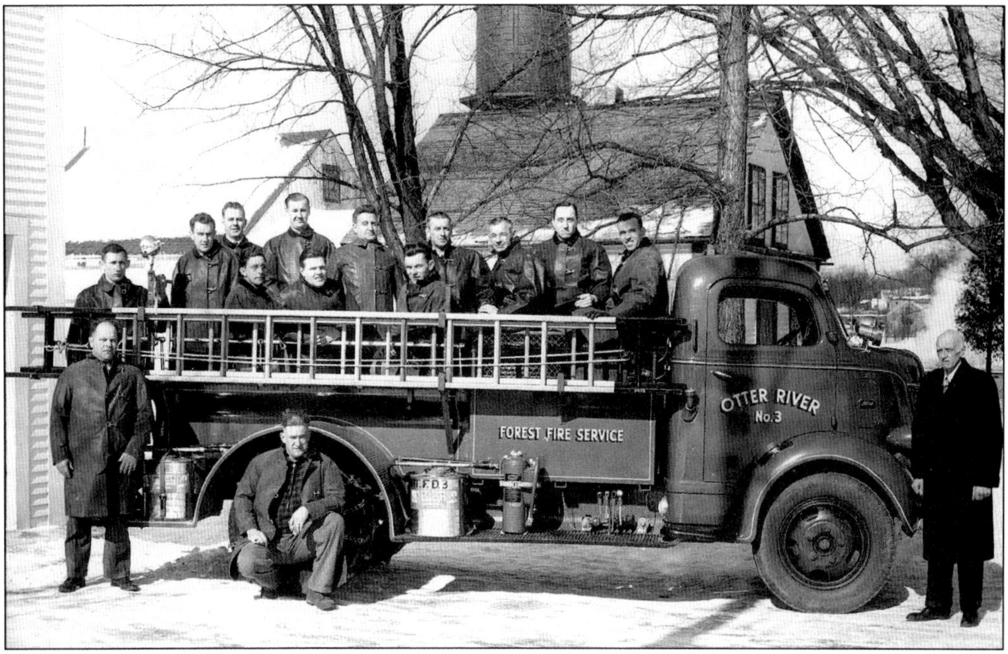

The Otter River firemen built this engine to fight forest fires. Years ago, it was not unusual for the firefighters to get together and build a piece of equipment. Sometimes this was the only way the village could afford it.

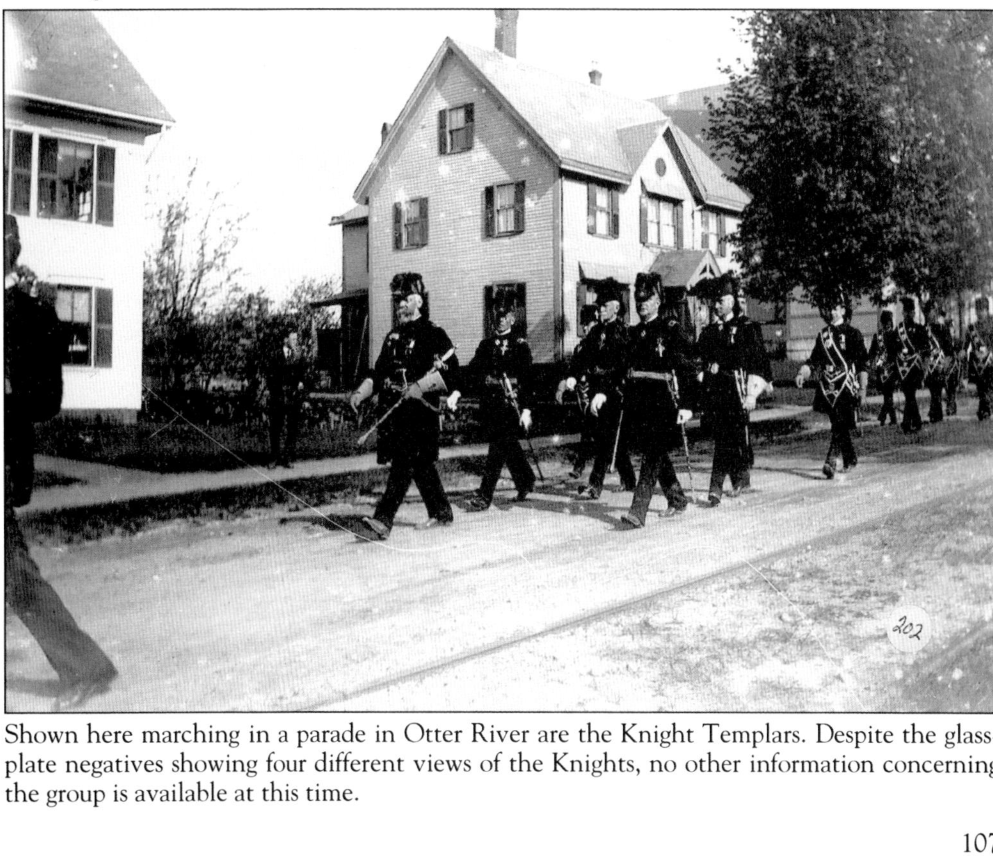

Shown here marching in a parade in Otter River are the Knight Templars. Despite the glass-plate negatives showing four different views of the Knights, no other information concerning the group is available at this time.

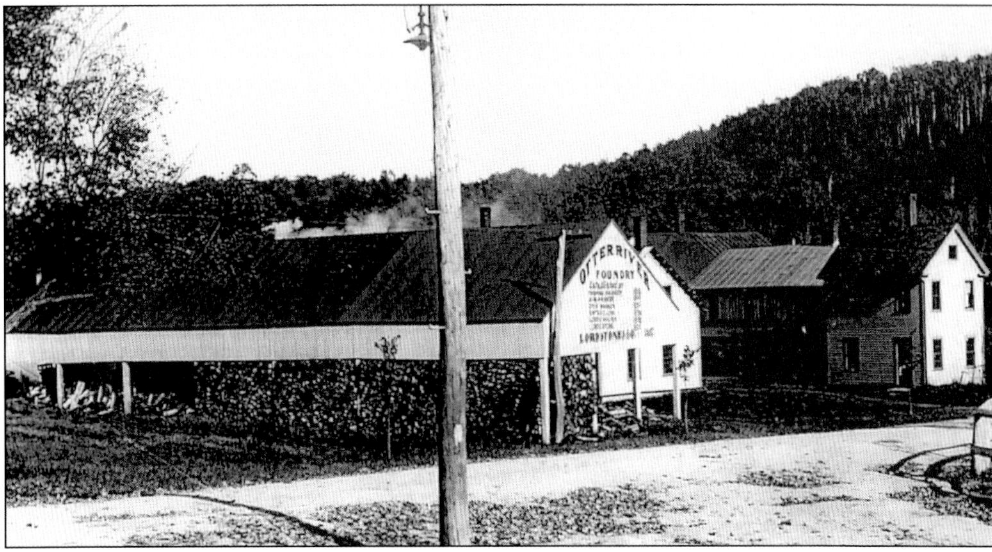

The Otter River Foundry was located where Otter River Green now is. The Parker family started it in 1833. Charles Lord and William Stone, and later Fred Stone, eventually operated it. They made small wood stoves, kitchen stoves, and some cookware.

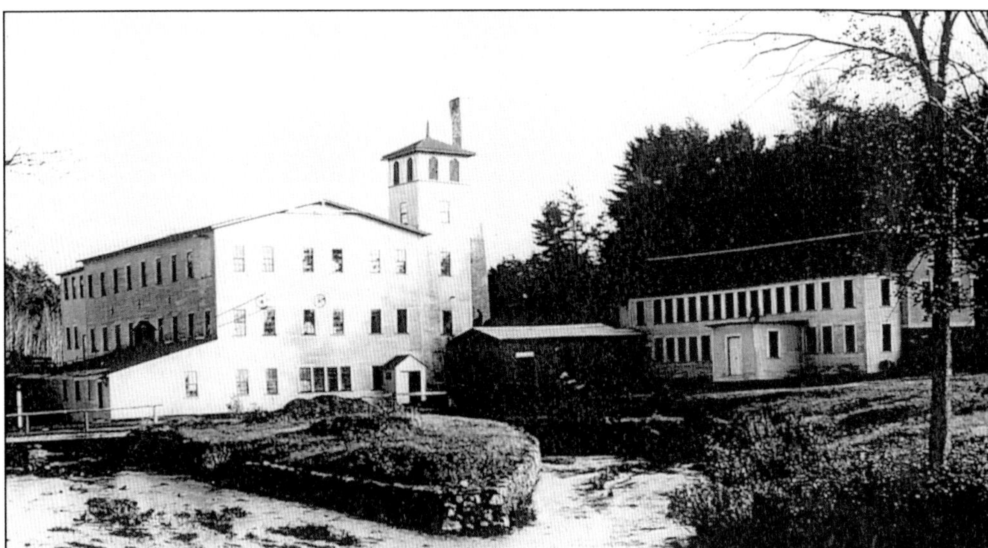

Shoddy Mill was located off Turner Street on the banks of the Otter River. If one stands on the bridge and looks east, one can see the dam where the mill stood. The company made horse blankets and blankets for the army during the war.

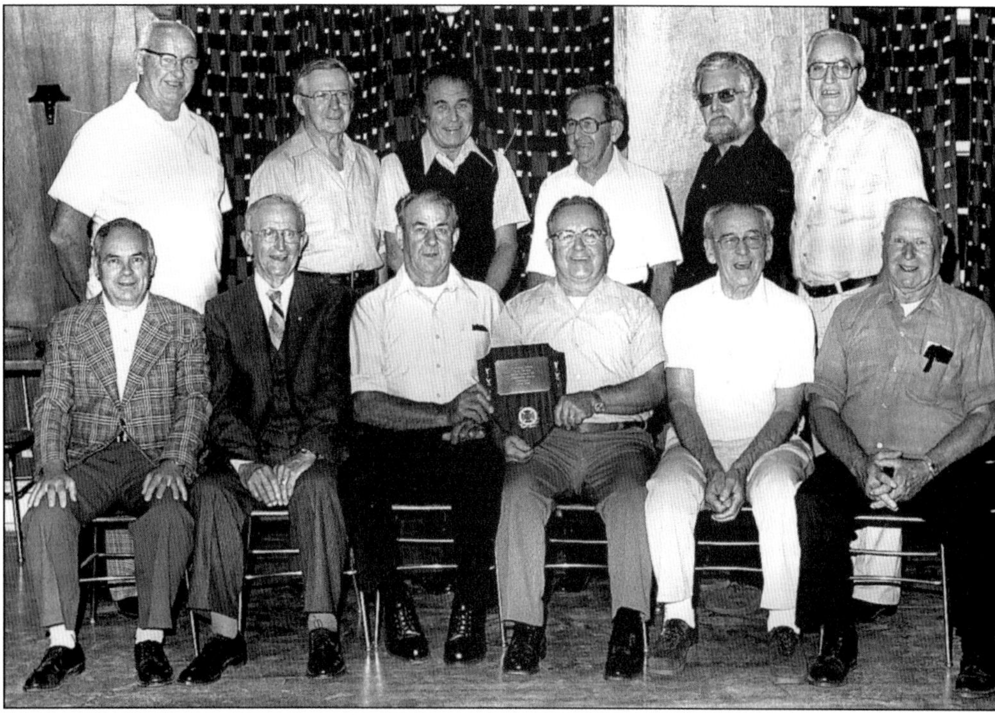

This group of Otter River firefighters appears to be receiving an award. Pictured are, from left to right, the following: (first row) James Columbus, William Conners, Alex Yackowski, Charles Valliere, Arthur Smith, and Edmond Jaillet; (second row) Francis Smith, Jack Kelley, Bernard Gronowicz, Eddie Valliere, Francis Perini, and Alex Zlotnik.

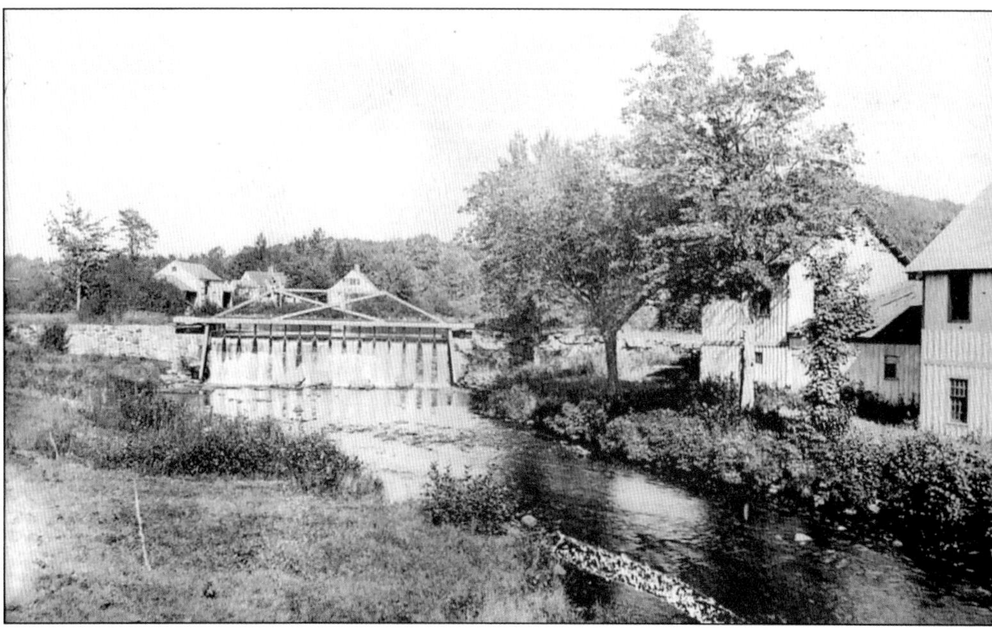

This dam was built to hold back water behind the Lord and Stone Foundry. The water flowed under Gardner Road and into the Otter River. This photograph was taken before 1938, and the dam was eventually removed.

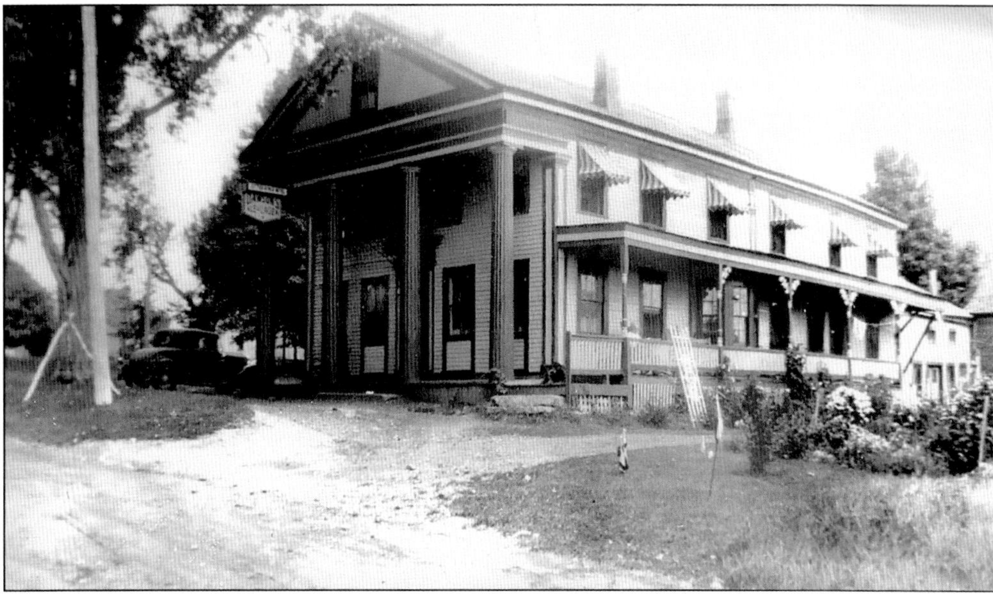

This is a picture of the Otter River Hotel, which was once located across the street from Leland's store. It was built in the mid-1800s as a home for the Charles Church family. Mr. Goldsmith acquired this property and converted it into a hotel after a fire in 1878 destroyed his hotel across the street. The Donegan family took over the hotel in 1903 and operated it until 1954. On November 29, 1963, a fire destroyed the building.

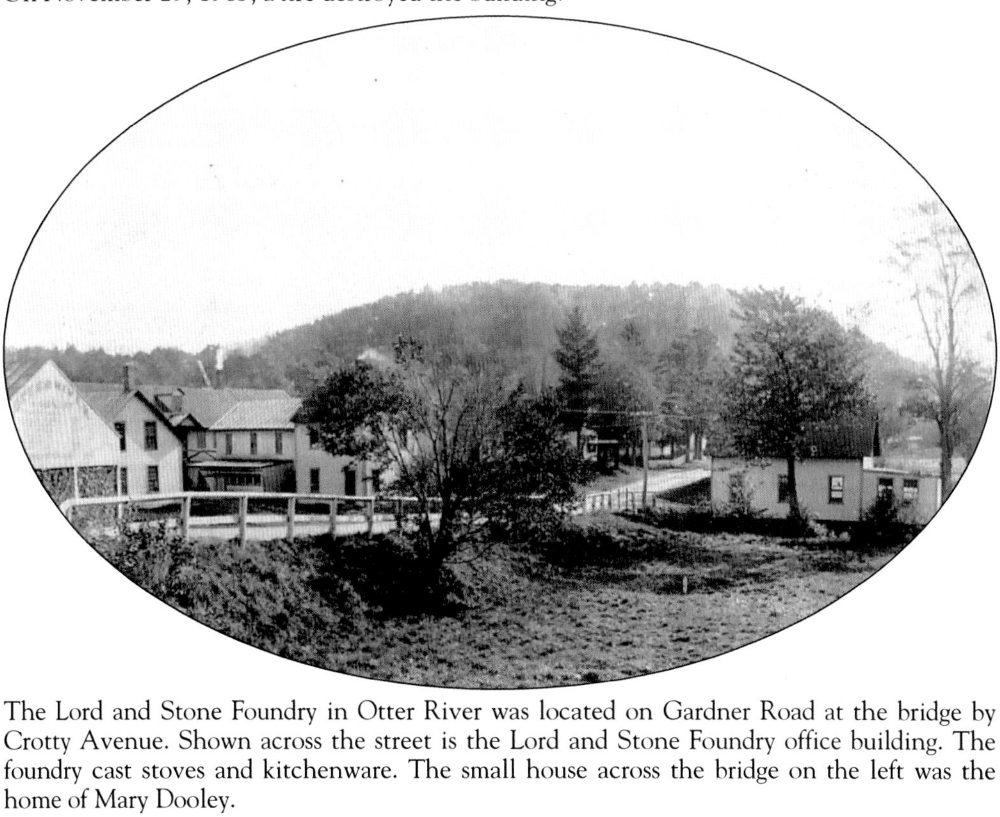

The Lord and Stone Foundry in Otter River was located on Gardner Road at the bridge by Crotty Avenue. Shown across the street is the Lord and Stone Foundry office building. The foundry cast stoves and kitchenware. The small house across the bridge on the left was the home of Mary Dooley.

St. Martins Church was built in 1853 and dedicated in 1854 by Rev. Matthew Gibson. This was the first Catholic church built in the town.

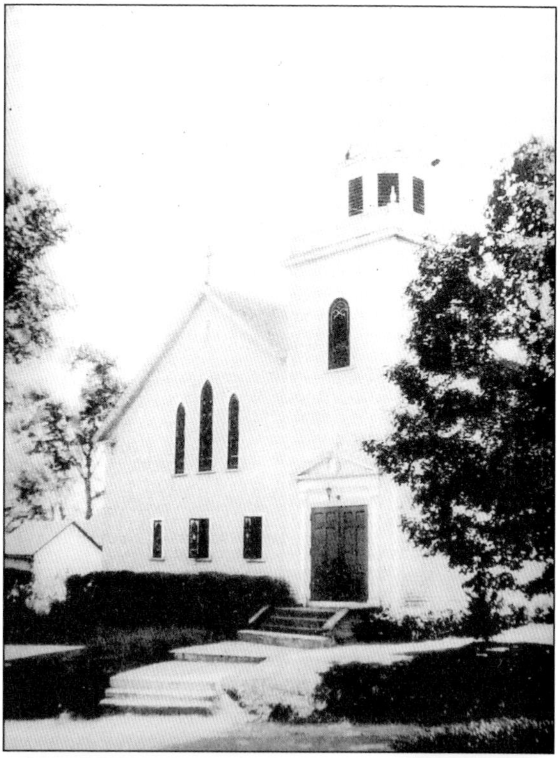

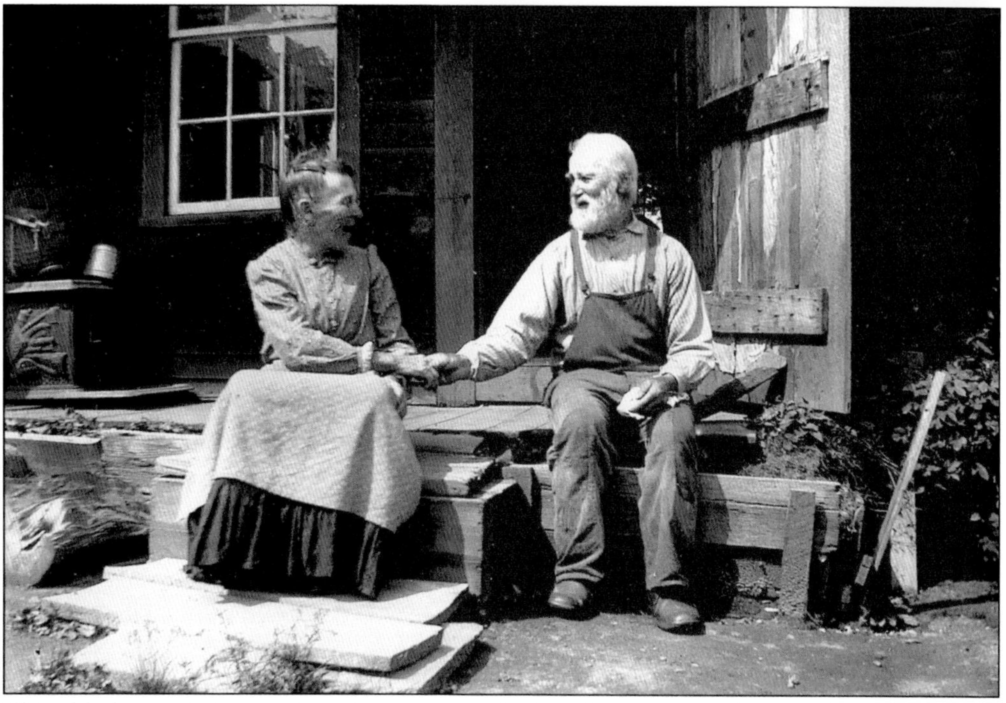

This elderly couple is enjoying a hot summer day by relaxing and talking on the steps of their home. The photograph was labeled, "Johnie and Mother-Me-Dear," although beyond that they are unidentified. One wonders if the stove on the porch was cast at the Otter River Foundry.

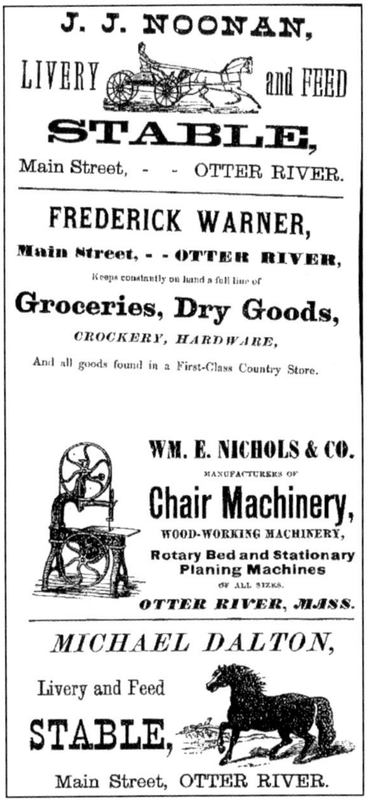

When the town was divided into nine districts, Otter River was known as Factory Village. These advertisements from 1880 show how prosperous the village must have been.

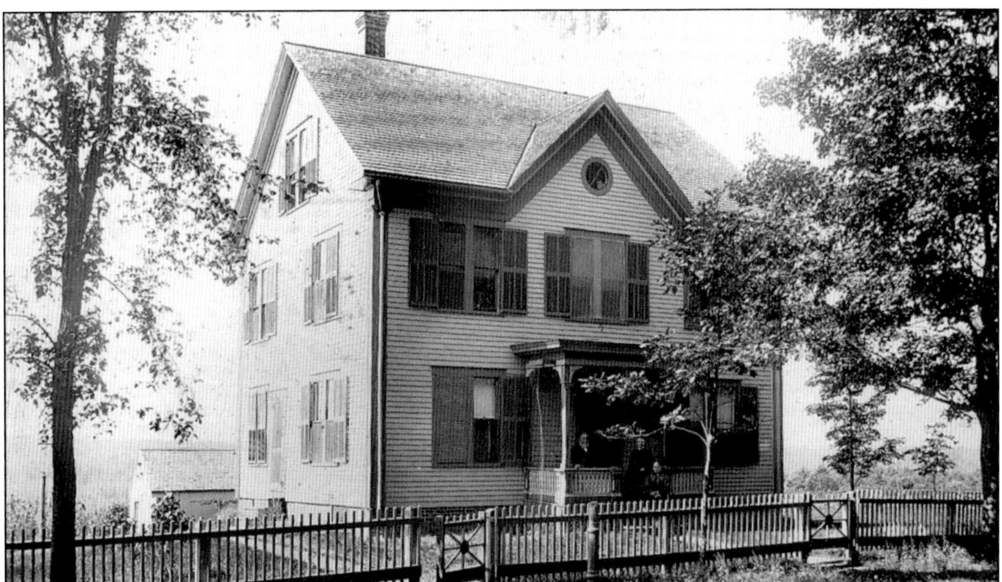

According to the 1898 map, this was the home of Henrietta Sawyer. It was later the home of Marion Greenwood. John O'Brien purchased the home in the mid-1900s. John moved here in 1906 with three of his brothers from New Jersey and purchased the paper mill. Today, the home is owned by John O'Brien's grandson James Columbus.

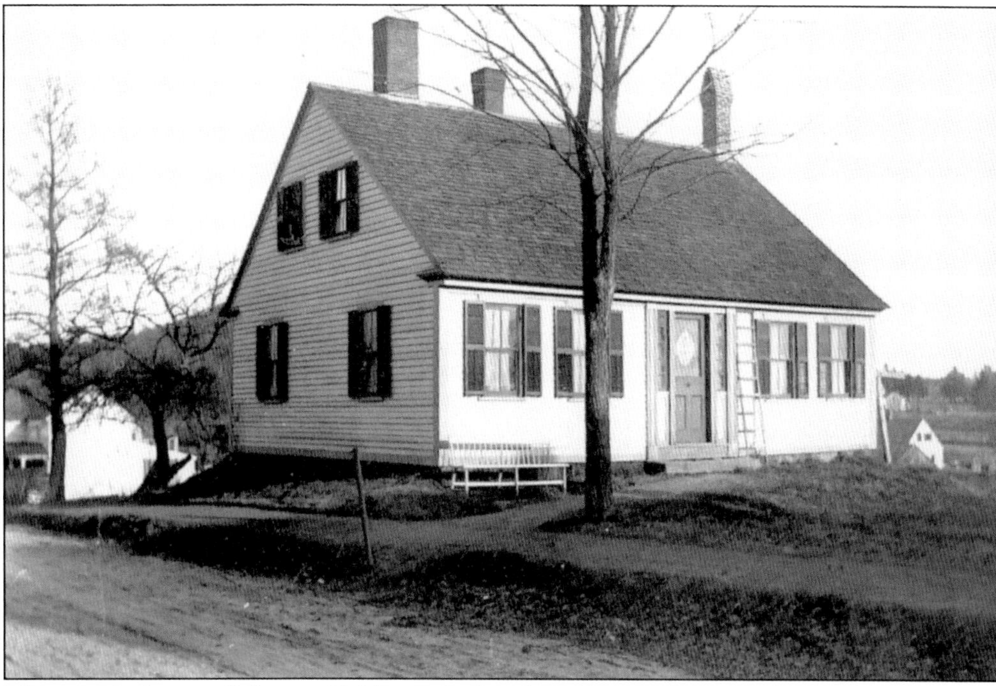

This was the home of Thomas T. Hare, who lived on Pleasant Street in Otter River in the late 1800s. The home stands empty today as part of the estate of James Higgins. The street has been renamed River Street.

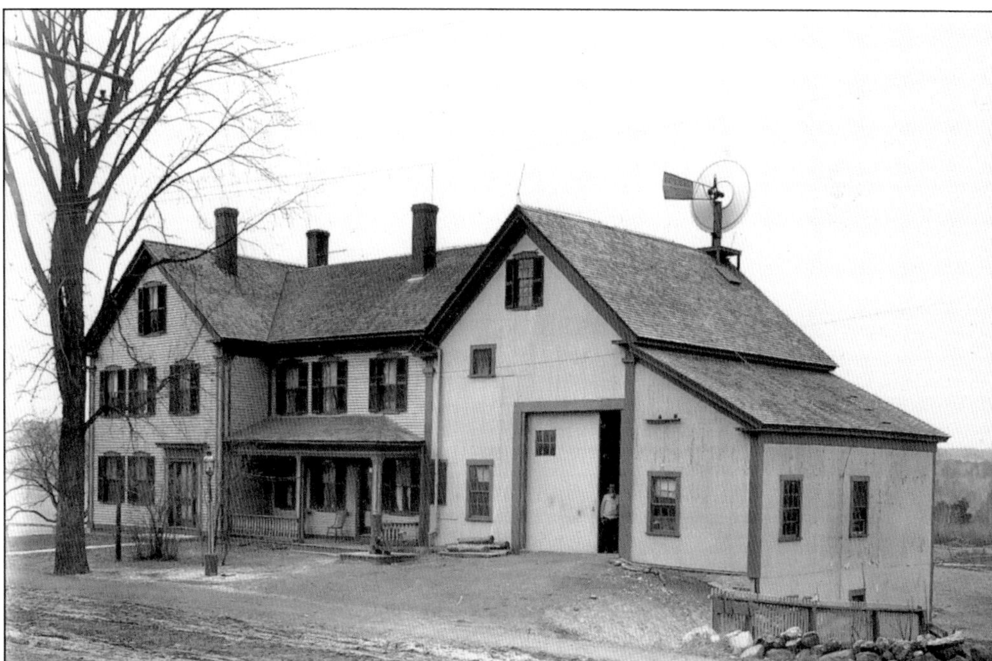

This house was the home of Charles Lord in the late 1800s. Notice the lightning rods on the roof. This picture was probably taken in the early 1900s, as there are wires for the trolleys overhead. Today, this house is the home of the Arthur Landry family.

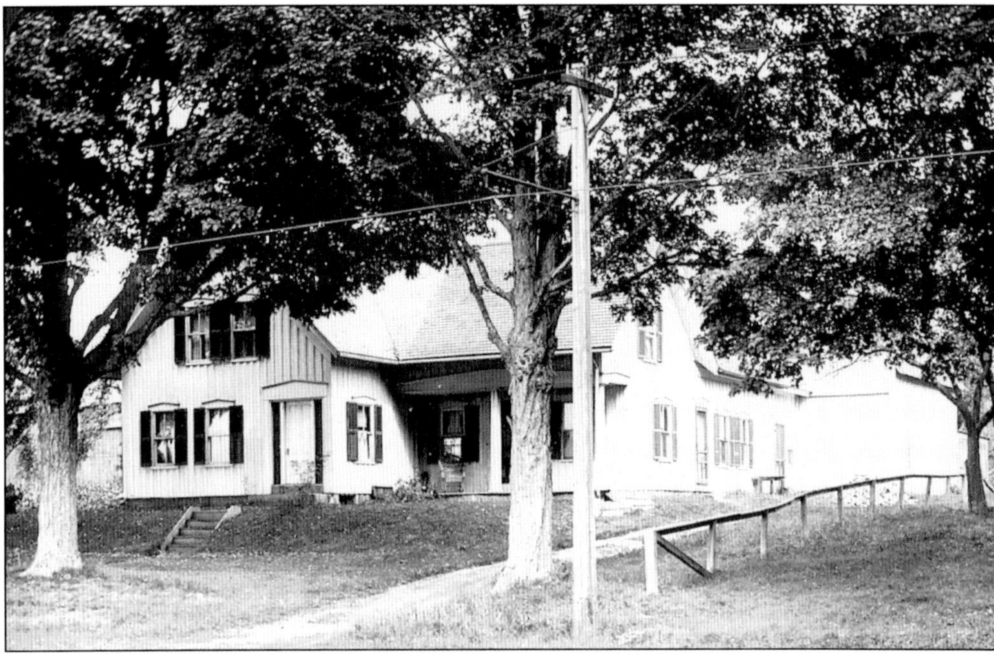

This residence located on Main Street in Otter River was the home of William Gray, who operated a farm here in the early 1900s.

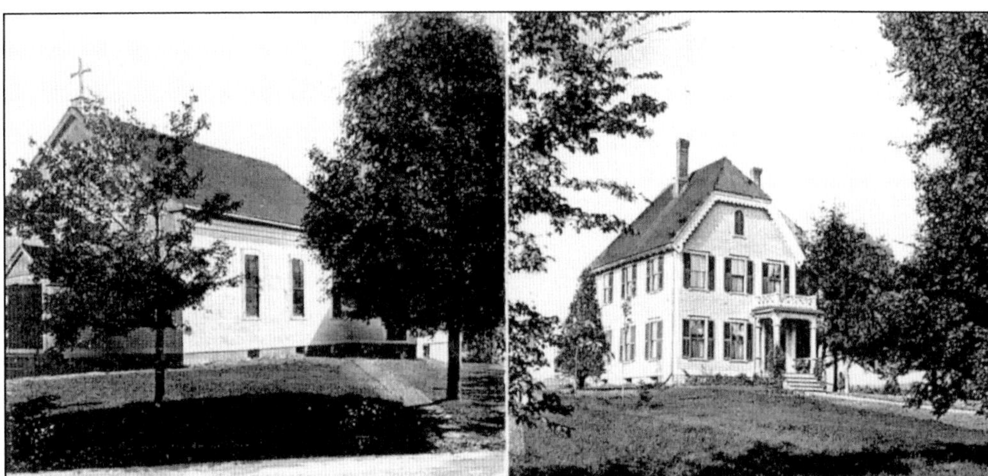

St. Martin's Church was the first Catholic church to be built in town. The church, located in Otter River, was built in 1853 and dedicated by Rev. Matthew Gibson. The parochial residence is located across the street from the church.

Five

Schools

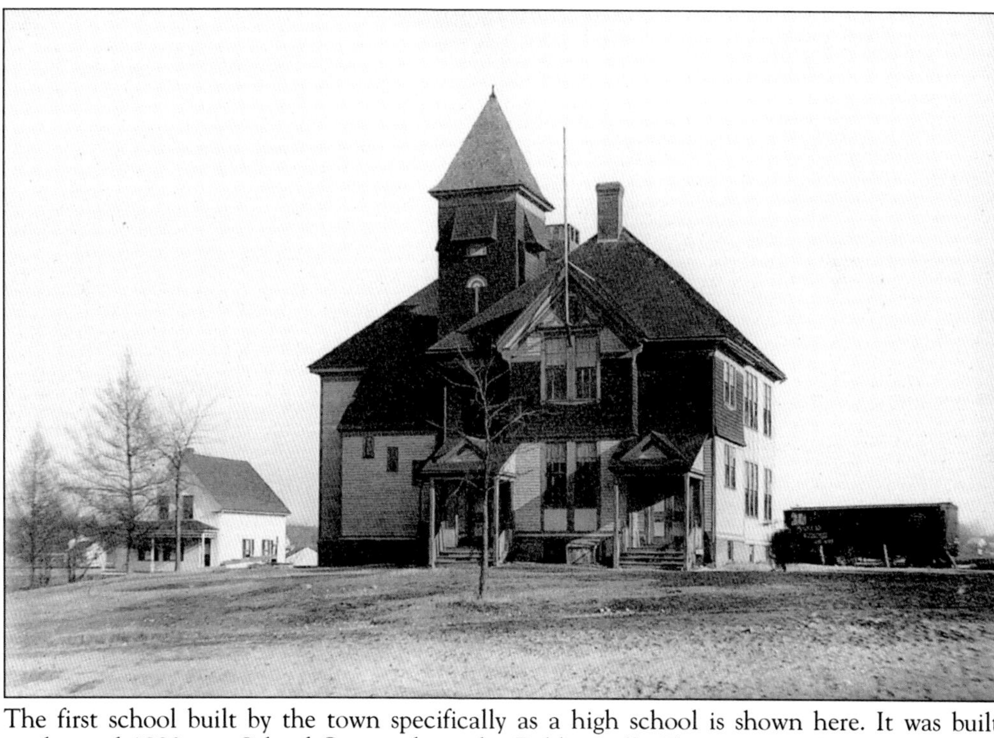

The first school built by the town specifically as a high school is shown here. It was built in the mid-1800s on School Street where the Baldwinville Elementary School now stands. The building was destroyed by a fire on December 18, 1921, and was replaced by the present elementary school building. In order to finish the school year, students were transferred to other village schools and the hall over the Otter River firehouse.

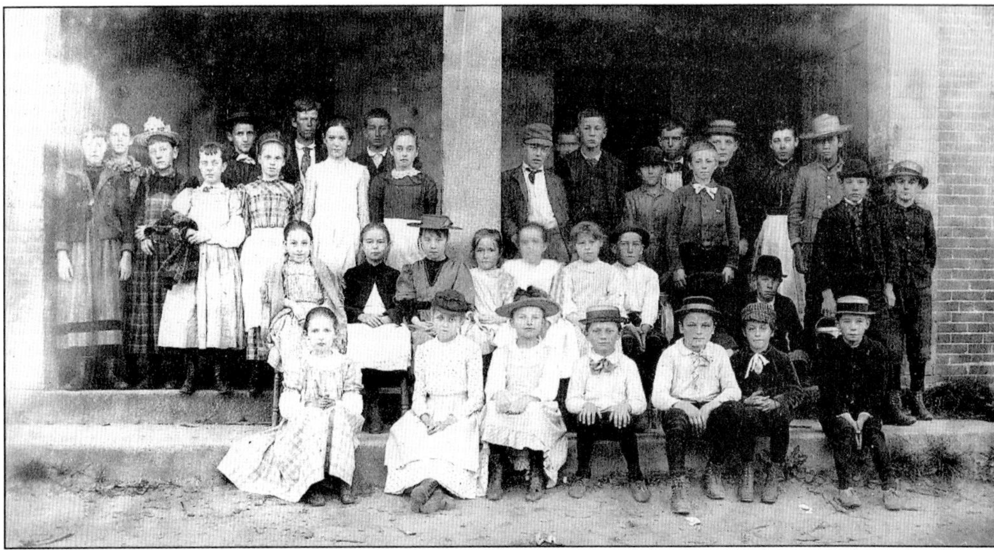

Students at the grammar school in Templeton Center during the 1892–1893 school year are, from left to right, as follows: (first row) Lucy Baker, Hattie Newell, Marietta Bryant, Walter Hadley, Stuart Winch, Dwight Seaver, and Fred Henshaw; (second row) Annie Scollay, Nina Ormsby, unidentified, Elsie Hayward, Nellie Doherty, Winifred Smith, Amos Valiton, and Waverly Oliver; (standing) Eva Gray, Carrie Woodbury, Bertha Manning, Edna Dudley, Lucy Bugbee, Elnora Woodbury, Louis Brown, Helen Maynard, Frank Robinson, Alice Heath, James King, Ernest LaClair, Clayton Knight, Ernest Bourn, Charles King, Charles Seaver, Harvey Winch, Edith Bates, Clarence Johnson, Ernest King, and Thomas Hawkes.

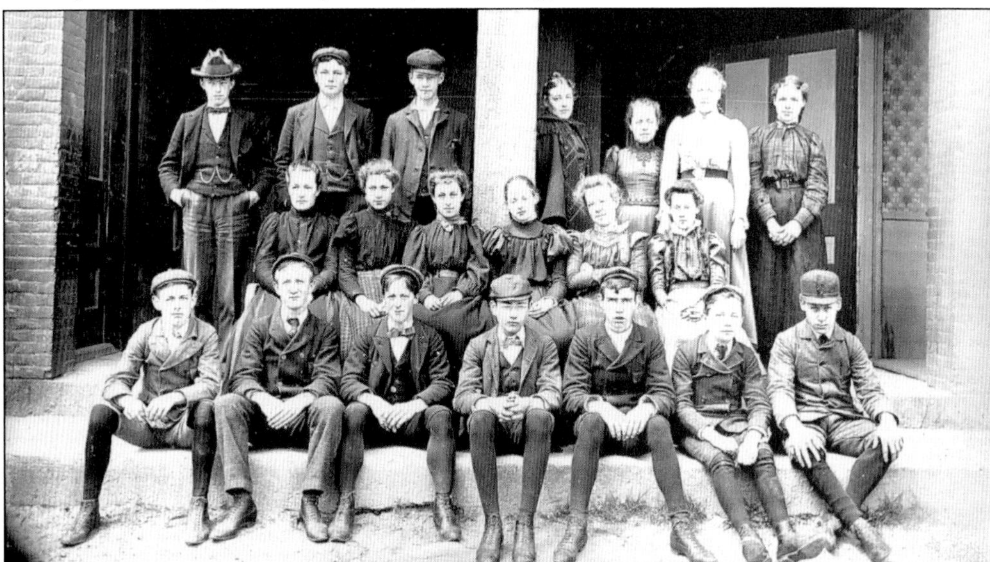

The Templeton Center School high school class of 1898–1899 are, from left to right, as follows: (first row) Harley Smith, James Hunting, Dwight Seaver, Charles Hersey, James Doherty, Walter Hadley, and Arthur Willoughby; (second row) Elsie Maynard, Ella Winship, Annie Scollay, Lucy Baker, Edith Braithwarte, and Chessie Whitney; (third row) Charles Seaver, Stuart Winch, Fred Henshaw, Mary Chandler Stone, Grace Blodgett, Martha Newton, and Mary Weir.

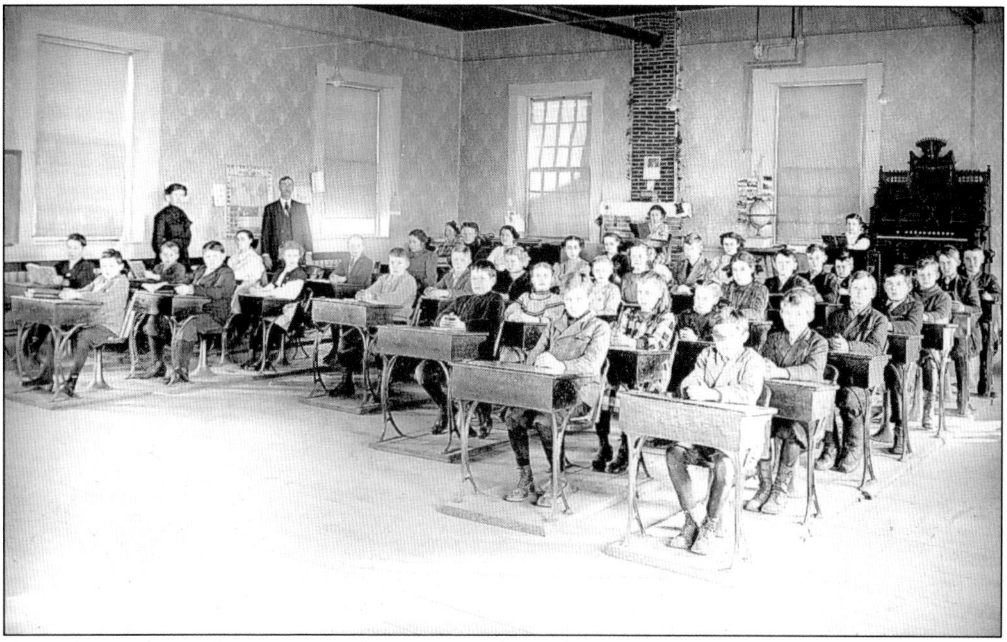

One of Templeton Center's two classrooms is shown here. The year is unidentified.

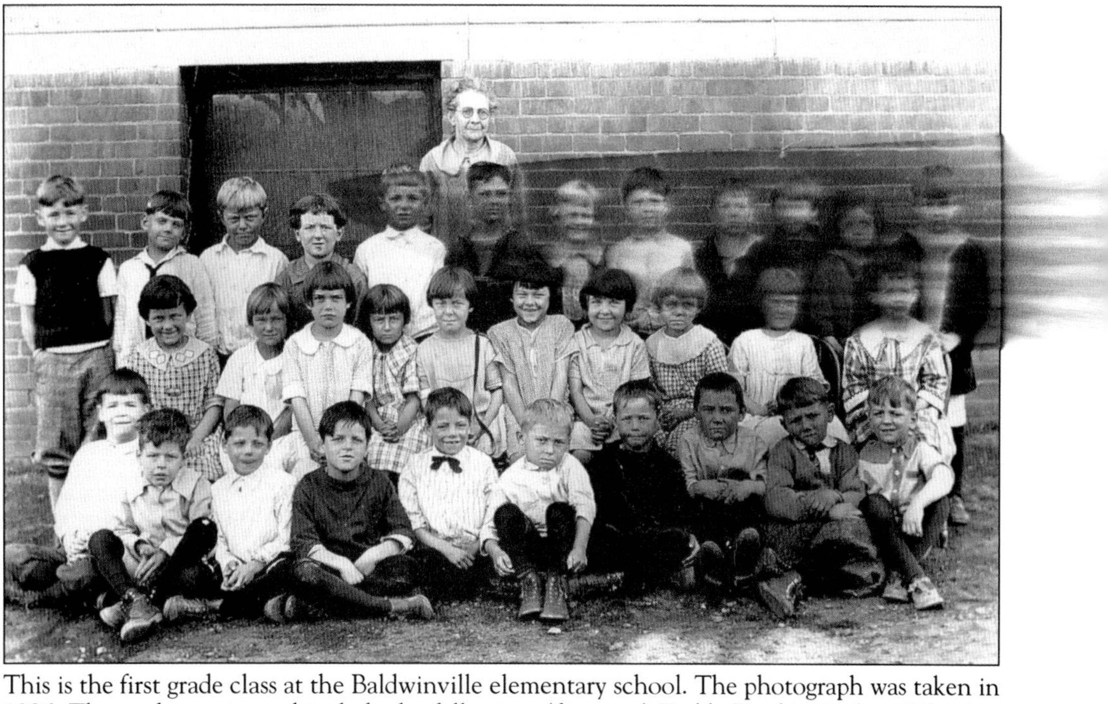

This is the first grade class at the Baldwinville elementary school. The photograph was taken in 1926. The students pictured include the following: (first row) Teddy Dunkin, Robert Wheeler, Frankie Vaughn, and Bob Stuart; (second row) Irene Carpenter, Jenny Green, Helen Smith, Rebecka Saveall, Gly Kenney, and M. Punzel; (third row) Richard Moore, Russ Adams, Eddie Mizereck, Alfred Stone, Martin Anderson, Roger Adams, Fred Davis, Marcel Nash, Madelyn Day, and John Kosakowski. Their teacher was Alice Martin.

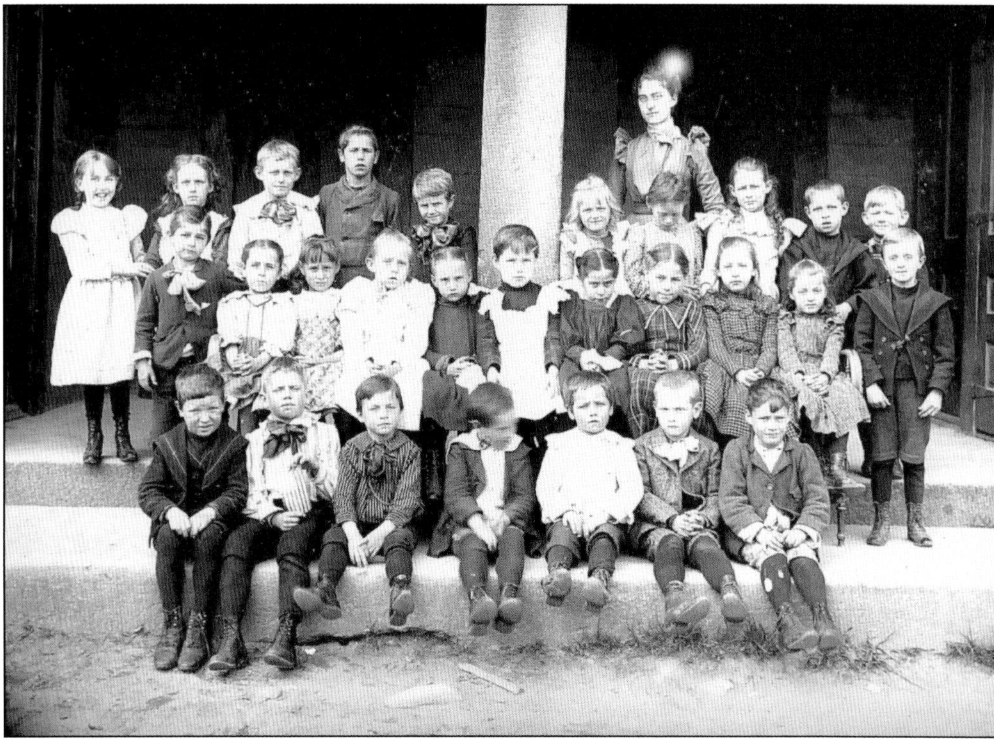

Mattie Goodrich was the teacher in this early picture of a class in one of the village schools.

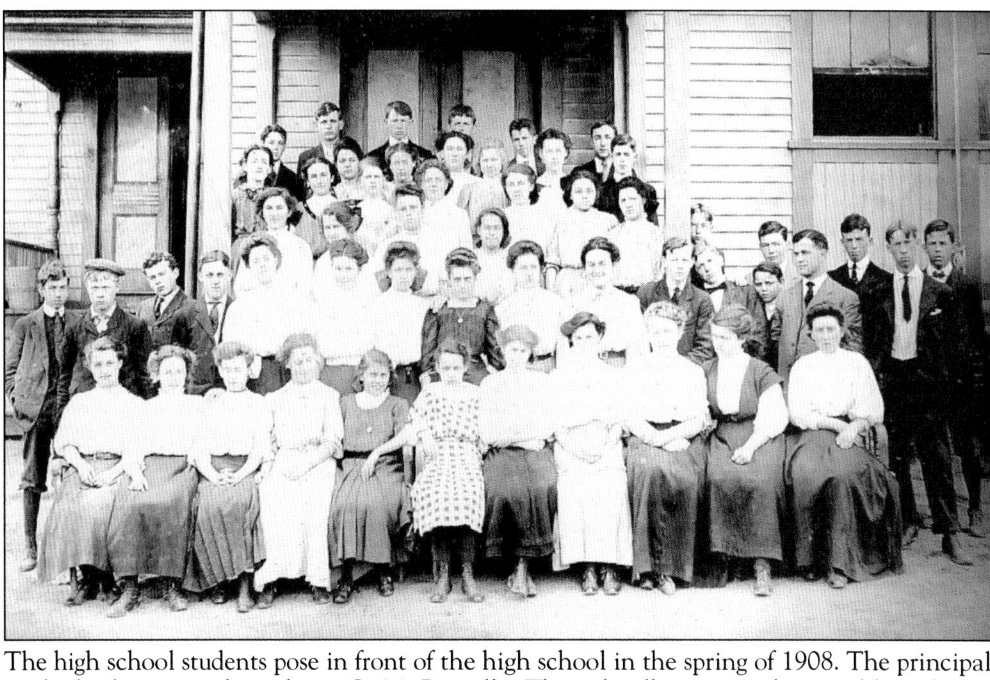

The high school students pose in front of the high school in the spring of 1908. The principal, in the back row on the right, is Q. M. Boutelle. This schoolhouse was destroyed by a fire on December 18, 1921.

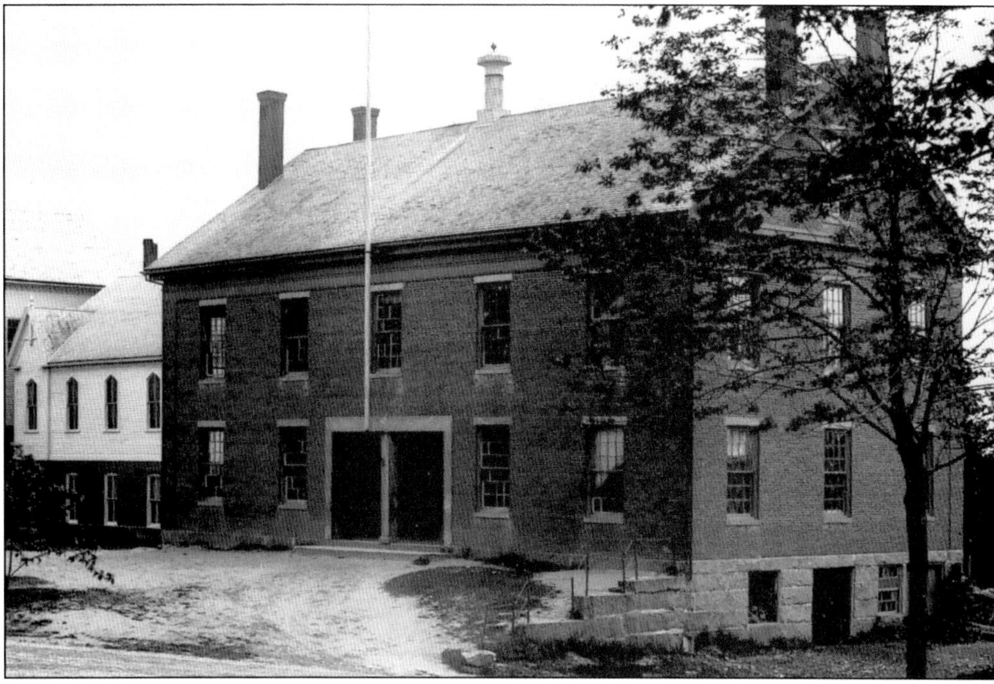

This schoolhouse, built in 1844, was the first in the town constructed of brick. It was located next to the First Church in Templeton Center and served as a town hall and school. Two rooms on the ground floor were used for the school, and the second floor was used as the town hall. The town hearse was stored in the basement. The school abandoned the building in 1942 and tore it down in 1948.

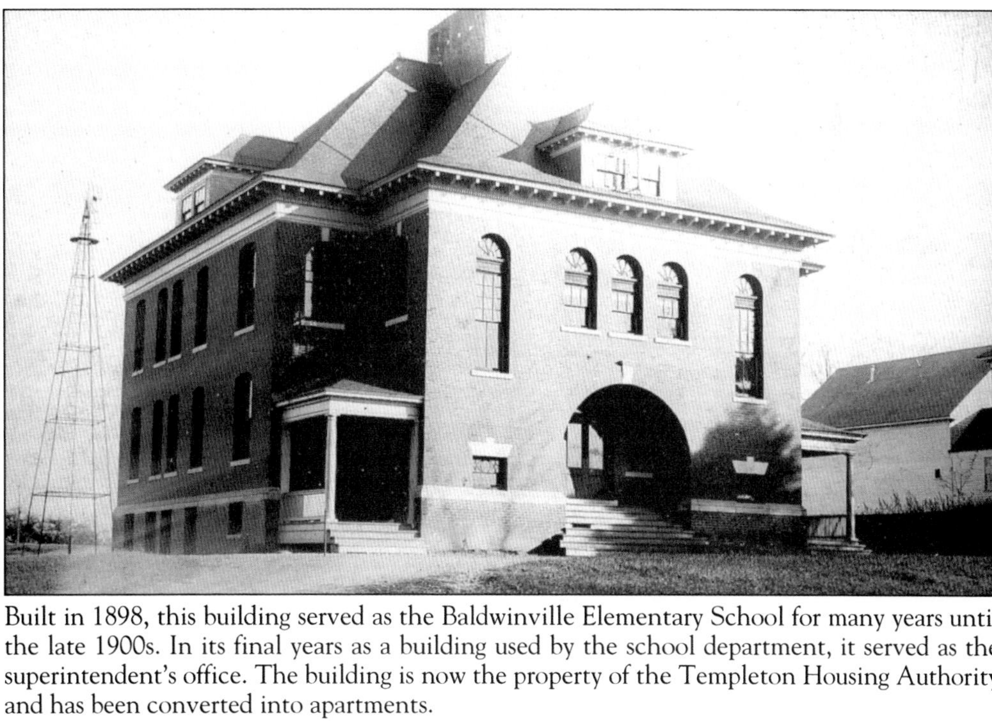

Built in 1898, this building served as the Baldwinville Elementary School for many years until the late 1900s. In its final years as a building used by the school department, it served as the superintendent's office. The building is now the property of the Templeton Housing Authority and has been converted into apartments.

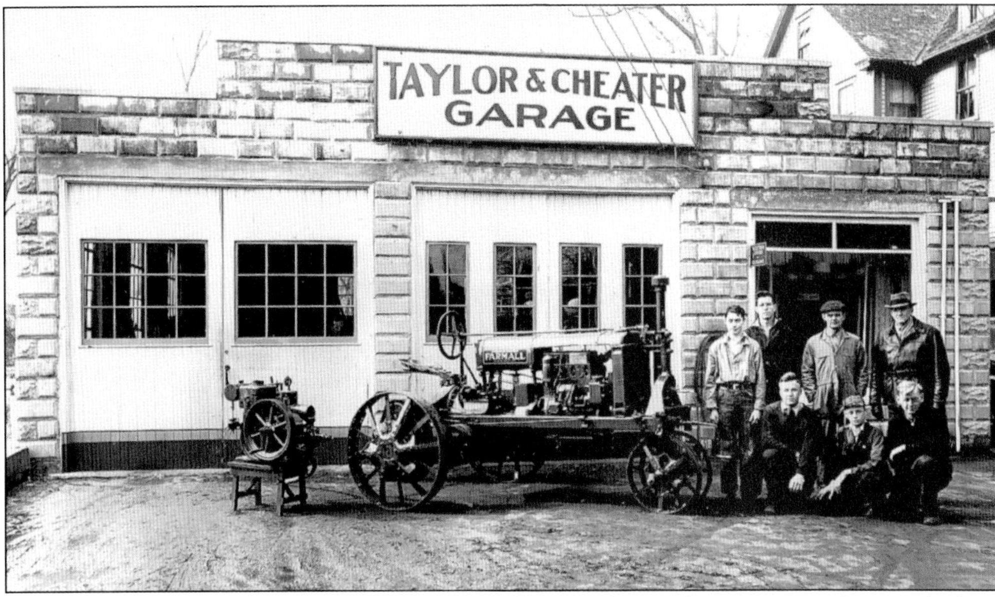

An early vocational agriculture class poses with their teacher and two projects they worked on. The teacher is believed to be William E. Curtis. The school did not have a shop when the class first started. Charles Cheater allowed them to use part of his garage for the mechanical part of the class until the school had a shop.

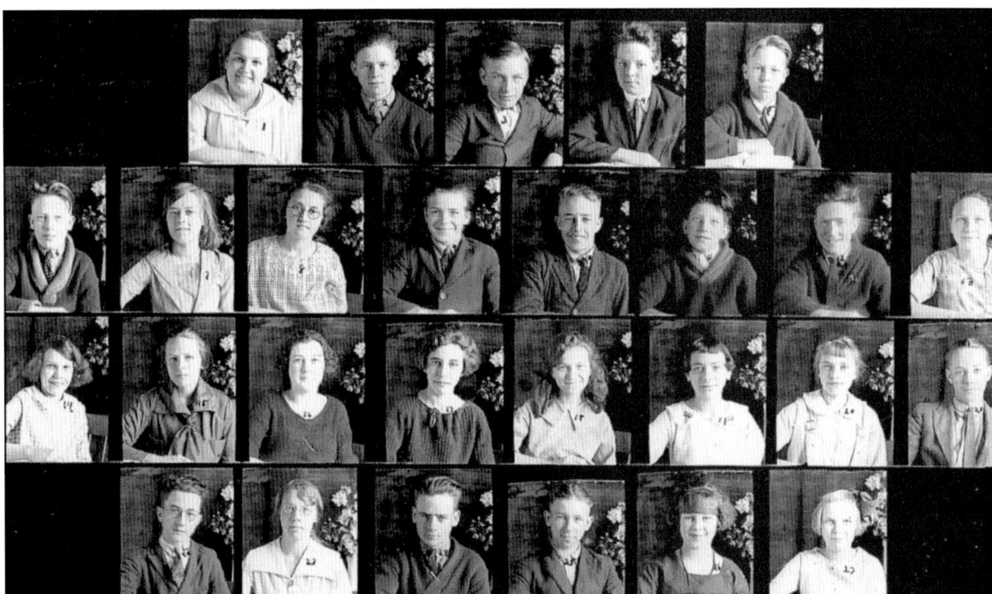

This c. 1907 class picture was probably taken in Baldwinville. The students are, from left to right, as follows: (first row) Richard Treacy, Edith Taft, Lawrence Leroy, John Stone, Mildred Saveall, and Margaret Morse; (second row) Blanche Morse, Myrtle Lewis, Beatrice Kenney, Majorie Snow, Mildred Piercy, Bernice Rousseau, Olive Duquette, and Uno Ronnie; (third row) James Murphy, Anna Szymick, Sophie Aponel, Raoul Cloutier, Oscar Tissari, John Cummings, George Kenney, and Georgianna Vachowski; (fourth row) Helen Gingras, Richard Sanders, Stanley Nasiatka, Charles Shaw, and Milton Gleason.

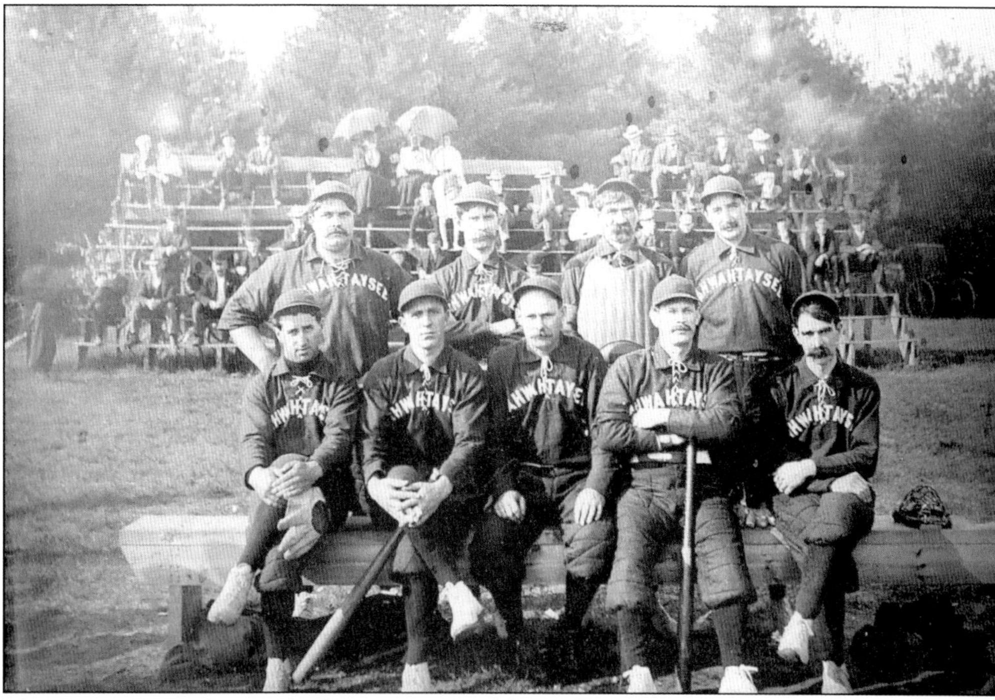

This picture was taken in the late 1800s in Baldwinville. The players are, from left to right, as follows: (first row) Frank H. Hunt, Harry E. Rowe, Albert E. Hager, and two unidentified men; (second row) unidentified, Dr. Carleton A. Fletcher, unidentified, and Alanson R. Paine.

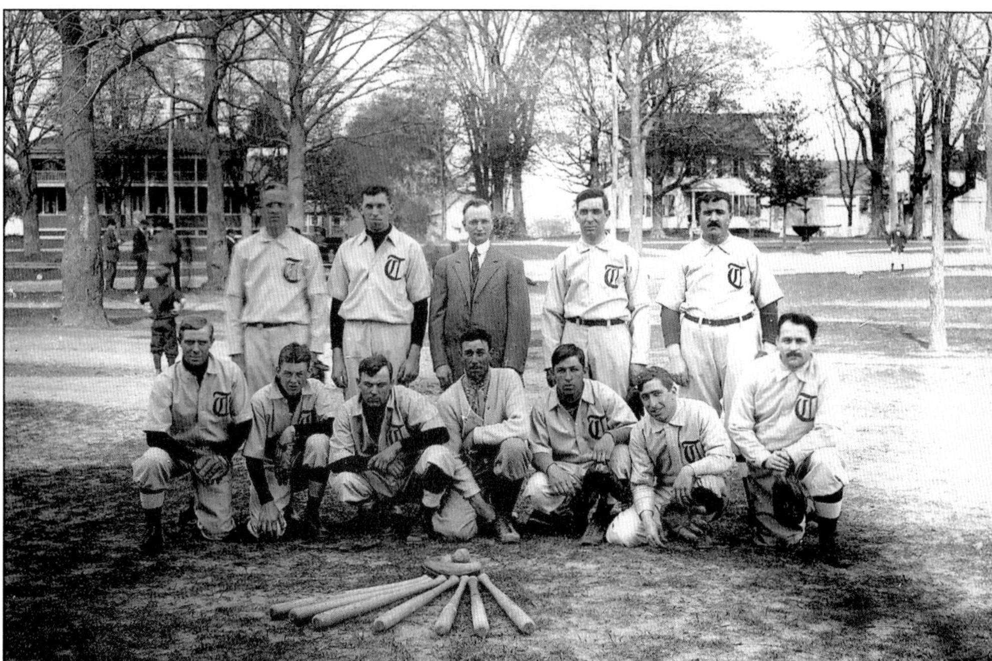

This is an early Templeton High School baseball team. The teacher and coach is Jay Stanley.

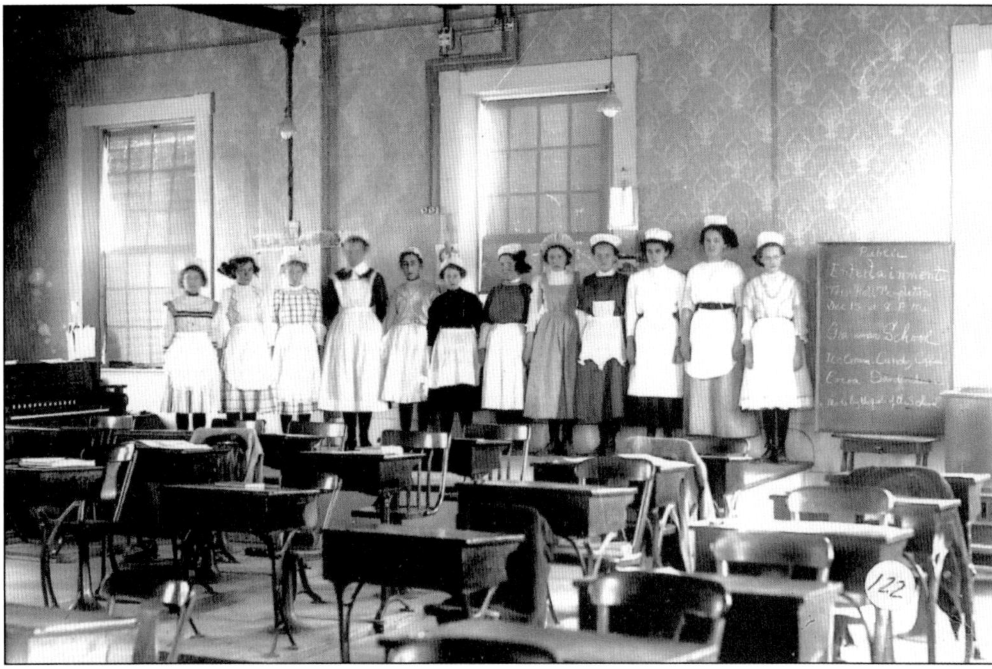

This is a picture of a group of students in the old school next to the First Church prepared to serve food at some type of function in the building. The writing on the blackboard states, "Public Entertainment, Templeton Town Hall, Dec. 15 at 8 PM."

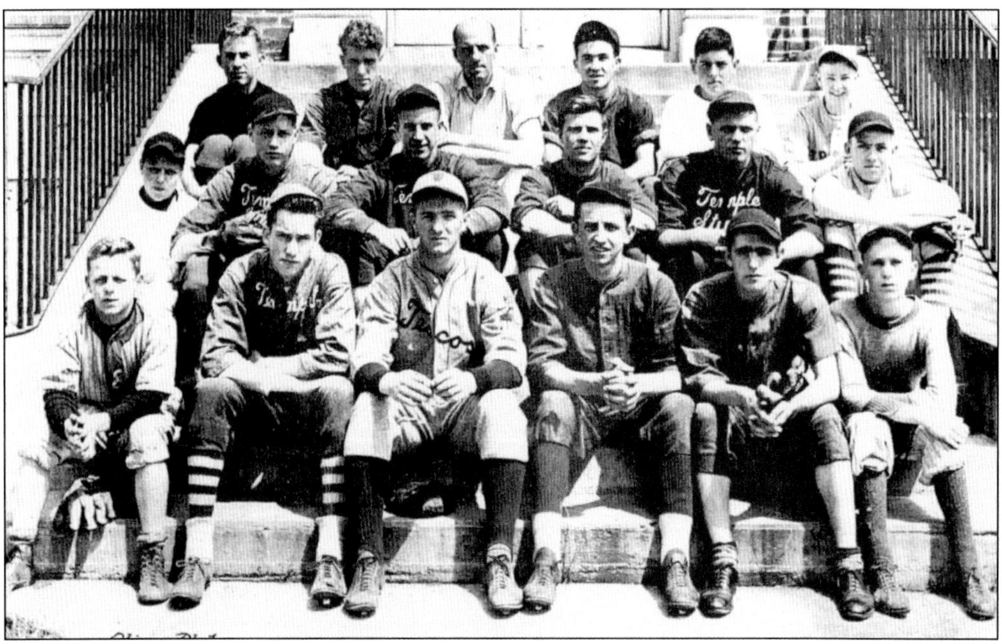

The Templeton High School champions of 1936 are, from left to right, as follows: (first row) Philip Mahoney, Carl Valiton, Eddie Mizereck, Eddie Savoick, Edgar Denis, and John Monahan; (second row) Joseph Spaulding, Leland Greenwood, Johnny Lendo, Mickey Baczewski, Eddie Bullock, and Ed Hawkes; (third row) Stephen Flis, Erwin Moore, coach Chet Poliks, Vinnie Valliere, Edward Welch, and Edward Saunders.

This school building, built in 1834, is now known as Scout Hall. It was a one-room schoolhouse until 1874, when a new school was built. The building is still used by the Boy Scouts as well as the town for functions.

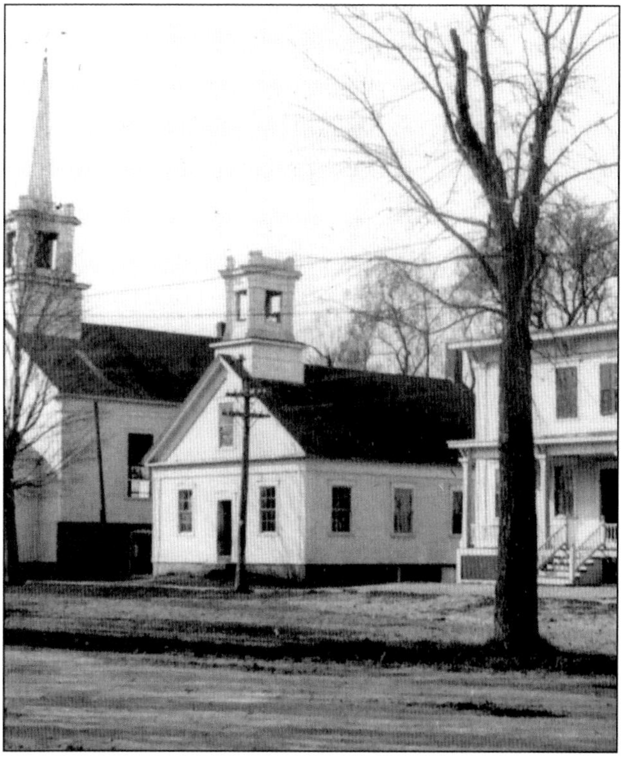

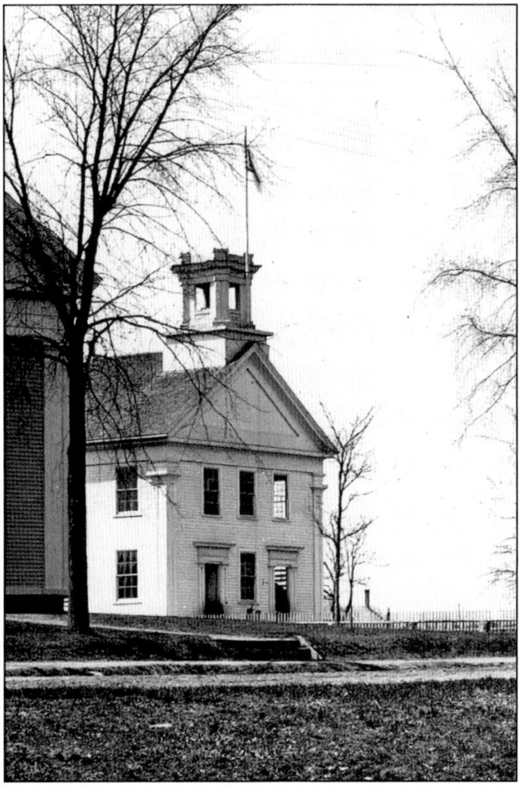

This old Baldwinville school was located where the Baldwinville post office now operates. It was built in 1850 and was used as a school until 1898, when the new brick schoolhouse was built as a replacement. At that time, this building became the Baldwinville branch of the Boynton Public Library. The second floor was used for lodge rooms.

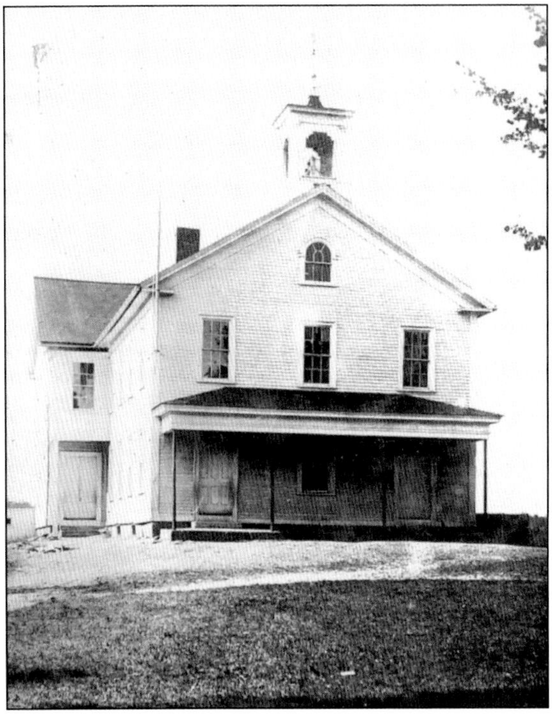

This schoolhouse was located on Old Winchendon Road in Otter River. Leonard Stone built this school in 1860 and constructed two classrooms on the ground floor. The second floor was used as a public hall for meetings. It is said that the teacher in this school had 81 students and her salary was $22 per month. The school was destroyed in 1933 by fire.

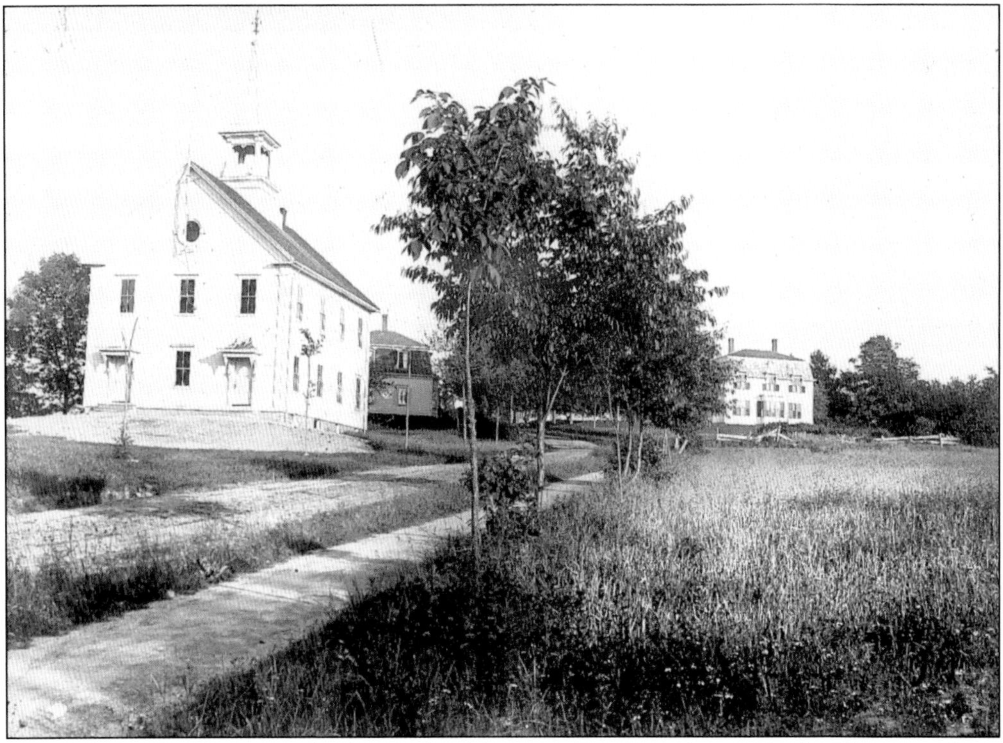

In 1874, this schoolhouse was built on School Street in East Templeton. The building served as a school until 1923, when a new brick schoolhouse was built. It was voted in 1940 to sell the school. The steeple was removed, and the former school is now the home of the Bernard family.

Six

MAPS

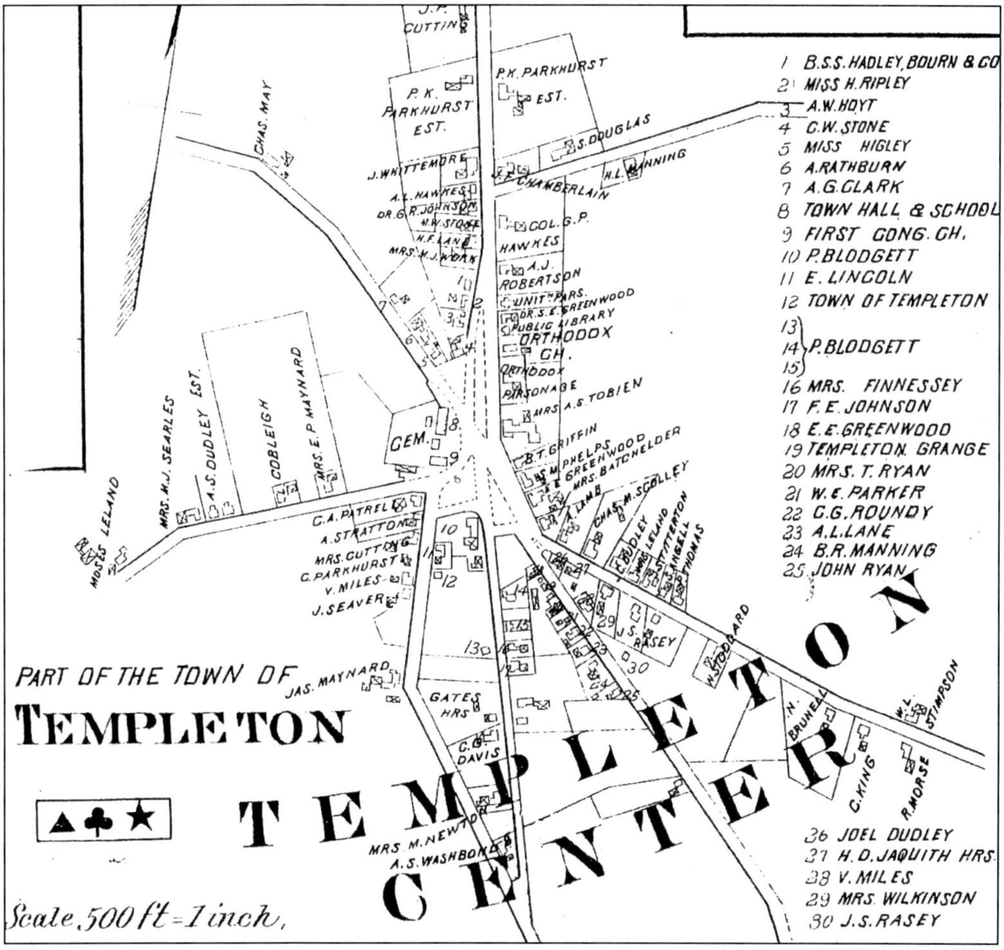

The following maps are taken from the *Worcester County Atlas* of 1898.

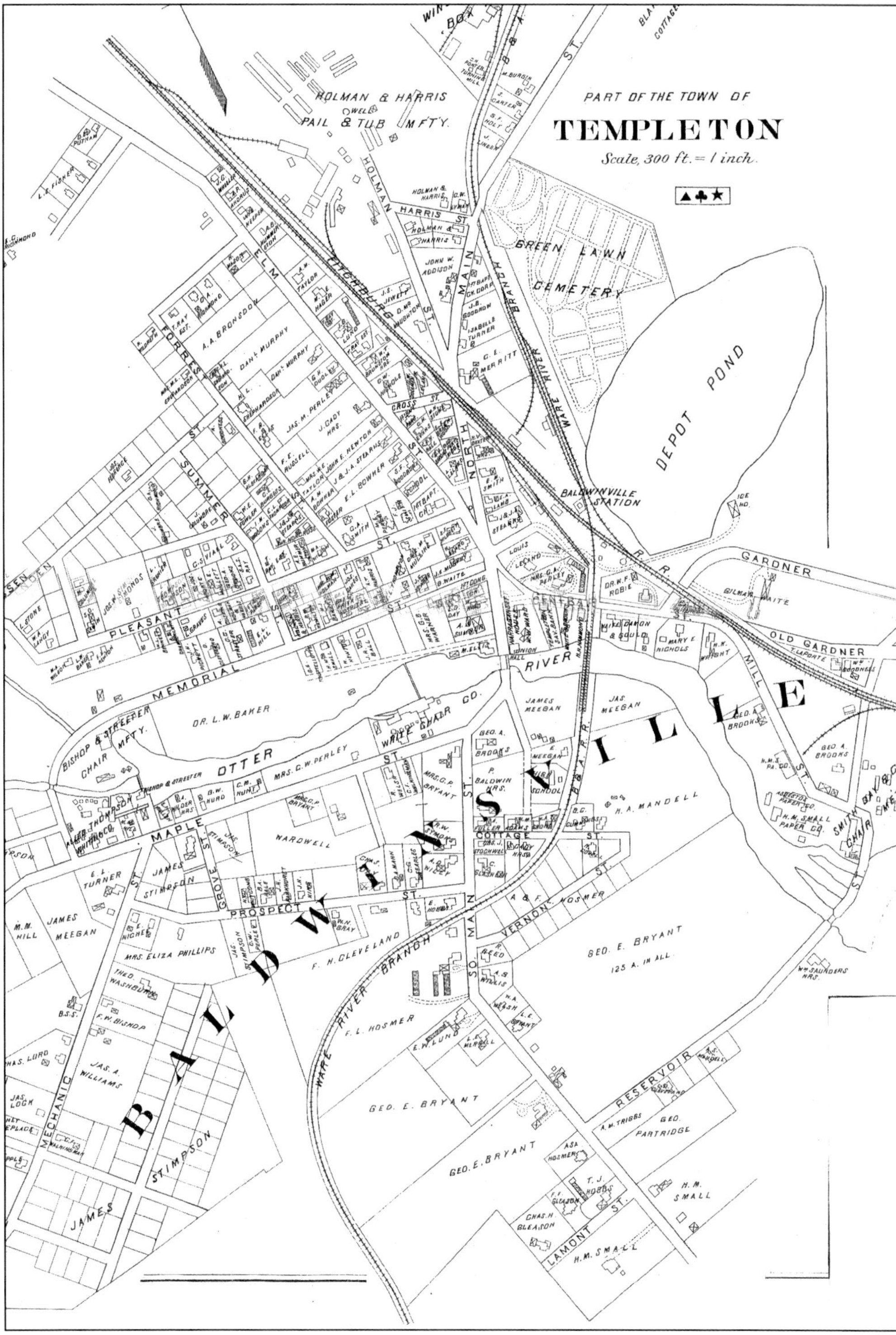

This is the map of Baldwinville that appeared in the atlas.

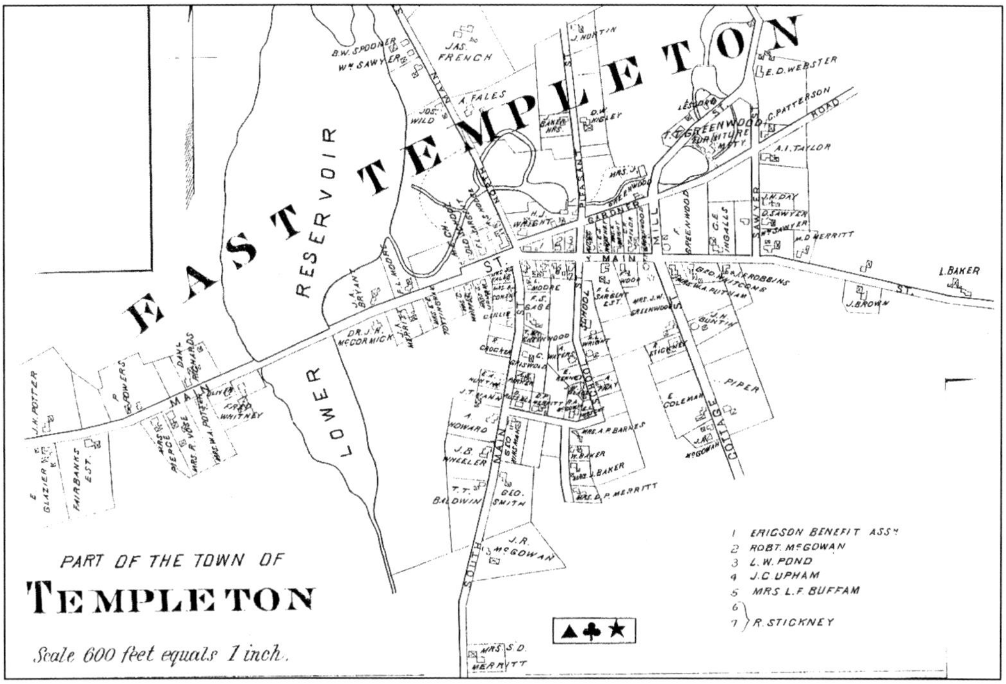

This is the map of East Templeton.

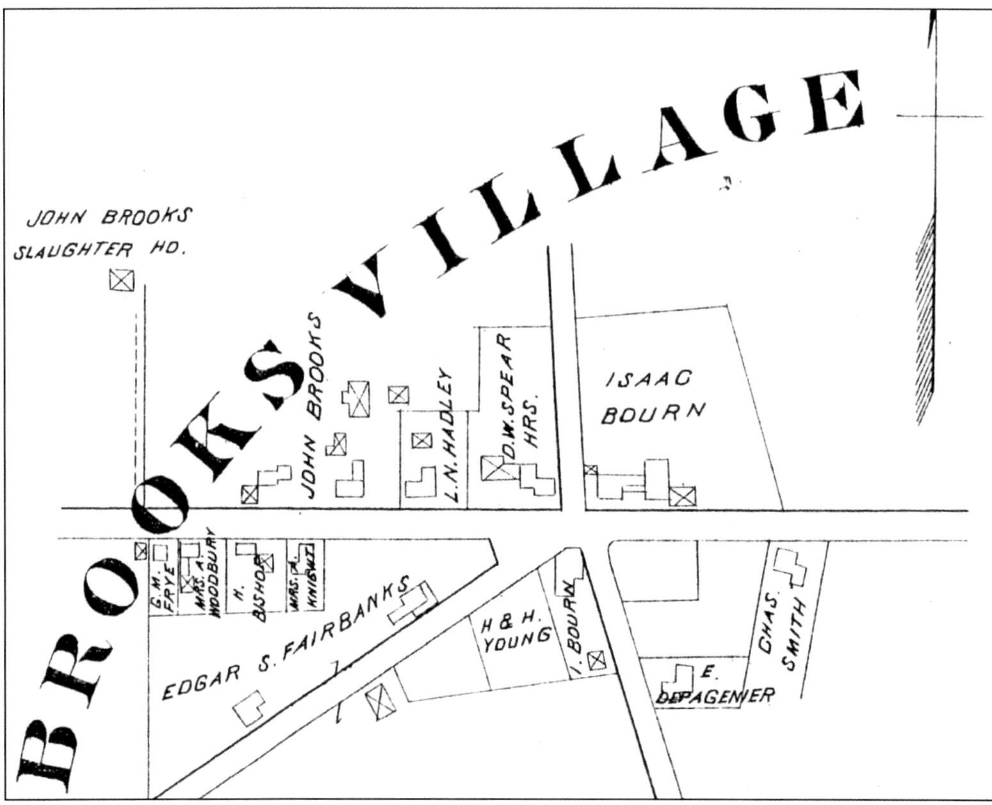

This is the map of Brooks Village.

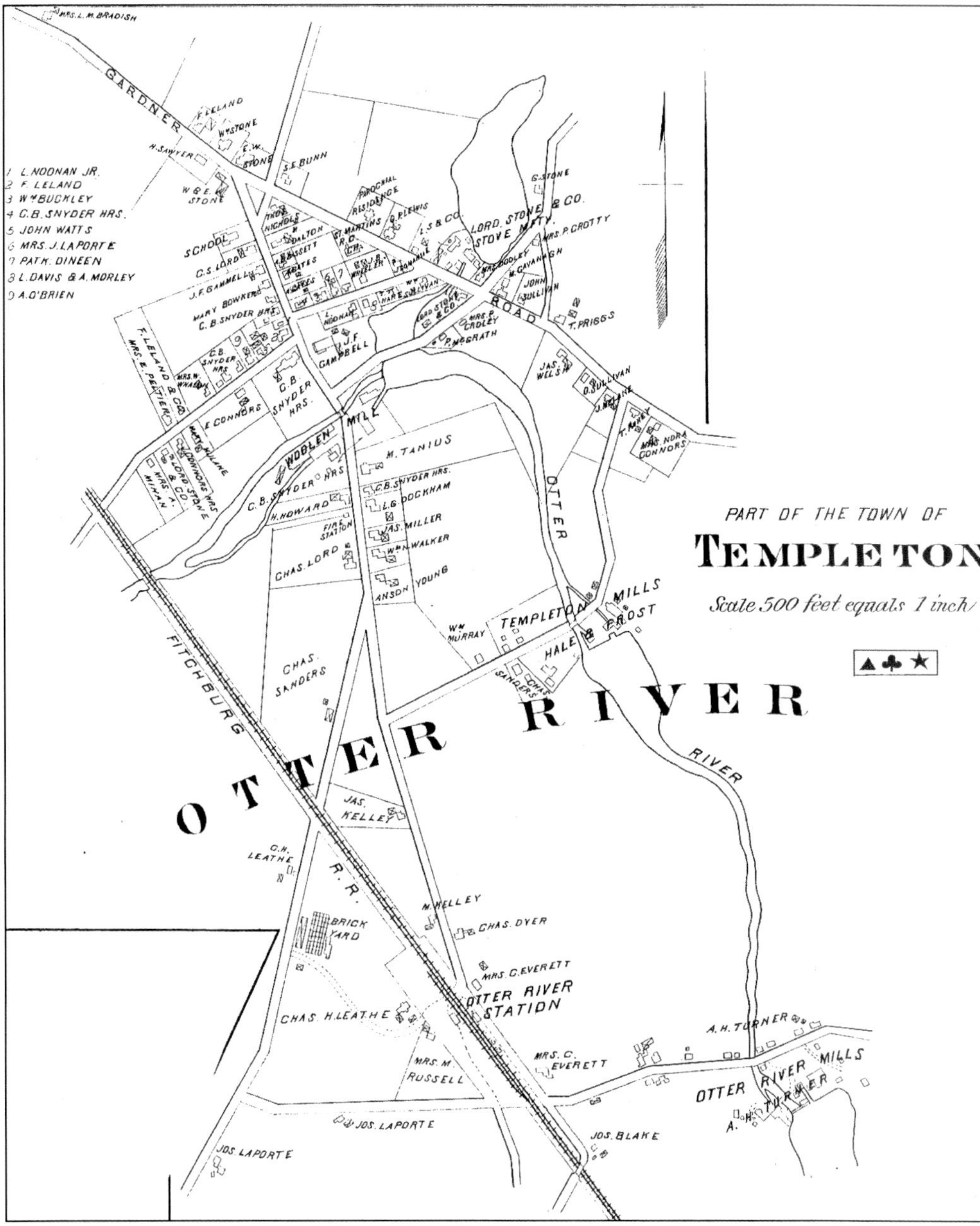

This is the map of Otter River.